To

Jack and Imogene

With Best Wishes

from a Survivor

of the Holocaust

Magda Herzberger

February 8, 2010

Survival

Magda Herzberger

1st WORLD
LIBRARY™
The World's Publisher

Austin, Texas

Survival
By Magda Herzberger
©Magda Herzberger, 2005
Survival

1st World Library
(an imprint of Groundbreaking Press)
8305 Arboles Circle
Austin, TX 78737
512-657-8780
www.groundbreaking.com

Library of Congress Control Number: 2005903331
ISBN: 0-9765821-1-2

First Edition

Senior Editor
Barbara Foley

Editors
Brad Fregger
Marjorie Smith
Katherine Bishop

Book Design
Amy Nottingham-Martin

Cover Design & Production
Ashley Underwood

Back Cover Photo of Magda Herzberger
Pro Photo - Fountain Hills, Arizona

Dedication

To all my loved ones:
My late parents, Herman Mozes and Serena Mozes
My uncle, Eugene Mozes
My husband, Eugene Herzberger, M.D.
Our son Henry
Our daughter Monica
Our grandchildren, Nathan and Mira Ma
And to all the victims of the Holocaust

Acknowledgements

I owe a deep debt of gratitude to all the people who were influential in formulating my story.

Special gratitude to:

My beloved husband,
Eugene Herzberger, M.D.
My daughter, Monica Wolfson, M.E.D.T.
My son, Henry Herzberger, Ph.D.
My best friend, Evelyn Vondran, Ph.D.
My dear friend, Maggie Smith, C.D.T.

My special thanks and gratitude to my teacher at the Jewish Gymnasium (high school) in Kolozsvár, Hungary, Professor Moshe Carmilly-Weinberger, Ph.D., for advice and for writing the foreword to my book.

I am most grateful for the constant support of my publisher, Brad Fregger, and for the hard-working, dedicated editors of my book:

Senior Editor:
Barbara Foley

Editors:
Brad Fregger
Marjorie Smith
Katherine Bishop

My deepest appreciation to Amy Nottingham-Martin and Ashley Underwood for the layout and cover design of my book.

Foreword

"Write, Jewish Children!" (*"Schreibts, Jidische Kinder!"*) were supposedly Simon Dubnov's, the famous Jewish historian's, last words from the death-train before it left the railway station of Riga. He was the author of an excellent Jewish history entitled: *Die Weltgeschichte des Judischen Volkes (The World History of the Jewish People)*. He knew the value of the written word. He cried out as his last testimony: *"Schreibts, Jidische Kinder!"*

"Verba volant, scripta manent!" Words have wings, fly away easily, but written words have everlasting power. Are we able to put in words our deepest feelings, pain, and suffering?

Expressionist painters tried to demonstrate anguish, torment, and agony in their artistic works. For example Kaethe Kollwitz in her drawing, "Sorrow," was able to express, with a few brush strokes, a woman's grief. Can we forget Edward Munch's famous painting, "The Scream", a young man standing alone on a bridge under a turbulent, red sky calling for help? In the far distance the silhouette of two people is visible. It appears that they walked away as if they didn't want to hear the tremendous call for assistance. The Jewish people were the lonely ones, who stood alone in the world when nobody was willing to hear the bitter cry which reverberated all over Europe and America. Six million Jews, including one and a half million innocent children, were annihilated.

What a miracle that a few escaped death and tried to rebuild their lives. Slowly they regained their human feelings and revitalized their strength. The Holocaust survivors started to reconstruct the tragic events of the past and to place it in historical perspective.

"Schreibts, Jidische Kinder!"

A storm of unbelievable, inhuman attacks, torment, and misery came alive on paper as hundreds of survivors took pen in hand and started to write and to publish their memories. Each personal report is not only a personal communication, but a confession, too, in order to get some relief from the unbearable past. The distinctness in these accounts is natural.

It is not an easy task to relive, to bring back the terror of Auschwitz. But they courageously followed the bibilical command, *"Zakhor al tishkah!"* (*"Remember! Do not forget!"*).

Magda Herzberger, an excellent student of the Jewish Gymnazium (Jewish High School) in Kolozsvár in the years 1940-1944, fulfills that task. She understands the power of the written word. A multifaceted, talented poet, writer, and composer, shaken by suffering experienced in the death camps of Auschwitz, Bremen, and Bergen-Belsen, was able to write lyrical poetry. Human voices are heard in her poetic works: *Songs of Life, The Waltz of the Shadow,* and *Will You Still Love Me?* With her poetic talent and her musical ability she composed a "Requiem" for solo and choir, in memory of those who perished in the death camps. The suffering of Job can be heard in this musical composition.

Before us now is her "magnum opus" called *Survival* (1st World Library, Austin, Texas, 2005). Magda Herzberger describes in her book the fight between life and death. It is a "death-dance" (known as *"Totentanz"*). The naked reality of the death camps is before our eyes. Total lack of compassion, inhumanity, and despotic harshness is the daily reality of her and her fellow inmates. Magda Herzberger looks in vain for human understanding among her captors. In that unbelievable hell, she finds human voices only in her sensitive heart. She prays. She believes in a better future.

In October 1945, Magda returned to her city (Kolozsvár-Cluj). She rang the bell of her home. "A window opened. I heard my mother's voice, 'Who is there?' 'It is your daughter coming home!' "

It would have been a great loss if Magda Herzberger's *Survival* had not been written. In a dark world it provides a profound insight.

Moshe Carmilly-Weinberger
New York, March 2005

Magda Herzberger

On the Way to the Grave

We were hauled
into the somber freight cars
and placed behind bars.
Then, the doors were locked,
our freedom was taken;
we were left in the darkness,
doomed and forsaken,
ready to be shipped
to our place of execution.
The slow puffing
of the steam engine
grew faster and faster,
as the locomotive
pulled us further and further
into the unknown.
As the train rolled on and on,
our last spark of hope was gone.
Some of us cried,
others tried to rebel,
in vain.
Sorrow and pain
crept into our hearts,
chilling our bodies,
clouding our minds.
But gradually
most of us succumbed
to the strong power

of destiny,
sitting silently,
hour after hour
on the cold, wooden floor,
lamenting no more.
Only a few
were still pounding
the heavy door
with their fists,
and shouting, "Open up!
Why are we here?"
No one could hear
our desperate outcry.
Then suddenly
the train stopped.
We were in Germany,
facing the barbed-wire fence
of Auschwitz.
Humiliated, heartbroken,
waiting for the judgment
of guilt
to be pronounced
on the innocent.
Each of us
was possessed by fear.
We were so near
to death
that we could feel
its breath.

We were robbed, trapped.
And with horror,
into the German concentration camp
we stepped!

We entered the gate of the greatest annihilation camp in Germany: Auschwitz, situated forty miles from the Polish city of Krakow occupied by the Germans. A large sign on the gate declared *"Arbeit macht frei"* ("Work gives you freedom"). Crammed into railroad cattle cars, we had traveled for three days and three nights from my childhood home in the city of Kolozsvár, Hungary.

It was the intention of our captors to completely erase our identities. I decided not to let them. Who was that eighteen-year-old girl who stood before that ominous gate that May morning in 1944?

Part One

Chapter 1

*I*t was a cold, clear night on February 20, 1926, in the city of Cluj, Romania, in the northern part of Transylvania. This mountainous territory in the heart of Romania is surrounded by the Carpathian mountains in the east, the Transylvanian Alps or Southern Carpathians in the south, and by the Bihor mountains in the west. On that particular starlit night, my parents, Herman and Serena Mozes, were expecting my arrival, their first child.

It was 8:00 p.m. My mother had been in labor for several hours at our residence. In those years it was customary for physicians to make house calls and for women to deliver their babies at home.

Our competent and well-regarded family physician, Dr. Weisz Fülöp, had assisted at many births. He assured my parents that everything would be all right and a natural birth was expected. There would be no need for any special intervention.

Nevertheless, there was lots of agitation at my parents' home on that night. There were family members present, among them my mother's Aunt Rivka, her sister Rachel, some of her cousins, and my paternal grandmother, Rose. All of them were assisting her, giving her moral support and comfort.

My father was very concerned. My mother's Aunt Rivka was especially worried, being an anxious person. She wanted to do something special for my mother in order to help her in some way.

An orthodox rabbi was my parents' next-door neighbor. He was well acquainted with my parents and with many of my family members. He conducted services at the big orthodox temple where my parents and much of my family had been members of his congregation for many years. On that particular night, the rabbi was at his home, performing a prayer welcoming the new moon, which had appeared in the starlit sky. Ten other men, members of his congregation, were present, joining him in the ritual. The new moon had a special significance, being associated with renewal and good tidings.

Aunt Rivka went to the rabbi's home and knocked on the door. The rabbi was surprised to see her at such a late hour. Aunt Rivka explained her great concern about my mother's plight and asked him to include my mother in his prayers to God, that she be granted a smooth, healthy, and speedy delivery.

The rabbi liked and respected my parents and he offered his help. He said that he would perform a special prayer for her, called *Misheberach* in Hebrew, meaning "special blessings."

He volunteered to do more than that. He told Aunt Rivka that he would bring something for my mother from the synagogue which would be of help to her. So, after the prayers were performed and everyone else left, the rabbi went to the synagogue which was located nearby. He opened the door of the synagogue, went in, walked up to the pulpit, and opened the sacred enclosure by the pulpit called the Holy Ark where the sacred Torah scrolls were enclosed.

The Torah scroll is a sacred scroll containing the five books of Moses: Genesis, Exodus, Leviticus, Numbers, and Deuteronomy. Torah means teachings and law. The Torah is the heart of Judaism. It is also called *Etz Chaim* in Hebrew, meaning "Tree of Life." The Torah is taken out from the Holy Ark at religious services every Sabbath and holidays, and the rabbi reads excerpts from it to the congregation.

In every Jewish synagogue there is at least one Torah scroll enclosed in the Holy Ark, but in larger synagogues there are several Torah scrolls in the sacred enclosure. The Torah scroll is wrapped with a Torah binder. Then it is covered with a Torah mantle that is usually decorated with different Jewish symbols, among them the Star of David or the Burning Bush.

The rabbi took out one of the Torah scrolls from the Holy Ark, lifted the Torah mantle, and removed the Torah binder.

Then he wrapped the Torah scroll with one of the reserve Torah binders kept in the sacred enclosure. He replaced the Torah mantle and placed the Torah scroll into the Holy Ark, closing it up. He picked up the original Torah binder, closed up the synagogue, and returned to his home with it. He then gave the Torah binder to Aunt Rivka, instructing her to wrap the Torah binder around my mother's abdomen and let her keep it there until she delivered her baby. He told Rivka, that in his experience, the Torah binder could produce miraculous effects which could facilitate the delivery of the baby.

The rabbi was a kind person who went out of his way to help my mother. He wanted to provide her with the protective Torah binder as a shield and comfort while she was giving birth to a new life, thus giving her strength, confidence, and faith in God.

Aunt Rivka placed the Torah binder on my mother around 10:00 p.m. following the instructions of the rabbi. Two hours later, I was born. It was midnight, ushering in the onset of the happy Jewish holiday of Purim commemorating the liberation of the Jews by Queen Esther, from Haman, an evil chief minister of King Ahasueros of the Persian Empire, who wanted to kill all the Jews living there. Queen Esther, being Jewish herself, persuaded King Ahasueros to let the Jews defend themselves against the planned massacre by Haman. The Jews fought and defeated their enemy. The holiday is celebrated with masquerades, distribution of gifts, and donations to the needy.

In the Jewish synagogues on that holiday, the readings of the Megillah scroll of Esther (the biblical Book of Esther) are performed.

Purim is a meaningful holiday for me because it marks the time of my birth. And since my birth occurred on the onset of that special day, I was given the Hebrew name of Esther Malka (Queen Esther).

After I was born, the rabbi told my parents that all the special circumstances at the time of my birth—the Torah binder placed on my mother, the appearance of the new moon (*Rosh Hodesh* in Hebrew), and the coinciding happy holiday of Purim—would make me a lucky person and the new moon would have a significant beneficial influence in my life. This was proven in the future, considering all the miracles which were to come later on in my life, keeping me alive and helping me to survive all of the awful challenges which destiny cast upon me.

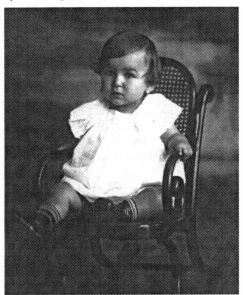

Photo 1 – Magda in her second year of life

I had a happy childhood, growing up in a home where I experienced much love, gentility, and harmony. My parents were wonderful people.

My mother, Serena Mozes (maiden name Serena Daszkal) was a beautiful twenty-five-year-old at the time of my birth. She had jet-black, wavy hair; a light, clear complexion; dark, expressive, and lively eyes; and a shapely figure. She was neat and organized, took pride in her appearance, and had a pleasant personality. She was a loving, compassionate, and generous person. On many Friday nights when my mother was cooking our festive Sabbath meals, she invited poor people to join us and eat dinner at our table. My relatives told me that Serena's mother, Malka Daszkal (maiden name Malka Salamon), was also a charitable woman. She died of a kidney infection when Serena was only fifteen years old. At that time, there were no antibiotics to treat infections of that kind.

Although my mother was such a young girl when her mother died, she took upon herself the responsibility of nurturing a family of nine people. They included two sisters and three brothers. Her oldest sister died of a complication after she delivered her first child, a son, leaving behind the newborn baby. Then there was the deceased sister's widower husband to be taken care of—very lonely and depressed after his wife's death—and Serena's father, Shlomo Daszkal, who was a businessman engaged in cattle trading.

Serena did her best to care for her family. Her sister Rachel, who was older than Serena, helped her in all the many household chores, and they also had some hired household help occasionally. But it wasn't easy to take care of a family of nine people, especially with a baby to look after.

Photo 2 – Serena (left)
with two of her cousins

My mother's grandmother, who was a widow at the time of my Grandmother Malka Salamon's death, moved in with the family in order to give assistance. There were lots of chores to do, lots of canning to prepare, because there were no canned foods to purchase then. Everything had to be bought and carried in baskets from the market and from the stores. There were no cars, no dishwashers, dryers, or washing machines. Neither were there any ready-made clothes.

Clothing had to be made by hand at home. By this time sewing machines became available and were very popular. My mother had three uncles and one aunt on her mother's side and one aunt and two uncles on her father's side. They were especially helpful when her grandmother died two years after she moved in with the family.

From a very early age, Serena was intelligent and hard-working, always taking her responsibilities seriously. She was a fabulous cook and she had great talent in handcrafting. She loved to read, listen to music, and sing, which she did beautifully.

My father, Herman Mozes, was twenty-nine at the time of my birth. He was a handsome, slender man with chestnut-brown hair and blue eyes. Gentle and sensitive, he believed in the power of words, not of blows. I never received any corporal punishment. I loved and respected my parents; they were my friends. I was never afraid of my father. If I did something which was not right or misbehaved like any child occasionally does, he made time to sit down with me and ask why I behaved in that fashion, and I had to explain my conduct. Then he would explain why such behavior wasn't beneficial, calmly guiding me in the right direction.

I could always communicate well with both of my parents, sharing my feelings and thoughts with them without any reservation or fear. From very early childhood I was taught the value of love, tolerance, and understanding.

When I was three years old, my father taught me the greatest lesson in love that I have never forgotten. It was my mother's birthday. I went to my father and said, "Daddy, I want money."

My father asked, "What do you need money for?"

"Because I want to buy a present for Mommy's birthday."

"You can give your mother the most precious present that no amount of money can buy."

"What can you buy without money?"

My father's answer was, "Love. Go to Mommy and give her a kiss and a big hug and tell her how much you love her."

I did just that. I ran to my mother, embraced her, gave her a big kiss on her cheek, and told her, "Mommy, I love you, I love you, I love you!"

Even now after so many years, I can still feel the happiness I experienced. I was so proud that I could give my mom the greatest, most valuable gift of love and I didn't need any money for it.

My parents didn't have to explain to me with words what love is. They demonstrated it by their actions. They manifested so much love towards each other by being affectionate, considerate, and attentive in their relationship.

My father Herman was an avid reader and a very educated man. He graduated from the business academy and helped my grandfather in his business. He loved music and played three musical instruments: the cello, the clarinet, and the violin. At one time, he played in an orchestra. Herman also was an astute chess player, almost unbeatable in that game. His strongest competitor in chess was George (Geza is the Hungarian name), the husband of my mother's Aunt Ilona. Herman liked to play chess with him because he also was an expert in that game. Aunt Ilona and George lived in the center of our city of Cluj. While Mother chatted with Ilona, my father played chess for hours with George.

I liked to go along with my parents to visit them. I wasn't interested in either the chess games or the discussions between Mother and Aunt Ilona. My interest was in the rich wood cabinet in Aunt Ilona's living room. I liked all the figurines enclosed there. I was about four years old at that time. My mother and Aunt Ilona were reluctant to let me stay by myself in that room, being afraid that I might break something in that cabinet. I was told that I could only look at the figurines, but I couldn't touch anything. I wanted, of course, to explore and touch the objects. I begged to be left alone in the room and promised that I would not touch anything.

I was a very well-behaved child. My mother trusted me. At first they watched me closely, but when they saw that I was just standing in front of the cabinet on my tiptoes, totally mesmerized by the miraculous objects inside the cabinet, they left me alone. They wondered why I was not bored looking at the objects for such an extended period of time, but they didn't know that I was fascinated by them, and left by myself, I was transported into a world of imagination where all the porcelain dolls and the figurines came alive interacting amongst themselves. I made up fantastic stories about them in my mind. There was a writer born within me at that very early age.

Every time we visited Aunt Ilona, I ran into the living room to the rich wood cabinet to invent my stories. Those figurines became actors in a puppet theatre I devised. I always had interest in acting, and making up stories. I was always a dreamer and still am.

I am a dreamer, let me dream and cross over fantasy's silver stream.

Photo 3 – Three-year-old Magda with family

Although I was an only child, we were a big family, and we had an unusual family history.

My paternal grandmother's maiden name was Rose Katz. She married David Mozes, a businessman, when she was twenty years old. Later on, she gave birth to my father, Herman Mozes, and to my uncle, Eugene Mozes. When my father and my uncle were still young children, Grandfather David died, leaving Grandmother Rose a widow at a young age.

One day Rose Mozes met Moritz Salamon, who was the brother of my late Grandmother Malka who died when my mother Serena was fifteen. This was an interesting twist of destiny.

21

At that time, Moritz Salamon was a widower. He had ten children (five girls and five boys) with his late wife who had died of some complication after the delivery of her tenth child.

So Moritz Salamon was left with ten young children, one of them being a baby. Naturally, as he was my mother's uncle, all ten children were cousins of my mother.

My grandmother, Rose Mozes, and my mother's uncle, Moritz Salamon, fell in love and got married. Grandmother, a beautiful and intelligent woman whom I adored, told me the following story about her second marriage to Moritz Salamon.

"When I decided to marry your mother's uncle, my family members considered me unreasonable and foolish. They said to me, 'Do you really want to take the responsibility of marrying a man with ten children, a baby among them? You have two children of your own. Do you want to be a stepmother for ten children, taking care of twelve children?'

"My answer to them was: 'I love the man, he loves me. I will take care of him and of all his children, including my own. I will be the loving mother to all his children and to my own.'"

I admired my grandmother's strong personality. She didn't shy away from any challenge. She was brave, intelligent, and strong, with a big heart filled with love. She took excellent care of her entire family. She became a loving stepmother to all ten children of her husband, and her husband became a caring stepfather to my father and his brother Eugene. I always called my grandmother's husband, Moritz

Salamon, "Grandfather" because he was a stepfather to my father, although, in reality, he was the uncle of my mother.

Moritz Salamon was a small businessman. It wasn't easy for him to provide for such a big family, but somehow they managed, and in the course of time, they became very well-to-do, because Moritz had exceptional talent in business.

In addition to taking care of her family, a capable and ambitious Rose also helped with the bookkeeping for their business. By the time all the children in the family, including my father and his brother, grew up, my grandparents were well-to-do people. Moritz, being such a talented businessman, managed to own two estates or farms as well as an alcohol factory and a flourmill. He had a likeable and outgoing personality. Also a giver, he contributed money to many good causes and helped needy people.

My grandparents had a big house on the outskirts of Cluj, surrounded by a large yard filled with beautiful flowers and tall, impressive Linden trees, and an orchard containing pear, apple, and plum trees.

My grandmother also raised chickens, ducks, and geese. She always was a hard worker, even when they were doing well financially and could afford more hired help. It was simply her nature. To me, as a young child, it seemed that she never tired from all of her many activities, but instead looked lively and energetic.

There was a strong feeling of togetherness in the family. They were very helpful to each other, and worked together like a good team. The young men in the family, including my father and his brother Eugene, helped in Moritz's business.

Two of his sons managed the two estates and were living there. My father and my uncle did the bookkeeping, both of them being graduates of the business academy of the city of Cluj.

There was also hired help for the many household chores, and all the girls in the family helped my grandmother with the housework. There were also weekly traditional reunions, to which my mother and her family were invited as they were a part of the Salamon family.

It happened that my father Herman fell in love with my mother Serena. She was a lovely girl of twenty-three; Herman was twenty-seven. They got married in 1924, in a joyful, big, Jewish wedding. Two years later, in 1926, I was born.

Unfortunately, I never got to know my maternal grandmother, Malka Daszkal, since she had died when my mother was fifteen. My maternal grandfather, Shlomo Daszkal, also died of Spanish flu when I was three years old. I remember him only vaguely. He was a tall, slender man. At my young age, he looked like a giant. I have no other notable memory of him.

Chapter 2

When I was three and one-half years old, we lived in an apartment in Cluj. I have no recollection of the street of our residence, nor of the interior of our home. I have only a vague memory of our yard with its trees and fragrant flowers. But I remember the owner of the house. His name was Kirkocsa, a Hungarian name. He was short of stature and stocky. His wife was also a hefty-looking woman. They were friendly people and they liked me.

They didn't have any children, but they had a white dog called Gigi. They adored her and treated her like a family member. She got the best care and food you could imagine. She was a gentle dog, very much loved. Sometimes I played with her. She was my friend and she was very affectionate with people and with me, but you had to be careful around her because she had a jealous nature. She didn't like it when you got too close to her masters. She became aggressive and was even capable of biting. She wanted the entire attention of her masters. I was never bitten by her. It seemed that she was so fond of me that she could even control her jealousy in my presence. I could be a close friend with her masters and she would accept it. Then one day she got sick and passed away. Her masters and I were heartbroken. We missed Gigi. I felt that I had lost my friend, my playmate.

My other early childhood memory was when I was four years old. It was a beautiful day in summer. I remember sweet-smelling flowers blooming in our yard. I saw a commotion going on at our next-door neighbor's house with many people going in and out of the home. I asked my parents what was happening there. I was told that they were looking for the stork that was going to arrive shortly, bringing a baby to the family.

I remember my thoughts at that time: *I want to meet the stork before the baby arrives. I want to talk to her and tell her to bring us a baby with whom I can play.*

My wish was to have a brother or a sister so that I could have a playmate. I was usually playing with my dolls—talking with them. So I decided to sneak out of the house unobserved. I walked down two blocks and stopped at a street corner, waiting for the stork to come. My mother noticed my absence and became desperate. She started looking for me all over, calling my name, but there was no answer. She ran out of the house to our street and spotted me two blocks away, standing on the corner. Obviously upset, she ran to me and started scolding. I began to cry; tears were running down my cheeks. I told my mother that I didn't do anything bad. I was just waiting for the stork so I could ask her to also bring us a baby, because I would like to have a partner with whom I could play all the time. I was tired of talking only to my dolls. I wanted to have a real person who stayed with us all the time.

My mother was very touched and felt sorry for me. She told me, "Don't be sad; the stork will come one day and bring us a baby."

"Mommy, you really think so?"

"I will personally invite the stork to visit our house, but today she is too busy to stop and talk to us."

I trusted my mother and walked back with her, although I was frustrated and unhappy at not being able to put my request to the stork right away. However, it happened that my wish never came true and I had to accept being an only child.

But as I grew a little older, I started thinking that maybe there is an advantage to being an only child. That way, I got full attention from my parents and I learned to entertain myself. I got used to it.

I was still in my fourth year when my father decided to break off from the family business and be on his own. He got a job as manager of

Photo 4 – Magda at age four

a large engine factory named Energia, which manufactured motors of all kinds. The factory was located on the outskirts of Cluj. Its enclosure included a fairly large territory, part of which housed the factory, while another area included a residential section consisting of an apartment building with a few large units designated for some of the officials holding jobs at the factory, and a private home assigned to my father and his family.

Those were our best, most prosperous, and happy times. My father was earning well and we had a wonderful, comfortable home.

Our beautiful, big house at Energia consisted of many large rooms: three bedrooms, a large kitchen, two bathrooms, living room, dining room, and a pantry where all the canned jellies, cucumbers, preserves, fruits, and other food products were stored. There was a closed terrace we called the veranda where we had many greenhouse plants. We also had plants in our living room. My mother liked to take care of them.

I also remember the massively built, old-fashioned oak furniture throughout our home and the large mirrors with their ornamental frames. I recall the needlework done by my mother depicting biblical and other exquisite scenes, hanging on the walls of our living room, encased in gorgeous frames. I personally didn't have patience for the tedious, time-consuming needlepoint work. I also recall the family portraits hanging on the walls of our dining room, enclosed in elegant ornamental frames.

I particularly liked the portrait of my great-grandmother on my father's side, whom I never knew. It was a charcoal sketch of her done by a hunchback who worked in a local photo shop. He was never recognized as the great artist he was. My great-grandmother was in her fifties when her portrait was drawn. She looked so alive! I always admired it and believe that I bear a strong resemblance to her. Her whole personality was captured in her portrait. I would look at it at different stages of my life as I was growing up. She looked so pretty and had such a distinguished look about her, and she had a hairdo which actually looked like the one I am wearing now. She had long hair, put up in a big bun and fastened with numerous hairpins. Although I never knew her, I felt that through that picture she was living with us in the house.

I will never forget the beautiful hand-crocheted curtains hanging over our dining room windows, the matching hand-crocheted tablecloth displayed on our dining room table, the embroidered handmade curtains hanging over our living room windows, the colorful hand-stitched tablecloth on our kitchen table, and all the embroidered doilies on the night tables and on the coffee table. My mother handcrafted all of these.

I remember our old-fashioned sewing machine, which was used often, and our tall, wood-burning heating units made of decorative, square ceramic tiles placed in every room to provide heat during the cold winter months.

I also recollect the sturdy iron stove in our kitchen, fueled with wood, which rested on top of a solid brick structure and was equipped with a capacious oven. My mother used it for cooking all our tasty meals and for baking delicious cookies, cakes, and fancy tortes. I loved sweets as did my father. Very often during the day, I would raid the cookie jar and the plates where the sliced pieces of cake were placed. My mother always provided us with freshly baked treats. She took good care of my father and me.

There were many chores to do in the house. Naturally, my help was always requested. We also had a live-in maid named Elizabeth, who was very dedicated to us and was a great help to my mother. She was a peasant girl from a nearby village. I liked her because she was very nice to me. I was four years old when she came to work for us. Elizabeth liked to play cards and taught me different card games. She also told me all kinds of fairy tales which she invented herself. She seemed to have a rich imagination.

As a young child, I didn't have any playmates nearby because there were no other children living on the factory premises. My occasional playmates were my cousins, and I had a good number of them.

My mother's brother Jacob had two boys. One of them, Oscar, was my age, and the other one, Shlomo, was younger than I. My uncle Ernest, another brother of my mother, had a daughter Magda, who was close to my age. Some of the Salamon girls and boys, sons and daughters of Moritz Salamon, were married at that time and also had children. At the family gatherings, I had the best time because I could play with many of my cousins at the same time.

My mother's youngest brother unfortunately died at eighteen of peritonitis, since there were no antibiotics at that time. So I never got to know him. My mother told me that he had a great operatic voice. Like my mother, her brother Jacob also had a very good singing voice.

Mother also had aunts, uncles, and cousins so our family members were increasing as time went on. I vaguely remember my maternal grandfather who died of Spanish flu when I was three years old. His brother George looked like him. His daughter, Sari Daszkal, my mother's cousin, had a boy named Mishu. He was two years younger than I. Many times they visited us at our home at the Energia. Mishu loved to tease me, making me very angry, but I still liked him. But most of the time while we lived on the grounds of the engine factory, I had to play by myself.

My other friends were the three watchdogs of the factory: Caesar, a big German Shepherd, Albu—which means white in Romanian—a beautiful dog with snow-white fur, and Lupu— which means wolf in Romanian—a handsome German Shepherd which looked like a wolf. I loved those three watchdogs. They were my best guardians and were very loving and protective of me. They were magnificent animals, but people were afraid of them with good reason because they were trained watchdogs and could be dangerous to strangers. They were the protectors of the factory's premises. Caesar was my favorite. I took food on the sly from the kitchen to feed him, giving him snacks.

The factory grounds had a gate with a guardhouse. Everybody who came to the gate was stopped by the guard and couldn't enter without his permission. The guards wanted to keep track of strangers.

About the time I turned five, my uncle Eugene, brother of my father, divorced his wife due to her infidelity with his best friend. He couldn't forgive her for her betrayal. My uncle was an exceptionally handsome man and a great athlete. He was the fencing champion of Romania, and had a high position in one of the banks in our city. Just like my father, he broke away from his stepfather's business, looking for an independent position and career. He still loved his wife and went through a very hard time after his divorce, feeling lonely and depressed. My father, who loved him dearly, was very concerned about him and suggested Eugene move into one of the vacant apartments that were available at the residential area on the Energia grounds.

My uncle welcomed the offer and moved in there. He transformed one of the rooms into a fencing studio and gave fencing lessons to my father who eventually also became a competitive fencer.

I loved my uncle and was happy that he was close by. He didn't have any children of his own. I became like his little

Photo 5 – Magda with her parents

girl and naturally he was determined to give me fencing lessons, too. Then, in a way, I began to resent my uncle's idea.

It was summertime. He came over to our place in the morning, took me aside, and said, "The cold winter and the cool spring are over. Now we are going to start a physical exercise program. It is going to be fun. Starting tomorrow, we are going to do some exercises together every morning, some running, some gymnastics, and jumping rope."

In the beginning I thought that it would be lots of fun, but it turned out to be hard work. He would come in the mornings and find me covered with my warm comforter. Due to the nearby mountains, even in summer, the mornings were quite cool. He would wake me up. I objected, reluctant to leave my warm, cozy bed. So he would take off my covers, insisting I get dressed and go with him for a run, then for gymnastics, and jumping rope.

Complaining about it didn't help. He would ask me, "Do you love your uncle?"

I'd answer, "Yes."

"Then you have to listen to me. I will teach you how to fence and you will become a champion like me."

Fencing is a very challenging sport. My uncle taught me to fence with the foil because it wasn't as rough as the sword for a girl. He was the best teacher. When I complained of muscle soreness, he would say, "Pain increases your endurance and makes you stronger."

So in the course of time, at age twelve, I also became a competitive fencer, fencing with boy opponents, and I won gold cups. Uncle Eugene was so proud of me. I ultimately became a passionate fencer. Maybe I inherited some of his talent.

Whenever he entered our home he asked me, "How do you greet your uncle?"

I had to perform a cartwheel. But he taught me the value of persistence and endurance. He made me a good fighter, which in turn helped me to be a survivor, overcoming all the hardships I faced in my life.

My uncle's fencing studio became well known. More and more students wanted him to teach them, and in the course of time, he became a full-time fencing instructor.

Eventually my uncle moved out of the apartment at Energia and established a fencing school in our city, and he also became the fencing instructor at the Jewish sport club called Haggibor, which means the strong one.

During the summer Eugene was a tennis instructor. He also was an excellent skater and swimmer. He instructed me in all these sports in addition to fencing. He also was a great skier in the wild mountains. There were no ski lifts there. He climbed the mountains and came down them on skis.

When I was a young child I had dreams about my uncle in which he was a pirate with a red scarf on his head and one golden hoop earring dangling in one of his ears, and he was robbing me of my sleep. But I am glad that I listened to him. He taught me the great value of physical fitness. He often told me, "We have to be strong physically and also mentally in order to withstand life's tribulations and to survive under the adverse situations which we might encounter in our life."

My uncle pointed out to me the merit of fierce determination to attain our goals and that we must be willing to make every effort required. The courage to go on regardless of the difficulties we might face and the importance of endurance and persistence are the two strong attributes of our existence.

The positive attitude and the fighting spirit my uncle instilled in me in my childhood is still alive within me after all these many years.

Photo 6 - Magda's Uncle Eugene

Photo 7 - Eugene - August 24, 1930

When I turned six, I started kindergarten. I was happy because it gave me the opportunity to be with other children. I enjoyed playing with the children and I liked our teacher very much.

At that time, my dream was to become an actress. I enjoyed imitating the way people talked and acted, and I got pretty good at it. Sometimes I got carried away and began imitating my mother's aunt and other family members. They didn't like what I was doing and considered it disrespectful, although I had no intention of being offensive to anyone. I was doing it to test my acting talent. Finally, I had to stop because it was getting out of hand and my parents admonished me.

My Uncle Eugene was also good at imitating people. He had a great sense of humor and a genuine acting talent. He could have been a good comic actor. He would imitate people—often even family members—the way they talked and acted, but he could get away with it. In his case, what he was doing was considered funny and entertaining. I felt it was unfair that he got praise for it and I got admonishment. Many times I felt that my acting talent was not appreciated.

My uncle was exceptionally handsome and charming. At one time he also wanted to be an actor, but in those times, the acting profession was not looked upon favorably, and besides that, my grandparents needed him in their business. Therefore, he decided to choose a more practical profession and got a business degree. But, as I mentioned earlier, his true passion was fencing. He became Romanian fencing champion, Olympic athlete, and then ultimately a fencing instructor, the profession he liked best.

Meanwhile, my acting talent was discovered by my kindergarten teacher and I always got the lead roles in our kindergarten performances. I was very pleased that my teacher appreciated my artistic abilities. I loved her for that.

In 1933, at age seven, I entered the first grade of elementary school. The requirement then was that you had to be seven years old to start school.

Photo 8 - Magda, curtain call

At that time, Transylvania and my native city of Cluj were under Romanian rule. But before World War I, this territory was a province under the Austro-Hungarian Empire.

My parents grew up under the Hungarian government. My first language was Hungarian. My parents also spoke German.

When I entered first grade, my father took me aside and told me, "You should take your studies seriously especially because you are Jewish. You will find out in the course of time what I mean. Your education is very important. Your good grades will give you an opportunity to be accepted

37

more easily into the best schools. It is also important to choose a profession for yourself which is needed and, at the same time, one you would like to practice."

Photo 9 - Kindergarten Performance (Magda, extreme right)

Photo 10 - Magda, first row, right

Perhaps I didn't fully grasp the great meaning of my father's words, but I promised him that I would be first in my class academically at the end of my first year, even though I was totally unfamiliar with the Romanian language and I was enrolled in a Romanian school. But I loved school and I tried my best to succeed, not only for my father's sake, but for my own desire and pride. Fencing gave me lots of self-confidence. I thought that somehow if I worked hard I would succeed and manage to keep my promise to my father and, indeed to my great joy, I was first in my class at the end of my first year.

We were still residing at our big house on the premises of Energia, the engine factory, where my father was still the manager. Elizabeth, our live-in peasant girl, was still working at our home. Our house and the Energia factory were located near the railroad tracks. The tracks lay on the top of a steep hill. At some short distance below the front side of the hill was located the entrance gate leading to the factory's residential area. As you entered the gate there was a straight road leading to our home. The factory was situated at some distance from it on the other side of the area. Below the hill on the other side of the tracks there was a road leading to a bus station going to the center of our city.

In the morning, Elizabeth took me to the bus which took me to school. In order to get to the bus station, first we had to walk to the gate, then climb the steep hill, then cross the tracks and descend on the other side of the hill, and then walk a short distance to the bus station to catch the bus to school. This was quite a chore in winter due to the deep snow on the hills and the slippery surface of the railroad tracks. In springtime when the snow melted and the tracks had no deposit of ice, it was a lot easier going. We still had to watch out for mud spots which were slippery. Elizabeth was always my faithful guardian. She had also accompanied me during the previous year when I attended kindergarten. As I became older and was in the third grade, I asked my parents to allow me to go by myself to the bus when the weather was nice. They agreed because they trusted me and I had always been a good child.

Even though I loved and honored my parents, at this time I started to feel the need for some independence. One day on my way home from school, I had the idea of walking on the railroad tracks for an extended period of time, testing my ability to balance on them. Once I discovered that I was pretty good at it, I wanted to practice it more and more. I didn't realize that my mother was watching me and saw what I was doing. She and my father both scolded me, and I had to promise them that I would not do it again. They told me that otherwise, I would not be allowed to go by myself and that Elizabeth would accompany me again as she had before. Knowing how important it was for me to be more independent, they believed that the threat of losing that independence would keep me compliant.

But although I promised my parents not to do my balancing act on the tracks anymore, after a while I felt the need to again assert my independence, being confident that I could handle myself and watch out for my own safety. So I started my challenging game again. Sometimes I could hear the whistle of the train but I still kept walking on the tracks, confident that I could jump off the tracks anytime I wanted. Perhaps without realizing it, I did it because it represented my rebellion against the rules I was expected to follow in my earlier childhood years.

But one day I learned a lesson which prompted me never to engage again in my balancing acts on the tracks. Coming home from school, I climbed up the hill leading to the tracks. I had in mind to do my balancing act once again. But when I reached the tracks, I could see many people gathered around and I heard loud voices and mournful cries. Curious, I came closer and saw a mutilated, dead body lying before me on the tracks, with fresh red blood oozing from it. It was my first horrifying encounter with death. I was terrified. I felt numb, speechless, started crying, and ran home. Someone had committed suicide on that tragic day. I suddenly understood that this could have happened to me if for some reason I hadn't been able to jump off in time, or I had stumbled on the tracks when the train came closer.

This experience was a turning point in my young life. I felt guilty for doing what I had done and I suffered from my guilt. I felt that I was going to be punished in some way for being careless and disrespecting my parents' wish, for not keeping my promise, and not being respectful enough of my life.

On that particular night I was afraid of the dark. I felt uncomfortable in my room. Every time I heard the whistles of the oncoming trains I could see in my imagination the gruesome picture of the dead man on the tracks. I imagined that the punishment for my bad behavior would be that the dead man's ghost would appear at my window and would haunt me forever, telling me, "This could have happened to you, naughty girl."

Every night I would cover my face with my comforter to protect myself from that vision of the gruesome scene I saw that day coming home from school.

My parents helped me to recover from that shocking experience and I learned to accept in time that the victim's death had nothing to do with me, and it was not a punishment for what I had done. With the help of my parents I came to understand that I didn't cause the victim's death. He did it himself for his own reasons.

Even though I didn't know him, or what prompted him to take his own life, nevertheless, it took me a long time to overcome my fears and my anxiety. However, due to that tragic incident, I became much more mature in my behavior and, as it happened, I needed that maturity later on when I was still a young teenager.

I recall the joyful celebrations of our Jewish holidays. There was Rosh Hashanah, the Jewish New Year; Yom Kippur, the Day of Atonement, spent at the synagogue in prayers and fasting; the happy holiday of Purim, celebrating the liberation of Jews by Queen Esther; Succoth, celebrating harvest time; Chanukah, the Festival of Lights; and Passover, our major holiday, celebrating the liberation of Jews from the Egyptian bondage.

I grew up in the orthodox Jewish faith. My mother prepared for us strictly kosher foods and all the other members of my family also consumed only kosher foods at their homes.

I remember the festive dinners my mother prepared for the holidays. I will never forget the Passover ritual, the Seder. Seder is a Hebrew name for "order," and there is a certain order in which the ritual is performed. My father conducted it. During Passover ceremony, he read from the Haggadah, the book containing prayers for the ritual and the story of the liberation of Jews from Egyptian bondage. At the end of the prayers, dinner was served. It started with a blessing with red wine and the distribution of the matzo (representing the unleavened bread) by my father to his family. Then the traditional Passover meal was served, consisting of chicken soup with matzo balls (dumplings), potato pancakes, and special desserts and cakes. My mother was a great cook.

On our high holidays and also on Sabbath (Friday night and Saturday) we attended the services at the large orthodox synagogue in our city where we were members of the congregation. All the other members of our family attended the same synagogue.

But occasionally we also liked to participate in the services conducted in the magnificent, very large Neolog or conservative synagogue in our city. Neolog is a Greek word and means "new way." The Neolog synagogue looked like an opera house with balconies.

We went to that synagogue to listen to Dr. Moshe Carmilly-Weinberger, chief rabbi of the Neolog synagogue, who conducted the services. Rabbi Carmilly-Weinberger's services were very special. He had a great operatic voice which resounded throughout the entire synagogue and touched the hearts of all the people. He looked dignified and self-confident. His wife Sarah was a beautiful woman. He was a very inspiring and talented teacher. We learned a lot from him about Judaism. I will never forget it.

Fortunately, as I write, Dr. Moshe Carmilly-Weinberger is still living in New York City with his wife, Rhoda Carmilly. He got his Ph.D. at the University of Budapest in 1934. The same year he was elected as chief rabbi of the Neolog community in Cluj and served until 1944, when he arrived in Palestine on a refugee ship, Kazbek. He dedicated himself to education. From 1951 to 1953, he was the acting director of the department of education and culture of the city of Netanyah in Israel. From 1953 to 1957, he was the principal of the Tchernichovsky High School in Netanya.

Dr. Carmilly-Weinberger was a professor at the Yeshiva University in New York from 1957 to 1975, when he retired as professor emeritus of Jewish studies. He was and still is active in Jewish public life and is an authority on Jewish history and Hebrew culture. He is the author of 13 books. Most recently, he completed his latest book, the Hebrew version of *The History of Jews in Transylvania: 1623-1944* The first edition appeared in the Romanian language in 1994 in Bucharest. The second edition appeared in 1995 in Hungarian in Budapest. It was published in Hebrew in 2003 in Jerusalem, Israel. Among other things, Dr. Carmilly-Weinberger is also the editor of the *Memorial Volume for the Jews in Cluj-Kolozsvár* (New York, 1970; 1988). In 1996 he was awarded the Wilhelm Bacher Memorial Medal for sixty years of Jewish scholarship by the Research Institute of Judaica at the Hungarian Academy of Sciences in Budapest. In 1990 an institute was established in his name, the Dr. Carmilly-Weinberger Institute for Hebrew and Jewish History at the Babes Bolyai University in Cluj-Napoca, the capital of Transylvania in Romania. The institute has 400 students. His bio-bibliography was published in the jubilee volume dedicated to him on his eightieth birthday by the Hebrew University (Jerusalem, 1992).

After many years of separation, I had recent contact with Dr. Carmilly-Weinberger. I have great respect and admiration for him. I am happy that he is still around, still achieving great accomplishments regardless of his advanced age. He is surely young in spirit. I enjoyed talking to him. It evoked old memories of my youth.

Chapter 3

*M*y thoughts are constantly wandering on distant memory lanes. They leave behind our big, old home, the grounds of the Energia engine factory, the railroad tracks, and I travel through time and space to land at my grandparents' place.

I remember my grandparents' huge house with its many spacious rooms furnished with antique solid-wood furniture ornamented by hand carvings; the large, impressive mirrors hanging on the walls in fancy, decorative frames; the heavy brocade curtains hanging over the living room and dining room windows; the vast kitchen equipped with a multitude of cupboards and cabinets, holding the beautiful china sets, everyday dishes, pots and pans, all kinds of glasses, and other household items; the pantry room filled with home-canned jars of jellies, all kinds of preserves, cucumbers, and many other food items.

I was especially fond of the white room with its cheerful white walls and the attractive white furniture in it. But what

I most loved in that room was the black grand concert piano. It was the room of my mother's cousin Margot. She was the youngest of the Salamon girls, the tenth child. Her mother had died after she gave birth to her.

Margot was a pretty girl with a pleasant personality. She attended the music conservatory of the city of Cluj. She was a talented pianist and she played beautiful classical piano music on the black grand piano. Her favorite musical compositions were the Chopin waltzes and Beethoven's "Moonlight Sonata." I loved music in my early childhood. I would listen with fascination to Margot's performances of classical piano music.

As soon as we arrived at my grandparents' home I would run to the white room and if Margot wasn't there, I would sit for a long time at the black concert piano trying to compose my own songs by playing around and experimenting with the different melodies I invented. Those compositions were my personal musical expressions. Sometimes they had to pull me out by force from that room because I refused to leave it. All those happy childhood memories will haunt me forever.

Memories

In the white room
with the black grand piano,
I listened to a solo.
I watched the fingers
move rapidly

from right to left,
from left to right,
hitting the white
and black keys
firmly.
It was my aunt
playing.
The room was filled with
music,
and images started moving
in front of me:
a river, with its gentle ripples,
a quiet summer afternoon,
with birds chirping
and crickets singing,
here and there
a butterfly,
blooming flowers
stretching their stems
and turning their heads
toward the sky.
I saw a cat
through the window,
passing the hollow
old oak
with its shabby cloak;
the dog barked
and chased his enemy away.
I wish I could stay

once more
in the house
of my grandparents,
and meet again
all the friendly tenants
of the yard:
the orchard,
the flowers,
the grass,
the tall Linden trees;
to hear again
the buzzing
of the bees;
to relive
the happy memories,
and the curiosity
of the child.
Farewell
to all of these,
but they still live
in the hidden corners
of the past
where they will
forever last.

Certain childhood memories are imprinted deeply in our minds and they live on, projecting themselves at random times on the screen of our imagination.

I can still see after all these years the old pear tree in my grandparents' yard. It was an old friend delivering its fruits faithfully each year. I can still feel the joy and happiness I experienced in my childhood each September when I collected the big Bartlett pears in my small basket. I rejoiced in the harvest together with my cousins.

The Old Pear Tree

I still remember the old pear tree
standing majestically
in my grandparents' yard
when I, as a small child,
playing with my cousins in the room,
suddenly, flew out of the house fast
like a witch on a broom.
We shook the old tree violently,
waiting for its fruits to fall, impatiently.
We picked up the big pears quickly,
examining each one separately,
admiring their giant size,
uttering shrieks of surprise.
The good old tree
delivered us yearly
its produce faithfully.
We looked up to it with pride,
saying loudly,
"Here is the best friend

of Grandmother's yard."
After all these years,
our laughter mixed with tears,
still echoes in my ears.

My early childhood years were good times for my grandparents and our whole family. Everyone was doing well in their personal lives and also financially.

My grandparents were quite well-to-do. Business was excellent. Moritz Salamon became a highly successful businessman. As I said earlier, he was generous and much beloved.

My grandparents had an active social life. There were frequent parties at their home. At those social events not only my grandparents' clients were present but also our entire family. On those occasions they hired an excellent professional cook to help my grandmother prepare all the special meals for the guests, and it was all served with elegance and good taste.

I also remember my grandparents' estates (farmlands). There were many cows raised on the farms. There were also some chickens, ducks, and geese raised mostly for our family's use, as well as some vegetables. There were many fruit, maple, and Linden trees dispersed all over the farmlands. I recall the rolling green hills around the farmhouses of the estates.

The estates were administered by two of the Salamon sons who lived there. There were also hired workers on the farms. Milk and all kinds of dairy products like cheese, sour cream, yogurt, butter, etc., were produced there.

My grandmother ran a business in the city selling all of those products to the public. My grandparents had two horse-drawn carriages. One was reserved for transporting the products from the farms to their shop in the city.

The other one was a fancier horse-drawn carriage reserved for the transportation of our family members to the farm for our family reunions, which took place mostly in the summer when the weather was good.

I will never forget those reunions when our large family got together, when I could play and run around with my cousins, while we eagerly awaited delicious family meals. Those were good and happy times. There was outdoor cooking. I remember the delicious taste of the grilled meat; the freshly roasted corn on the cob; the fresh milk; and all of the wonderful cheese and sour cream; the delicious apples, pears, and plums picked from the fruit trees.

I can see in my imagination my grandmother preparing homemade ice cream, bringing fresh vegetables from the garden, fresh-baked bread, and cakes from the kitchen. There was lots of laughter and singing.

I loved those rolling hills, the beautiful and colorful wildflowers of all kinds, the luxurious-looking grass, the apple trees, the tall Linden trees standing majestically on the farmlands.

When I was about five, I was given a basket to collect wildflowers. I came back with an empty one. My grandmother asked, "Didn't you find any flowers that you liked?"

"I didn't want to break them because then they might die," I answered.

I was very romantic. My favorite fairly tales were "Cinderella" and "Sleeping Beauty." I remember times when I was running on the hills by the farmhouse imagining that a prince would appear on a white horse at the top of one of those hills and carry me away to his castle and I would become a princess like Cinderella.

Chapter 4

*I*n 1936, when I was in third grade at the elementary school, my grandfather, Salamon Moritz, died as a result of malignant skin cancer. Prior to his death he underwent several extensive surgical procedures. After he passed away, his businesses were taken over and managed by three of his sons. The other two sons were still administering the two estates (the farms) where dairy products were produced.

The big old house was eventually sold and my grandmother moved into an apartment in the center of the city of Cluj and ran the store where the products from the farms were sold to the public. Father tried in vain to persuade her to move into our house and not to work too hard. But she enjoyed working and she liked challenge throughout her life. She had a strong, independent personality and was endowed with lots of energy, self-confidence, and courage, as well as physical and emotional strength. She preferred to be on her own and to take care of the business as long as she could.

Grandmother had a live-in peasant girl, Aniko, who was very loyal and helpful to her doing many chores around the house. My mother also helped occasionally in the store.

My uncle Eugene stayed for a while with Grandmother to keep her company and to give her comfort during her grieving period.

So life went on. We still had our family reunions at the estates like before but we all missed Grandfather, especially Grandmother who grieved for him for a very long time.

As time went on, especially in the mid and late thirties, while Hitler was in power in Germany, the political scene in Romania changed. The Romanian government was drawn to Nazism and Fascism.

King Carol II was the ruling monarch of Romania at that time. In 1937 he nominated Alexandru Cuza, who was the leader of the National Christian, right-wing, anti-Semitic party, as prime minister. That marked the start of anti-Jewish sentiment in the country and in my native city; the beginning of the Jewish persecution.

I was completing fourth grade. Our school system consisted of four grades of elementary school and eight grades of gymnasium or middle and high schools. After completion of elementary school, there was an entrance exam which we had to pass in order to be accepted into the gymnasium. There was another tough exam to pass in order to be accepted in the fifth grade of the gymnasium. At that point, we had to decide whether we would continue in the direction of the sciences or the humanities. And then we selected the appropriate subjects for the school year according to that decision.

After the completion of the eighth grade of gymnasium, there was another very tough exam called the baccalaureate, which was a written and oral exam that lasted for several days. It was the nightmare for all the students. We had to pass this exam in order to be accepted at the universities.

In the gymnasium we had a very intense, difficult curriculum. We studied many subjects and we had several different foreign language requirements. The school was not coeducational; there were gymnasiums for girls and separate ones for boys. In our city there were two gymnasiums for girls, Regina Maria (Queen Mary) and Principesa Ileana (Princess Ileana). I was determined to attend the best one, Regina Maria. There was a hard entrance exam for these schools. You had to make a high grade in this exam in order to be accepted in any of them, especially if you were Jewish.

I was eleven years old when the first anti-Jewish law came into affect. It was called the Law of Numerus Clausus, which meant that only a limited number of Jewish students would be accepted in the gymnasiums, approximately six percent of the entering class. If you were Jewish, you had to have almost a perfect grade in order to be accepted.

I always took my studies seriously. I had high grades throughout all my elementary school years, and I had a very high score in the entrance exam, so I managed to be included in that small percentage of Jewish students.

When I entered Regina Maria Gymnasium, I experienced Jewish discrimination for the first time in my life. All my teachers, including the principal of the school, were strongly anti-Semitic.

On my first day of school, all of us Jewish students were told to stand at the beginning of each class so the teachers could familiarize themselves with the Jews in order to terrorize us. If a Romanian student couldn't answer some question, the Jews were called upon. We had to be well-prepared at all times because we couldn't afford to have any bad grades. We had to have a high grade point average in order to stay in school. Many times we didn't get the grades we deserved because we were Jewish.

We couldn't complain about the injustice we experienced because we would have been persecuted even more. Some non-Jewish students followed the example of their teachers and when we Jewish students came out of school at the end of the day, they threw stones at us and addressed us with humiliating limericks.

After my first day in school, I came home crying and asked my father, "Why do they treat us like that in school? We don't deserve this injustice just because we are Jewish!"

My father said, "I can't tell you why they hate us, but I will give you good advice. Ignore it. Do your best. Make the sacrifice of suffering in silence in order to get your education."

So, in the course of time, I had to accept what I couldn't change. I studied hard. We Jewish students became strong fighters for our education. I had wonderful parents and family. They gave me all the moral support I needed in order to bear the Jewish discrimination in school.

There was one positive aspect to my education at this time; the principal of our school was our composition and Romanian language teacher. Although she didn't like Jews, she always liked my compositions and encouraged me. Because of this, I started writing short stories at age eleven.

In the following years, in 1938 through 1940, anti-Semitism grew steadily in Romania, especially after Hitler annexed Austria to Germany in 1938 and occupied Czechoslovakia in the same year. In 1938, an extreme right-wing, nationalistic, and strongly anti-Semitic party called the Iron Guard became popular. The party recruited members from all over, even approaching students in the gymnasiums. Fortunately, they didn't last for long because King Carol II worried that their increasing popularity threatened his throne. The leader of the Iron Guard, Corneliu Zelea Codreanu, was ultimately arrested and assassinated in prison in 1938. Many Guardists were also killed at that time.

Hitler became even more powerful after the occupation of Poland in 1939 and after the fall of Paris in June 1940. King Carol and his government wanted to be on good terms with Germany, especially after the Romanian government was forced in 1939 to cede to Germany their petroleum production and the country's entire economy.

The Romanian government turned more and more anti-Semitic, trying to please Hitler by adopting his anti-Jewish policies. King Carol was worried about losing his power, his throne, and some of his country's territory if he didn't comply with Hitler's demands. In 1940, the anti-Semitic party, the Iron Guard, which had been vanquished in 1938, came to power again, and was admitted into the government. Their leader, Horia Sima, became undersecretary of state in the Ministry of Education. Anti-Semitism was fully adopted, resulting in the rapid increase of the Jewish persecution. Hundreds of Jews in the Jewish quarters of the capital city of Bucharest were massacred. Anti-Semitism grew stronger and new anti-Jewish laws like the following were introduced:

No marriages were allowed between Jews and Romanians. Breaking the law resulted in severe punishment, like imprisonment up to three years and hefty fines. Some restrictions were established against Jewish participation in public education. Jewish teachers and college professors lost their jobs, and also Jewish employees of public offices were fired. No Jews were allowed to hold important managerial positions. Due to that, my father lost his job at Energia, the engine factory. Our life changed dramatically. We had to leave our beautiful, big house on the Energia grounds and move into an apartment in the city, closer to my grandmother's place.

In late 1940, great political changes took place in Romania. On August 30, 1940, Hitler forced Romania to sign the Vienna Decree, initiated by Galeazzo Ciano, Italian foreign minister and son-in-law of Mussolini, and by Joachim von Ribentropp, German foreign minister. According to this decree Transylvania, a territory enclosed in the heart of Romania, was split in two parts. Its northern part with a population of two million people, including its capital city of Cluj (100,000 population) and seven other major cities were taken away from Romania and were annexed to Hungary. The southern part of Transylvania was left under Romanian rule. This political maneuver by Hitler resulted in Hungary's alliance with Germany.

When, how, and why did that alliance take place? Hungary suffered severe territorial losses after World War I, and this was very much resented, especially the loss of Transylvania. Before World War I, the whole territory of Transylvania had been a province in the Austrio-Hungarian empire. At the end of the war, after the treaty of Trianon was signed on June 4, 1920, in the Trianon palace in Versailles, Transylvania was taken away from Hungary—including its capital city (named Kolozsvár at that time)—and it was annexed to Romania because Romania was allied with the western allies who ultimately defeated Austria-Hungary. They renamed Kolozsvár the city of Cluj, giving it a Romanian name. In addition to that, Hungary also lost another part of its territory which was given to Czechoslovakia. Hungary, now a much smaller country, faced great economical and political difficulties.

Hitler was a shrewd politician and wanted to draw Hungary into the war on his side. He knew that the way he could attract the Hungarians to join him would be to restore some of Hungary's lost territories. After he occupied Czechoslovakia in 1938, he took away Southern Slovakia, which had a population of two million people, and restored it to Hungary in late 1940.

So, naturally, Hungary, being in alliance with Hitler, fully collaborated with Germany and adopted Hitler's anti-Jewish policies.

On September 14, 1940, Admiral Miklos Horthy, who was at that time Hungary's regent, entered the city of Cluj. He rode a white horse and was followed by the Hungarian army. Ironically, Miklos Horty had the title of admiral, while in reality Hungary had no navy. After the treaty of Trianon, Hungary's access to the Adriatic Sea was lost; nevertheless, Miklos Horthy maintained his honorary ghost title.

After the Hungarian occupation, our city of Cluj was renamed Kolozsvár, as it had been called previously.

For us Jewish people, the Hungarian rule brought more disasters, miseries, and worse Jewish persecution because the Hungarian government was strongly drawn to Nazism and Fascism.

Hungary's regent Miklos Horthy was welcomed by Transylvania's Hungarian population. They considered him their hero, responsible for the restoration of Hungary's lost territories. They received him with open arms and gratitude. But the Romanian population was very unhappy. Many people left and went to the southern part of Transylvania which was still under Romanian rule. Many Romanian institutions were closed. Unfortunately, all the Romanian gymnasiums were also closed, including the Regina Maria girls' gymnasium, which I attended.

I was now fourteen. Hungarian gymnasiums for girls and separate ones for boys were opened. The school year always started in September. But in the Hungarian gymnasiums, even fewer Jewish students were accepted; only three percent of the students in the school could be Jewish. If you were

Jewish, you were required to have an almost perfect grade point average in order to be accepted. I was fortunate because I mastered the Hungarian language. It was my first language at home, and Romanian was my second. I also had high grades throughout my two years at the Romanian gymnasium; therefore, I was accepted.

The very limited acceptance of Jewish students in the Hungarian schools posed a serious problem concerning the educational opportunities for other Jewish students. In the Hungarian gymnasium, which I attended for only a very short time, I encountered even worse Jewish discrimination than in the Romanian schools.

After about three weeks in school, another anti-Jewish law was announced, stating that no Jewish students were allowed to study in the Hungarian gymnasiums. Thus, the few of us who had been accepted were suddenly expelled from school, deprived of the opportunity to continue our education. It became crucial to provide continuous education for the Jewish students in our city.

Dr. Moshe Carmilly-Weinberger, chief rabbi of Neolog (Conservative) synagogue, came to our rescue. He approachd Mr. Homan Bálint, the Hungarian minister of education, who happened to be in Kolozsvár at that time, and asked him for an appointment in order to discuss the serious problem of the Jewish students. The appointment was granted.

Rabbi Carmilly-Weinberger led a delegation of the local Jewish communities, both Orthodox and Neolog, to meet

Mr. Homan Bálint. The meeting took place on October 8, 1940, and Rabbi Carmilly-Weinberger obtained written permission from the minister for the establishment of two secondary Jewish schools or gymnasiums, one for girls and one for boys.

After a month of preparation, the two Jewish gymnasiums opened on November 10, 1940. The opening of the schools was a very big event, considering that there had been no Jewish schools in our city since 1927 when the Tarbut Jewish gymnasiums, one for girls and one for boys, were closed by the Romanians. The Tarbut gymnasiums were the largest and best Jewish schools in all of Transylvania. They had been opened in 1921 by the Tarbut Jewish Educational Assocation.

All of the Jewish students were very grateful to Rabbi Moshe Carmilly-Weinberger, who made the reopening of the Jewish schools in our city possible.

I enrolled in the third grade of the girls' gymnasium at the newly established Jewish school. I was pleased because I didn't have to tolerate the discrimination and humiliation I had experienced at the strongly anti-Semitic Romanian and Hungarian schools.

Our school had a good reputation. We had many highly qualified teachers. Some of them were college and university professors who lost their jobs because they were no longer allowed to teach in any public schools. So, they accepted teaching jobs in the Jewish gymnasiums in order to make a living. Actually, over two hundred teachers applied to the schools but there were only forty teaching positions available.

Professor Antal Mark, an outstanding teacher, became the director of our gymnasiums. He had been the former director of the Tarbut Jewish Gymnasiums from 1921 to 1927. Winkler Janka was the principal of our girls' gymnasium. She was also a fine educator and former director of the Tarbut Girls' Gymnasium.

Photo 11 – Jewish Girls' Gymnasium (high school), Magda is back row, center (white bow in her hair)

Our school curriculum included: Bible, Hebrew language, culture, and Jewish History. Our Rabbi Carmilly-Weinberger taught bible and Jewish history. He was a wonderful and dedicated teacher.

We didn't have school on Saturdays. We had to attend the weekly sabbath services at the Neolog synagogue. The students conducted the services by themselves.

The majority of our curriculum was that of the Hungarian educational system and it was naturally conducted in Hungarian. We also had foreign language requirements, like Latin, French, and German. Chemistry, biology, physics, general history, mathematics, philosophy, geography, etc. were taught. The Jewish school became our second home! We were encouraged to participate in the Chaim Nachman Bialik literary activities for boys and the Beruria (Bible figure) literary

הרב דר. משה כרמלי-וינברגר
DR. CARMILLY-WEINBERGER MOSHE FORABBI

Photo 12 - Dr. Moshe Carmilly-Weinberger

activities for girls. Teachers guided all these activities.

We gained an insight into Hungarian history and literature. I enjoyed studying the great Hungarian poets like Ady Endre, Petöfi Sándor, and Arany János. I always loved poetry and participated in many poetry readings at school.

Chapter 5

My father got a job as an accountant at a small, private, Jewish textile factory which manufactured beautiful sweaters among other things. The owner of the factory was a kind man named Kassirer. He liked my father since he was an honest and responsible person. Father's salary was modest but we managed by living very economically. His workplace was some distance from our home, but he usually walked and in summer he rode his bicycle there.

My new school was also further away and I had to walk a good distance back and forth every day. Winter was a challenge because there was lots of snow and cold weather.

It happened that my father's boss was also living with his family at our same apartment house. Our home was on the second floor of the building and the Kassirer's family home was on the first floor. In the course of time, we all became good friends.

At that time I had a thirty-five-year-old piano teacher, Mr. Stern, whom Uncle Eugene discovered. He had become a concert pianist at age twelve, being exceptionally talented, but due to the new laws, Jewish artists could not perform in public. So he was forced to give piano lessons in order to make a living. He was such an outstanding artist but could not share his talents with the public because of his Jewish faith. It was a great privilege to have such a wonderful music instructor, although he was a strict teacher. I learned a lot from him and I respected him. I loved playing the piano and practiced for hours since I wanted to be well prepared for my lessons. This wasn't hard for me because I had a great passion for music. In the course of time, I became his favorite pupil. Unfortunately, Mr. Stern was later killed in the Holocaust.

Photo 13 – Magda , 16, with her piano teacher, Mr. Stern. Magda is in the center behind her teacher.

Music played a big role in my life and also in the life of my parents and family. From an early age I was introduced to the magical world of music. My parents were enthusiastic opera lovers. They attended performances at our magnificent local opera house where excellent singers performed. From October to May there were opera performances three nights every week and one afternoon performance every Sunday.

At age twelve I was introduced to my first opera which was *Carmen* by Georges Bizet. I loved it. After that wonderful experience, I also became an opera lover. During my teenage years I liked to go to the afternoon performances, which had reduced prices and affordable tickets for students.

Some of my favorite operas were: *The Barber of Seville* by Gioacchino Rossinni, *Madame Butterfly* by Giacomo Puccini, *Faust* by Charles Gounod, *Rigoletto* by Giuseppe Verdi, *Pagliacci* by Ruggiero Leoncavallo, *Cavalleria Rusticana* by Pietro Mascagni, and *Don Giovanni*, by Wolfgang Amadeus Mozart.

I also liked to listen to the musical programs aired on the radio and the ones performed at the concert hall in our city. My favorite musical compositions were: the *Fifth Symphony* by Ludwig Van Beethoven and *The Afternoon of a Faun*, by Claude Debussy. One of my favorite composers of classical music was Chopin. I liked to play the Chopin waltzes and mazurkas on my piano.

One day I was sitting at my piano and playing a Chopin mazurka. My father came in with his violin, stood behind me, and began to accompany me. He also liked this particular mazurka. I enjoyed playing music with my father. At one point, he stopped me and said, "Don't just follow the correct notes of this beautiful composition, but put more feeling into it and try to express what Chopin conveyed in his music." Then he demonstrated to me what he meant by performing the mazurka on his violin. He played it beautifully with much feeling. I will never forget that experience. I suddenly understood what he was trying to tell me. From that time on, I paid a great deal of attention to the interpretation of any of the musical compositions I performed.

I also frequented the theatre with my parents at the local opera house. Excellent actors performed there. I will never forget the performance of the play *Crime and Punishment*, based on the novel of the famous Russian writer, Fyodor Dostoyevski, or the wonderful performance of *The Tragedy of Man*, which was written by Madács Imre, a well-known Hungarian playwright.

My native city offered a great variety of cultural entertainment. We had a big university library where you could find a good selection of books of all kinds. Our city had both a university and medical school.

We also had our private library at home. Both of my parents loved to read. We had a sizable bookcase with a protective glass door and a lock and key. A wide selection of books was enclosed in that bookcase, purchased by my father through the years. Some of them had leather bindings. We had a fine collection of novels by the famous European writers, for example: *War and Peace* and *Anna Karenina* by Leo Tolstoi, the most famous Russian writer; the *Magic Mountain*, *Doctor Faustus*, and *Joseph and His Brothers*, by Thomas Mann, the leading German writer; and many other classics. Hebrew prayer books were also enclosed in our bookcase. Our library also contained a collection of books on history, science, philosophy, and psychology. In addition to all that, we also had poetry books of the great Hungarian poets like Ady Eudre, Petöfi Sandor, Arany János; as well as the French poet, Paul Verlaine; the works of the famous German poets, Johan Wolfgang Von Goethe and Cristoph Schiller; the poetry of Alexander Pushkin, Russia's greatest poet, author of *Eugene Onegin*, a verse novel; and the poems of George Cosbuc, the greatest Romanian poet. Many classical novels for young readers and the fairy tales of Grimm and of Hans Christian Anderson were also included in our library collection.

During my teenage years, I read with pleasure the great classic novels. Among my favorites were *The Count of Monte Cristo* by Alexander Dumas, *The Invisible Man* by H.G. Wells, *The Hunchback of Notre Dame* by Victor Hugo, and *Gone with the Wind* by Margaret

Photo 14 – Herman Mozes

70

Mitchell. I became an avid reader just like my parents who inspired me.

All these books enriched my life spiritually, which in turn enlarged my horizon, my thinking, and led to the development of my inner resources.

Reading also enhanced my cultural education. My father instilled in me a great interest in reading books from early childhood, a habit which has followed me through a lifetime.

I was fortunate to have such loving and caring parents who guided me and educated me to the best of their abilities. They set a good example for me to follow.

As for as my social life, I had some good friends and we spent pleasant times together. All of them were goal-oriented, serious, and ambitious young people. We had inspiring discussions about knowledge, music, and self-improvement.

In my teenage years I encountered hard times, great political changes, upheavals, and anti-Jewish discrimination. Due to all that I was also serious and goal-oriented. My highest goal was to go to medical school and become a physician so I could help people and be a useful member of society. I also began writing short stories and by the time I was sixteen I had a book-length manuscript of various short stories I had written through the years. Some stories had very somber subjects. Others were dreamlike. I created all kinds of characters in my stories and follow their lives. Dream and reality were intertwined to some extent in all my stories. I kept my manuscript locked in our library bookcase.

I also was quite involved with my fencing training. I was a tough fighter like my instructor uncle, who gave me a good example, and I won many gold cups in competitions.

In addition, I had to spend time on my academic studies and on piano practice. It was time-consuming to walk back and forth to school and to my other activities, because we didn't have a car. I also had to set aside time to help my mother in the many chores at home.

In winter, I liked to ice-skate on a lake which was located at one of our city's most beautiful parks. But it involved forty minutes of walking to get there.

In summer, I loved to swim and play tennis, as my uncle was also a tennis instructor. We had a big public swimming pool in our city. Near the swimming pool flowed the river Szamos. Often I also swam in the river and thoroughly enjoyed the challenge. The summer in our city lasted only for about six weeks, during which time we encountered many cool days, so I tried to take advantage of every warm, sunny day that was favorable for swimming. It was also customary to hike on pleasant days. We had mountains close by.

In 1941, when I was fifteen, Grandmother had a serious heart attack. After she recovered, my father insisted that she move into our home and give up her apartment and the management of the store where dairy products from the farmlands were sold to the public. He thought it would be too stressful for her, considering her health condition. Our family physician was very concerned about her. He said that Grandmother should have lots of rest and not much exertion if she wanted to stay alive, because she had a serious heart condition.

I adored my grandmother and cherished the wonderful times we had together. She was my great friend. We took wonderful care of her. She loved my mother and Mother was also attached to her, especially since she had lost her own mother at fifteen.

The year 1942 brought additional hardships to us Jewish people. New severe anti-Jewish regulations were introduced. Jewish people could not employ any Hungarian household help. So Aniko, Grandmother's peasant maid, wasn't supposed to help my mother anymore. There were lots of chores in the house, including the washing of clothes by hand and carrying products from the markets and stores in baskets. We didn't have cars so we had to walk back and forth. Also, help was needed in the store where the products from the farm were delivered.

But regardless of the restrictions, Aniko remained loyal to us. She was a good person and she came occasionally to help us out. The Hungarian authorities could have punished her if they had found out that she broke the rule. But Aniko was willing to take the risk. She couldn't let us down.

Another painful anti-Jewish regulation was the confiscation of Jewish properties and businesses. A Jewish owner could not keep his business unless he hired a non-Jewish Hungarian trustee who practically had control over it. Sooner or later the business was taken over by the trustee and he became the owner. Due to that kind of arrangement, many Jewish people lost their businesses, their assets, and the source of their income.

Mr. Kassirer, the Jewish owner of the textile factory where my father worked, was forced to hire a non-Jewish, Hungarian trustee and later on ended up losing his business, which was, of course, taken over by the trustee. Due to that, my father lost his job.

Another very disturbing anti-Jewish regulation was the confiscation of our radios so that we ceased to have any communication with the outside world and were kept in darkness, not being informed about the fate of the Jews who were under Hitler's rule. If we had known what horrible crimes were being committed against the Jewish people, perhaps we would have done something to prevent being caught in the web of disaster.

Towards the end of 1942, when I was sixteen, my grandmother died. She was seventy-two years old. She passed away at our home. I remember that day. It is still fresh in my memory.

How could I ever forget my dear grandmother? We were such good friends. She always took time to listen to me and give the best advice and guidance she could think of. Now that I have grandchildren of my own, I understand fully the deep affection she felt for me.

I admired her keen intellect, her exceptional physical strength, her ambitious yet kind nature, and her great love and devotion to her family. She was a hard-working woman, tireless, charged continuously with high energy.

Unfortunately, at age seventy-one, she was struck by a debilitating heart ailment. She spent the last year of her life at our home, confined most of the time to a chair. It was painful for me to see her suffer so much. She had frequent, serious heart attacks, sometimes accompanied by a high fever. She often told me that the reason she kept on fighting for her survival was to be with her family and me a little longer.

A week before her death she knew the end was near. The following dialogue took place between us at her bedside on the day she passed away.

The Last Hour

"Come, my child,
can you see that black shadow
by the window?"
"No, there isn't anything there,
dear Grandmother."
"I can see distinctly a dark figure
waiting for me ...
There he sits on the window frame.
He knows that he will win his game."
"Grandmother, dear Grandmother,
it is only your fever."
"No, there is no mistake.
I can see death's outline
even when I am wide awake ...
He waited for me a whole year.

Sometimes he was so near
that I could hear him whisper in my ear.
'Soon you will be mine.'
Come here, my dear granddaughter,
sit upon my bed.
Put your palm upon my burning head.
I know this is my last day,
so listen to what I have to say ...
I was once young, pretty, and strong,
and filled with so much energy.
I thought the whole world was just for me.
I married early,
and dedicated my life to my family.
I loved my husband dearly;
we were happy.
I raised your father
and your uncle decently.
Now I will join your grandfather, finally.
And even after death,
love will keep us company ...
Give me your hand, my loved one.
Let us say to each other, 'Good-bye.'
Keep me always in your memory
as the years go by."
"Grandmother, Grandmother,
Please don't die!
I love you so ..."
"My dear child, don't cry,
someday we all must go."

In 1943, the situation for the Jewish people became even worse. The Hungarian government proclaimed severe new anti-Jewish laws: the confiscation of estates and businesses owned by Jews.

As a result, a special Hungarian police called Gendarmes appeared at both estates of my late grandfather, Moritz Salamon, where two of his sons lived and managed the farms. The Gendarmes forced them to leave the farmlands at gunpoint, telling them: "Either you get out of here or else we will shoot you if you resist!" So both sons of my late grandfather were chased away and the police confiscated the two estates with everything in them. In just one day, everything was lost, representing many years of hard work and effort.

What right did the Hungarians have to treat us like that? We were citizens of that country. Even my great-grandparents were born in Kolozsvár (formerly Cluj), the capital of Transylvania. They robbed us like bandits. My late grandmother's store in the city was taken away. Many Jewish landowners faced the same fate as our family.

Many times I have thought that at least my grandparents, who had passed away, didn't have to experience those painful events. Life became more and more difficult for us. The next phase of Jewish persecution was the confiscation of Jewish businesses. This was the time when the so-called trustees, whom the Jewish owners had been forced to hire, took over the Jewish businesses. The government allowed, even encouraged, this wholesale robbery of these businesses. The other two businesses of my late grandfather, the alcohol factory and the flourmill, were confiscated as well. After that happened, the three Salamon sons who were running those businesses moved with their families to Bucharest, located in the southern part of Romania and still under Romanian rule. They established themselves there, having somehow managed to take along some money with them. Later they emigrated to Latin America and settled in Buenos Aires. In the course of time, they became very well-to-do and established a joint banking business. They inherited my grandfather's talent in business.

Toward the end of 1943, we faced very hard times. My father was forced to take three poorly paying jobs in order for us to exist. Very often he worked at home until late at night. He provided bookkeeping and accounting services for some of his Hungarian friends who owned businesses. Those were very kind people. They wanted to help my father by giving him work but he had to do his work at our home, because as a Jew he couldn't work in public anymore. This rule was spelled out in the text of the anti-Jewish law.

What his Hungarian friends were doing was illegal. They were not supposed to give any financial assistance to Jews. But they knew my father and our family well and they felt great compassion for us. They were willing to take the risk of being punished if it was discovered that they were helping us. They were decent and honest people who didn't like what was happening to us. Their actions were commendable. Fortunately, the authorities never found out what they did, so they escaped punishment. Yet there were others among the population who hated Jews to such an extent that they rejoiced in our misery. They didn't mind taking over properties created and developed by Jewish owners through many years of hard work. Often, the efforts of a lifetime were invested in those businesses.

It was convenient to attain instant wealth by robbing others and it was done with the approval of the Hungarian government. I call this *stealing in grand style*. The government also committed other terrible injustices toward us by dismissing the Jewish people from their jobs in order to give jobs to the unemployed non-Jewish citizens of the country. We were also citizens of that country, yet we were deprived of our rights because of our religion. Anti-Semitism became popular, approved, and justified.

It was convenient for the Hungarian leaders and Nazis to blame all of the political and economic difficulties existing in their country on the Jews and this way, distract the public from the truth by using us as scapegoats.

There were many Jewish professional people in the country—physicians, lawyers, businessmen, artists, writers, musicians, scientists, college professors, etc.—who had contributed a great deal to the country's economic and cultural life, who were wronged by being deprived of their livelihood and of their rights to practice their professions.

We Jewish people who experienced persecution and discrimination learned to excel in our education and in the professions we selected for ourselves. We strove to be successful. Persecution made our lives harder, and therefore we developed in ourselves a strong, fighting spirit and a determination to rise to the top despite all the obstacles we faced. We became successful in our professions. We also tried to select professions which were needed so that we could become useful to people and offer our help to society.

Maybe our inner strength, our strong fighting spirit, and our willingness to work hard and put maximum effort into all of our endeavors and education stirred up envy in many people. And when those people had the opportunity to take away from us the fruits of our labor, they did it without any guilt or conscience. They ignored all of our contributions to our native country. They were the silent contributors to the tragedy of the Jewish people.

Chapter 6

*T*he year 1944 brought catastrophic events to us Jewish people, starting the prelude to the Holocaust. On March 19, 1944, Hitler occupied Hungary and his troops marched into Budapest, the capital city. Then on March 27, 1944, the German troops entered the northern part of Transylvania, including the city of Kolozsvár. It was a horrifying event. We Jewish people were terrified, wondering what would happen to us next.

Why did the German occupation take place? What were the political circumstances that led to the German occupation of Hungary? Hungary made an alliance with Germany during World War II when Hitler transferred the northern part of Transylvania including the city of Cluj and seven other major cities to Hungary.

Thus Hungary participated in the Russian offensive in 1941, helping Germany in that war. But in 1943 when the German troops surrendered in Stalingrad and the Hungarian

Army was also defeated, having had serious losses, and when later on, in early July of 1943, the Allies landed in Sicily and brought about the end of the Fascist regime of Mussolini in Italy, Hungary wanted to get out of the war and establish a peace treaty with the Western Allies. Eventually, the secret of Hungary's planned peace agreement with the Allies was discovered. Hitler was angry with his satellite and in order to keep Hungary from making any such arrangements, he invaded the country. At that time, Miklos Horthy was still Regent of Hungary.

Hitler planned to establish a pro-German, puppet government in Hungary under total German control. He demanded that Horthy form a new government. Horthy complied and set up an extreme right-wing anti-Semitic government which fully adopted Nazi Germany's policies.

The head of the government was former Hungarian Ambassador Sztójai Döme, a great anti-Semite. Other key members of the government were Jáross Andor and Endre László, who later was called the Hungarian Eichman. He was a terrible anti-Semite who passionately hated the Jewish people.

The anti-Semitic, Nazi-controlled government and the presence of the German troops was a hellish and frightening experience for us Jewish people. No one was prepared for what was coming. On March 28, 1944, just one day after the occupation of our city, 150 wealthy, local Jewish families were arrested by the Gestapo and by the Gendarmes (Hungarian special police). Their homes were looted. They were also tortured and forced to reveal the secret hiding places of their other assets. The Gendarmes assisted the Gestapo in their criminal acts. They had lists with the names and addresses of the victims. It was also sad that some of our local German anti-Semites were leading the Gestapo and the Gendarmes to some of those Jewish homes.

The Gestapo set up their headquarters at the luxurious New York Hotel, and also in the villa of a wealthy Jewish family.

They arrested twenty-eight members of the administrative boards of the Jewish congregations and some of the leaders of the Jewish communities. They also arrested Dr. Joseph Fischer, a lawyer and the president of the local Neolog Jewish communities. He was also the president of the National League of the Transylvanian Jews and former Romanian parliamentary representative.

But after a few days, Dr. Fischer was released form jail. Dr. Strohschneider, the Gestapo commander, set him free so that he could form a Judenrat (Jewish Council). Fischer was also ordered to present himself daily to Dr. Strohschneider and to Dr. Roeder in order to get instructions from them. He was not allowed to have any communication with the Hungarian authorities.

Dr. Fischer, following the orders of the Germans, established the Jewish Council and became its chairman. The Jewish Council members who were selected were prominent local professional people of the Jewish communities who were dedicated participants in Jewish education and welfare.

Among them was Dr. Moshe Carmilly-Weinberger, chief rabbi of our local Neolog community, and Chief Rabbi Akiva

Glasner of our local orthodox community. Other members included Dr. E. Marton, chief editor of our local, leading Jewish newspaper *Uj Kelet* (New Dawn); Dr. Joseph Fenichel, chief physician of our local Jewish hospital; Engineer Gyula Klein, chairman of the Education Committee of the Jewish Community, and Zsigmond Léb, president of the orthodox Jewish congregations.

The role of the Jewish Council was to keep in touch with the local Jewish communities and with the Jewish population of our city, keeping them informed about what was going on and relating to them the instructions given to Chairman Joseph Fischer by the Gestapo commander.

The office of the Jewish Council was established at the Neolog Jewish community's office. The council had a well-organized system of communication with the various Jewish communities through district representatives. The council divided our city into forty districts and for each district, one Jew was assigned to be the district representative. The representatives received the news and instructions from the council's office and shared the information with their districts.

Meanwhile other anti-Jewish regulations came into affect. Jews were not allowed to travel on trains or any other public transportation. That way, we were denied any escape from the hellish environment soon created.

Shopping at the market was also curtailed for us. Jews were allowed to shop at the market only for a period of one hour daily for their alimentary products and exclusively in the afternoon. By that time, the best selections were gone. The non-Jews had bought them up earlier.

Posters were distributed announcing that there would be curfews applied to Jews. After 6:00 p.m. no Jews were allowed to be on the streets.

The Hungarian police chief, Hollosy Kuty, announced that Jews must submit lists of their jewelry and the amount of money they owned. He declared that all silver and gold jewelry would be confiscated except for wedding rings. He also said that we would only be allowed to keep a specified amount of money—another robbery. Gradually we were separated from all our assets.

When we heard that decree, my father was determined to save some of our heirloom pieces of jewelry including a necklace with a locket decorated with miniature rubies and diamonds. It had belonged to my great-grandmother on my father's side. He also wanted to save my mother's engagement ring, some gold watches and bracelets, gold chains, a silver pocket watch, and my first earrings with their small diamonds which had been given to me by Grandmother Rose. In order to be on the safe side, my father also included his and my mother's wedding rings. He placed all this jewelry in a metal safe and late at night when everybody was asleep, he buried it in the yard next to a big tree hoping that nobody would discover it. Miraculously, it remained there until the end of World War II when my mother unburied it. I am fortunate to have all these heirloom pieces of jewelry.

My father also wanted to preserve some of our family photos. He selected among them the fourteen most meaningful ones and gave them to his Hungarian friend, Mr. Rimotzi, for safekeeping.

Mr. Rimotzi was my father's favorite chess partner. Both of them were excellent and passionate players. My father enjoyed playing chess with people who were astute, and Mr. Rimotzi was one of his most challenging opponents. His daughter, Viola Rimotzi, was the main ballet dancer at our local opera house.

My father was wise to entrust Mr. Rimotzi with our photos. I am deeply grateful to have them, considering that our house was looted after we were deported to the Ghetto in our city. All the beautifully framed photos in our home were taken and all the others placed in our drawers were also gone, along with all of our belongings.

While all these tragic things happened to us, I had to keep my spiritual strength and bear all our trials and awful challenges, focusing my attention as best I could on my studies. It wasn't easy to do that.

It was also getting difficult for my parents to pay for my piano lessons. Mr. Stern, my piano teacher, didn't want me to discontinue them and offered to reduce to half-price the payments for my lessons. I was his favorite pupil and progressing so well. I was very happy that I could continue taking lessons from my wonderful teacher. I loved music and my piano.

Through all the years of my childhood and young adolescence, I continued my fencing training with my uncle. Until 1943, I participated in many fencing competitions, competing with boys and winning gold cups. My uncle was so proud of me.

◆　◆　◆

As we lived with great fear and anxiety, an unexpected humiliation hit us. In April, 1944, all Jewish people, above six years of age, were forced to wear a yellow Star of David, the symbol of Judaism, attached to our clothing. We were instructed to cut out the star from a yellow canvas material. It had to be about ten inches in diameter. We had to sew it securely on our clothing and walk on the streets with that sign of discrimination, so that everyone could see the stamp of our religion. The yellow color of the star, selected by the Germans and Hungarians, symbolized the "dirty Jew," the tarnishing of our religion. We also were obliged to write in the middle of the star in big capital letters, "JEW." Public authorities circled the streets to make sure that the yellow stars were well secured on our garments. It was highly punishable to walk the streets without wearing the Star of David. If it was found that the star was not securely enough sewn to our clothing, according to the regulations, we had to pay a stiff monetary penalty for it, yet another way of robbing us.

It was emotionally painful and very humiliating to be discriminated against in such a cruel way. It was also dangerous because some Jewish people were beaten up by the Gendarmes, the German SS soldiers, and by some anti-Semitic factions of the population. Many times we were also laughed at and ridiculed.

We lived in constant fear from that time on. We were scared when we left our homes, shopping for necessities. We tried to severely limit our ventures to the streets. Sometimes I dared to go outside and walk the streets for one hour without wearing the Star of David. My parents were very concerned about this. But I wanted to experience freedom, even risking my life for it. If I had been stopped on those occasions and asked to show my identification card, I would have been in great trouble because our cards listed our religion. Fortunately, I always got away with it and that pleased me. Why did I do it? Because it was extremely painful to be treated so unjustly and cruelly just for being Jewish and I felt that it was inhumane and evil.

The Yellow Star

With tight lips
we had to bear
our humiliation.
Upon our chests
we had to wear
the yellow star
of discrimination,
so that everyone could see
from afar
the stamp of our religion.
We were avoided
like the plague.
In the eyes of the wicked
we were a disgrace
to the human race,
the cancer of society
destined to be excised
from the face of the earth.

We were accused to be the cause
of all the ills,
pain, and misery
of the country we lived in.
Our sin was our belief in God,
our guilt was our passion
for harmony.
We were condemned
to annihilation
without justice, mercy, or pity.
Compassion and love
were dead,
hatred and cruelty
ruled instead.
This is the story
of the yellow star;
the prelude
to the mad ambitions
of an insane barbarian.
To hide the truth,
to contaminate with lies
the heart of youth,
and to sentence to death
six million
innocent Jews.

But the Yellow Star was just the beginning of a much more severe and awful discrimination, which was directed towards us in the following months.

The local Hungarian newspapers were full of anti-Jewish articles, trying to instill hatred against us. All the propaganda writings were full of poison. The main articles in the papers concerned the Jews. We became the scapegoats of the government. We were constantly victimized. The worst thing was that we had to keep quiet and endure all the pain and humiliation because otherwise we would have been persecuted even more. As a young person, I suffered a great deal not being able to fight back. It was too dangerous to open my mouth and protest.

If I had not mastered some restraint, I could have been put in prison, beaten up, or killed. As a Jew I ceased to have any rights. Anti-Semitism was perhaps popular as it offered to the unemployed the jobs and income taken away from the Jews. Therefore, some part of the population had seen some benefits in hating Jews and enjoyed material gains by persecuting them. It represented instant wealth, instant income. The injustice was therefore justified. But what about the plight and sacrifices made by the Jewish people in order to build up their businesses, to get the necessary education to qualify for high managerial positions, and to achieve success in their respective careers and professions? How would all those anti-Semites have felt if all that hatred had been directed towards them? They forgot to think about not doing to others what they wouldn't have wanted done to themselves. While there were also many good people among the population who didn't like what was happening to us, unfortunately, there were also lots of silent collaborators who had seen an advantage for themselves in the suffering and the robbing of the Jews. The inflammatory newspaper articles incited and encouraged them to become hateful, losing their human decency.

Many doctors, lawyers, journalists, artists, scientists, and other professional people were Jewish in our city. They were no longer allowed to offer their services to the public. What a loss to humanity. Hatred is such a destructive, evil force.

While all these things were happening through April 1944, I was in the seventh grade of gymnasium, and I was eighteen years old.

There were rumors that in the following month, a ghetto would be established for the Jewish people living in our city and in the surrounding area. The Hungarian anti-Semitic newspapers announced joyfully that this kind of arrangement was occurring already through other cities in Hungary, but we didn't believe that it was true, nor that it would happen in our city. But we were very wrong in our assumptions.

The Jewish Council tried to intervene and prevent the formation of a ghetto by sending a petition to the mayor soliciting his help and asking him to oppose the creation of a ghetto.

The Jewish Council also entrusted Dr. Carmilly-Weinberger, chief rabbi of the Neolog synagogue, to contact some Christian church leaders, asking their help. Rabbi Carmilly-Weinberger approached Imre Sándor, the representative of the Roman Catholic bishop; Miklós Józan, Unitarian bishop and member of the Hungarian Parliament;

and János Vásárhelyi, Bishop of the Reformed Church. Rabbi Carmilly-Weinberger asked all these spiritual people to persuade the mayor and the town council of Kolozsvár to come to our assistance, but unfortunately nothing helped. All the efforts failed because the Hungarian government of Endre László was strongly determined to follow their Nazi policies and carry through the establishment of the ghetto at the outskirts of our city at the site of an old, abandoned brick factory near the railroad station.

At that time, changes also occurred concerning the Jewish Council. The Gestapo didn't want to deal anymore with rabbis and didn't approve of their presence in the Jewish Council. As a result, Chief Rabbi Carmilly-Weinberger and Chief Rabbi Glasner were removed from the council and replaced with other members approved by the Gestapo. Dr. Joseph Fischer maintained his position of Chairman.

The Jewish Council warned the Jewish population about the serious possibility of the establishment of a ghetto and advised them to be prepared for that, but the Jewish people in Kolozsvár didn't believe that it could happen to them.

However, the Jewish Council took it seriously and made arrangements for food and drug provisions in case the ghetto was to be erected. We couldn't believe that discrimination would take such proportions. Maybe we believed in miracles. Maybe we believed that we were going to be spared from that ultimate humiliation, and anyway, even if it was true, what could we have done? Our movements were already so limited at that time. Maybe we should have left

Hungary before all that happened, but it is not easy to leave everything behind. We always hoped that things would change somehow for the better. We had been born and had lived in our city for generations. It was our home.

Because of all the insecure, difficult, and trying situations which all of us Jewish people were facing, our school principal and our teachers in our Jewish gymnasiums decided to conduct all our final exams earlier than usual. They were scheduled for the middle of April. I took all my exams at that time and completed my seventh grade of gymnasium.

I didn't know that the awful tribulations I would shortly be subjected to would delay the continuation of my education until the end of fall 1945. In May, terribly shocking and devastating events happened to us Jewish people.

The Hungarian Gendarmes appeared, going from street to street, from house to house, forcing Jewish people out of their homes. The Gendarmes carried along their lists of Jewish people, and their addresses. Our street was one of the first ones they came to.

It was the fourth of May, a beautiful day in spring with sunshine and blue sky. I was at home with my mother. My father was away. He had gone with his bicycle to pick up some accounting work from a Hungarian friend's office. The friend was a good and kind man who was sad to see what was happening to us Jewish people. It was early afternoon. We heard a commotion in the yard of our apartment house. We looked out through our dining room window and were terrified to see the Hungarian Gendarmes chasing our Jewish neighbor from his apartment downstairs, together with his wife and their two little girls. It was my father's former boss, Mr. Kassirer, the one-time owner of the textile factory where my father used to work. We were surprised at the rough behavior of the Gendarmes who were brutally pushing the family outside.

At that moment, I wanted to believe that somehow miraculously they would bypass our place, and we would be exempted from such rough treatment, that we would not be driven out of the home where we had been living for a number of years, that we would not be robbed of all our belongings.

But then, I heard the footsteps of the Gendarmes climbing up the stairs, heading for our apartment. The special Hungarian police collaborated totally with Hitler. They wore helmets decorated with cock's feathers. Small bells were attached to the heels of their highly polished boots. I could hear the sound of their bells as they climbed the stairs. My mother and I were horrified, possessed by fear. They broke into our home, pushing us around and giving us only a few minutes to pack some clothes. We had a small suitcase into which my mother threw some underwear and a few pieces of clothing. I tried to tell one of the Gendarmes that my father was not at home and suggested they should wait; he should be home any minute, but I met deaf ears. They were hollering, "Hurry, hurry, fast, fast, out!" I was so shocked. I was thinking, *What should I take along which would be most precious?* I had to make a fast decision. I pulled out from our library bookcase my book of short stories, which I had started to write when I was eleven years old. My book was my spiritual friend. I considered it a part of myself. I was holding my book close to my chest, protecting it from harm.

One of the Gendarmes looked at me and asked, "What are you holding there?"

"It is my book of short stories which is very dear to me and I would like to take it along."

"Can I see it? Let me look at it."

I was naïve and innocent. I thought that he might have some decency. He took it from me and tore it into pieces. I could see the title page lying on the floor— *Short Stories*, by Magda Mozes. I was speechless. I felt that a part of me was torn apart and had died. I was appalled at the cruelty of the malicious act. I didn't dare voice my indignation and the anger I felt. I had to control my emotions. I was thinking, *You can kill my book, but not my spirit or thoughts. I will reconstruct my book in my mind. One day, I will have my own book again.*

I never can forget the emotional pain and suffering I felt. We were pushed out of our home and our house was looted. Everybody could go in and take what they wanted, including our non-Jewish neighbors. Outside, the open trucks were waiting for us. Already a number of people were on it, including Mr. Kassirer with his family and others. I was praying to God that my father would show up. It would be terrible to leave him behind. My prayers were heard. I saw my father coming home on his bicycle. He spotted us on the truck. He threw his bicycle to the side of the house and jumped up on the truck. He didn't have a chance to take any extra clothing along, except what he had on. But at least we were together.

As I was standing on the truck, a gentle breeze was teasing my hair. I felt the sweet scent of some blooming spring flowers. Spring was my favorite season. Everyone enjoyed the month of May which brought warmer weather after the harsh, cold winter months. But on that beautiful, much-awaited spring day, my heart was filled with sadness. I looked at our house and I said good-bye to my childhood and young teenage years. I felt that my life would never be the same. I was scared and worried about what other tragic surprises and emotional tortures were waiting for us in the future. I was concerned about my parents and family members in our city who also were taken along on that nightmarish, horrifying journey.

Finally our trucks and the other ones loaded with Jewish people from the street, also chased from their homes, started moving along, taking us to the ghetto located at the outskirts of the city.

Chapter 7

The ghetto presented a serious health hazard to all of us. Primitive tents were hastily erected for us. We were 18,000 people concentrated in the territory of the ghetto, including Jews from Kolozsvár and the surrounding areas. We slept on the bare ground in those tents.

The camp was surrounded by a barbed-wire fence and by armed Hungarian Gendarmes. There was a gate at the entrance to the ghetto. Across from the gate was an office with Gendarmes dressed in civilian clothes. Well-known, wealthy Jewish people whose names were on the lists of the Gendarmes were taken into that office. They were tortured and forced to reveal their hidden assets. There were women, men, and old people among them. They were badly beaten and asked to confess where they were hiding their valuables from the authorities who wanted to rob the Jews before the Germans could do it. Fortunately, our family and many others didn't fall into the wealthy category. We had already been robbed previously by the Hungarians of our very modest means and incomes. Therefore, we were totally impoverished when we entered the gate of the ghetto. Nevertheless, everyone was checked and robbed, even of the small things we took along. No money or jewelry could be kept. My father was pleased that he had buried our jewelry earlier.

There were some people who had created secret compartments in their clothing long before the Gendarmes took them from their homes. They had cut slits in their coats or in other clothing, creating small pockets where they could hide some jewelry pieces or some money. The pockets were then closed with a number of stitches. Others tried to hide valuables in their shoes, having had secret places built into them.

Life in the ghetto was almost intolerable. The Gendarmes were rough and brutal towards us; they used foul language, physical and mental abuse, and torture. Beatings were not uncommon. They behaved just like the Nazis in Germany.

The Gestapo assigned the Jewish Council to distribute the food to us in the ghetto. Our food consisted of half a bread loaf for a family and a bowl of bean soup per person. We had to stand in line to receive it at the assigned distribution locations in the camp. We also had to stand in line to use the outdoor toilets, which consisted of holes in the ground with primitive wooden seats. Sometimes the Gendarmes derived some sadistic pleasure from singling out a person who was standing in line for the toilet and forbidding that person to use the facility.

I remember the day when an old lady was standing behind me, waiting in line. The Gendarme pulled her out. She was begging him to let her go because she had an urgent need to use the toilet. He yelled at her, telling her, "You dirty, Jewish old hag, piss and shit in your pants." The poor woman did just that. She was terribly embarrassed and terrified while the Gendarme made fun of her.

When I saw such humiliation inflicted upon an innocent person, I felt anger, rage, and deep sadness. Tears rolled down my face. It was so hard to keep silent and yet, silence was my only protection from harm.

We had no running water in the ghetto. Twice a week we were given pails and were accompanied by the armed Gendarmes to a water faucet on the outskirts of the city where we filled our pails with water, carrying them back. The water was precious to us because of its shortage. Therefore, we had to use it sparingly. Only a very minimal amount was used for washing our clothing or ourselves. Most of it was reserved for drinking in order to quench our thirst.

I had long, thick braids of chestnut-brown hair. For hygienic reasons, I put up my braids, twisting them around my head, and fastened them to my scalp with bobby pins. That kind of hairstyle was called the Gretchen Hairdo. It became very difficult to wash my hair because of our water shortage. Using soap was impractical. Sometimes a good, strong rainfall was welcomed for washing purposes. We could collect the rain to some extent. The problem was that we didn't have enough reserve clothing. If things got wet, it was difficult to dry them.

Considering all those circumstances, we could not maintain adequate hygienic conditions.

We didn't have any facilities for people who became seriously ill. Neither the Gestapo nor the Hungarian police were very helpful in situations like that. It was extremely difficult to obtain permission from them to let the people who needed immediate medical assistance be taken out of the ghetto in order to get help. Neither was the ghetto equipped with sufficient medication. By the time you got help, you could find yourself half dead.

The Jewish Council appointed Endre Balázs, a Jewish lawyer, as commander of the ghetto. There were a number of Jewish professional people and leaders of the former local community centers participating in the Jewish Council of the ghetto. But it was very hard for them to deal with the German or the Hungarian authorities in order to improve our situation. They got their orders from the Gestapo and they had to notify us of what was happening—about the next steps assigned to us by the German authorities.

We all were upset living under such conditions and under such inhumane treatment. The fear of the unknown was devastating. We asked ourselves: *How long will this situation last? What will ultimately happen to us?* We were living under circumstances that deteriorated everyday.

I told my parents that maybe we should try to escape, to do something instead of just enduring in silence all the terrible treatment. I told them about a plan I devised for escape, which in my opinion could have been feasible. My plan centered on the times when we left the ghetto twice a week to get our water. When we were marching accompanied by the guards, we always had to form rows of ten. I noticed that there were fewer guards stationed by the rows in the back of our columns. I figured that if we could place ourselves in the back rows, we could somehow sneak out at some point and run away. I also knew that the seamstress, Miss Mancy, who had worked for our family for many years and who liked us so much, was living in the area where the water faucet was located. I suggested to my parents that she probably would be willing to help us and hide us at her place. But it was not that simple and my parents were more realistic than I.

It was highly illegal for any Christian person to hide Jews and there were plenty of anti-Semitic people who would announce to the authorities the hiding places of Jews. That would be followed with grave punishment for the people who were involved in hiding Jews and for the Jews found in the hiding places. It was a very dangerous enterprise. My father and Uncle Eugene from that time on kept a very keen eye on me. They were worried that I might implement my plan for my personal escape and run away, in which case I could face being shot. At this point, all of us were trapped. It was too late to do anything anymore—it was very risky and likely not to succeed. What can you do when you are surrounded by armed guards who hate you? They wouldn't hesitate to shoot you if you tried to escape.

Then after two weeks in the ghetto, the Gestapo headquarters instructed the Jewish Council to inform us that things were going to change for the better; that the ghetto situation was just a temporary stage. Endre Balázs, the ghetto commander, announced that according to the news from the Gestapo headquarters and the Hungarian authorities, we would be taken out from the ghetto to slave labor camps in the city of Kenyérmezö in Hungary, where families would be staying together, and we would have better accommodations in the barracks, and also that we would receive better food and medical assistance. We believed this terrible lie. Anything seemed better than the environment we were in. It was evil and cruel to give us false hopes.

The Jewish Council, their leaders, and the ghetto commander, Endre Balázs, were instructed to organize gradual transports of 3,000 Jewish people to be taken out of the ghetto. The first transport left the ghetto on May 17, 1944. They were accompanied by the armed Hungarian Gendarmes and by the armed Gestapo troops. We didn't know at that time that they were put in locked cattle railroad cars and they were not taken to the so-called Kenyérmezö city. That place was non-existent. Instead, they were transported to the German concentration camps. We found out the truth only when our turn came ...

Transports of 3,000 people left the ghetto regularly. Within a month, the entire ghetto was vacated of 18,000 Jewish people.

Meanwhile, the Jews were also taken from other ghettos established in other cities throughout the northern part of Transylvania and from all over Hungary. Documents show that 160,000 Jews were deported from the ghettos in the northern part of Transylvania, and 400,000 Jews from the rest of Hungary.

In the third week of our stay in the ghetto the weather changed. The temperature dropped, it was raining a lot, and it got quite cool, especially at night. It was very unpleasant to lie in our tent on the bare ground. We could feel the cold and humid air all around us. It was early morning. My mother got very sick. She complained of having similar pain that she used to have when she had problems with her gallbladder. During my early teenage years, my mother used to have gallbladder attacks. Eventually, the small gallstone she developed was eliminated thanks to the treatment she got at that time. But it seemed that our poor living conditions, the stress to which she was subjected, and the poor nutrition were very hard on her and reactivated the problems which she had suffered years earlier.

Later on in the morning, she started having severe pain. In the ghetto, it was very difficult to get even a painkiller, not to speak of the serious help that my mother needed. As the day went by, my mother's pain increased, and by night she developed a high fever. We were desperate and very worried about her condition.

In the morning, my father tried to get some professional help for my mother. I prayed to God for assistance. It happened that on that particular day an inspector from our city's health department was sent to the ghetto in order to inspect and to report on the living and health conditions in our camp. He first stopped at the office of the Jewish Council of the ghetto. As my father entered the office to solicit help for my mother, he recognized the inspector. He was a Hungarian man whom my father had known before and he was a decent person. The inspector also recognized my father. When Father related to him my mother's serious condition, he was compassionate and came immediately to our tent. He grew concerned about the gravity of my mother's health problem and immediately made arrangements for an ambulance to come and take her to a hospital in our city. This was a true miracle. By the time the ambulance arrived, my mother was semiconscious and in almost intolerable pain.

The inspector was kind enough to allow Father to accompany Mother in the ambulance. I was hysterical. I jumped up on the ambulance, wanting to accompany my mother. To me it looked like she was dying. I was forcibly taken down and not allowed to go along. My Uncle Eugene and his

fiancée Pere tried to console me. I will never forget the terrible emotional pain and desperation I felt.

Photo 15 – Eugene with his fiancée

I felt so helpless and desolate as I cried. Father asked Uncle Eugene to take good care of me and to keep a watchful eye on me until he returned. For two days we didn't know what had happened to my mother. It was agonizing. On the third day, Father was brought back, looking very tired and depressed. He told us that Mother was very ill. She had been taken to the University of Kolozsvár hospital and fortunately, she was under the care of Dr. Hainal, who was professor of internal medicine and chief physician of the internal medicine department of the University of Kolozsvár hospital. He was well-known and a reputable and respected physician.

Without the help of the inspector who knew my father, all that would never have happened.

Dr. Hainal, besides being an outstanding physician and professor, was also a great humanitarian who risked his life to save Jewish people. He told my father that my mother had gallbladder stones and, in addition to that, she also had developed a kidney infection by being exposed to trying conditions in the ghetto. He also mentioned that Mother was predisposed to that, considering that her mother died of a kidney infection at an early age. Dr. Hainal assured Father that he would do anything in his power to save my mother's life. She was in too weak a condition to be treated surgically to remove the gallbladder stones, and at that time there were no antibiotic drugs available for the treatment of her kidney infection. So there was no certainty that my mother would survive, but there was still a slight chance for it.

Dr. Hainal also suggested to my father that he should not return to the ghetto. He offered to hide him in the hospital, where he was hiding several Jewish families. He also offered to keep me in the hiding place, if I could somehow get out of the ghetto. So Father came back to the ghetto with the idea that he would try to somehow find a way to escape with me and go to the hospital to be hidden by Dr. Hainal. But that didn't happen because by that time it was too late. We were totally trapped and two days later we were taken out of the ghetto with our family, along with 3,000 other Jewish people, and deported in railroad cattle cars to the German concentration camps.

Our departure took place towards the end of May 1944. Accompanied by the Hungarian Gendarmes and some German Gestapo, we marched by foot to the railroad station.

I was marching with my father, my uncle, his fiancée Pere, and some other members of my family. Other members of my family had left earlier with previous transports. We wondered how we would find them among such a large number of people. We were carrying our small suitcases with our few belongings.

We arrived at the long rows of railroad cattle cars assigned for our transportation. From there on, it was like a madness descending on us. ...

We were pushed forcefully into those cattle wagons by the Hungarian Gendarmes and the Gestapo. So many people were pushed into each compartment that we could hardly move. There was so little space for each person. It was difficult to lie down on the wooden, barren surface of the cars. We tried to sit down on our suitcases. There were small children among us who were crying, terrified of what was happening. There were also old people having difficulty coping with the nightmarish environment.

And then the heavy doors of the cattle cars were shut and bolted from outside. It got pretty dark and dreary inside. Not much light seeped through the narrow slits of the wooden-boarded walls. We were placed behind bars and imprisoned in that frightening environment.

The train finally started moving. The slow puffing of the steam engine grew faster and faster as the locomotive carried us further and further into the unknown. We couldn't believe that something so awful was happening to us.

We traveled for three days and three nights. During all that time we didn't receive any food or drink, and there were no toilet facilities whatsoever. We were locked up day and night. They didn't let us out of the cattle wagons to be certain that there was no chance for us to escape. We had to use our compartments for toilet purposes. Some people brought along some pots from their homes and we used them for restroom purposes. Little kids had difficulty in understanding what was going on.

At night we tried to lean towards each other so that we could have a few minutes of rest, maybe a short nap, which would allow us some brief escape from our awful predicament.

I remember the first night. At some point late at night, I fell asleep. I was exhausted from the emotional shock of being treated so unjustly, and from experiencing the ultimate humiliation and disrespect towards us Jewish people. It seemed that our situation had become even more critical than expected. I wondered what other unforeseen miseries, unexpected changes, and painful losses destiny would cast upon us.

Suddenly I woke up and felt drops of salty water rolling down my face. I realized that my head was resting on my father's shoulder and the salty drops of water were tears my father was shedding, tears born out of grief and suffering. I lifted my head and felt a great sadness descending upon me. I had never seen my father crying like that. I asked him, "Daddy, what is wrong?"

He answered, "We made a grave mistake. We should have run away in time. Now we are trapped. It is too late." He had a premonition that something terrible would happen to us and unfortunately he was right about that.

Everyone from my family who was in the cattle car with us joined in. "Your father is right. We should have left Hungary and our native city of Kolozsvár and gone to Turda in Romania where some of our relatives are living. Despite the strong presence of anti-Semitism there, the Jews from Romania are treated better. Anything is better than what we are facing now. But we didn't realize that such terrible things would happen to us."

I said, "We should have escaped from the ghetto. Maybe we could have found some people who could have hidden us. We also have relatives living in Bucharest. Why didn't we go there?"

But it was too late to think about it now. Anyway, it wouldn't have been easy for my parents or for many of my family members who also were caught in the web of disaster to run away. First of all, it would have been dangerous if we had been caught escaping. I don't know what would have happened if we had been arrested by the Gendarmes or the Gestapo. Who knows what tortures or even death could have been in store for us? Secondly, it was hard to leave everything behind. We didn't have much money to sustain us elsewhere. There were those who were well-to-do people who had left much earlier and perhaps went to Switzerland or somewhere else before their wealth could be confiscated. Maybe they'd had better foresight of what was coming.

Other people in the cattle car were waking up and starting to talk. They were wondering what we could have done. What actions should we have taken in order to not fall victim to history's monsters?

But finally, all of us realized that no matter how much we fretted about the things we didn't do, or the steps that we should have taken, it would not change the situation. So we figured that we would have to accept the things that we couldn't change if we wanted to go on with our lives, if we wanted to be survivors. So after a while, silence fell. Some people in the cattle car cried constantly and had a hopeless attitude. Others, like the orthodox rabbi, prayed to God, asking for His help for His chosen people.

In the daytime, it was very warm in the car and at night, it was cold. There was no comfort or peace for us. There was agitation, desperation, and resignation to the inevitable blows of fate.

The worst part was the lack of water. That presented great hardship, especially for the children, who had much less patience and tolerance. It was also hard on the old people, who got sick from lack of food and drink or other health problems.

It was agonizing to not know what was happening outside our compartment, and we feared more painful, emotional shocks in the future. Would destiny be merciless for us Jewish people?

None of us locked up in those cattle cars could foretell the even more horrible and painful suffering we would be subjected to at the end of our miserable journey. We felt that our awful trip was planned for our demise and that we were helpless, desperate prisoners on our way to the grave.

After three horrible days and nights, the train finally stopped. It was midmorning. We heard many loud voices coming from outside. All kinds of commands were shouted in the German language. I realized that we must be somewhere in Germany, but I wondered where. Then the locks and the bolts of our cattle car compartments were opened. The SS guards came in with their short, hard rubber sticks and hauled us out of the cattle cars. They yelled at us, *"Heraus, heraus, schnell, schnell!"* ("Out, out, fast, fast!"). They beat us if we didn't jump down fast enough from our cattle cars, totally inconsiderate of the elderly, the young children, the pregnant women, and the sick people.

I encountered true violence and evil cruelty in its worst form on that day.

We were not allowed to take any of our baggage or suitcases along with us. We were told to leave everything in the cattle cars. The final robbery took place.

While standing on a platform, I saw men dressed in blue-and-white-striped prison clothing remove all of our belongings from the railroad cars. We found out later that they were Polish prisoners who worked in the big warehouses in Auschwitz called the Canada warehouses where all the belongings of the victims were stored: children's toys, clothing, jewelry, shoes, human hair, eyeglasses, artificial limbs, baby carriages, etc. These items were continually shipped to different cities throughout Germany for public use. They deprived us of the most basic and minimal assets, and of everything else they could put their hands on.

At the time of our arrival we didn't know that we were at Auschwitz-Birkenau, which was the largest and most infamous German concentration camp. It was located in Poland, which had been occupied by Germany in 1939. The camp was forty miles west of the city of Krakow in the midst of a birch forest (*Birkenwald* in German).

The railroad tracks which we faced while standing on the station platform were the separation points between the main camp of Auschwitz and the camp of Birkenau, which was actually a part of Auschwitz. The left tracks led to Birkenau and the right tracks led to Auschwitz.

Standing on that platform facing the tracks, I could see the vague silhouette of an extensive building complex on the other side of the tracks. Looking ahead some distance, I could see tall chimneys with great flames belching from them. The air was filled with the strange, sickening, sweet odor of burning flesh. Even in my worst nightmares I couldn't have imagined that these flames were rising from the crematory ovens of the killing facilities. There were four crematory units and gas chambers at Birkenau where the bodies of those not considered useful were consumed after they had been killed in the gas chambers shortly after their arrival at Birkenau.

Birkenau was an extermination camp. Jewish prisoners from surrounding camps who were not considered useful anymore were sent to Birkenau for extermination. We, the freshly arrived prisoners, were totally ignorant of these horrible arrangements.

No wonder Germany never mentioned Birkenau being connected with Auschwitz. They didn't want to reveal the existence of the crematory units and the gas chambers. They kept it a secret. Therefore, the facilities were hidden from view in the midst of the birch forest. The killing facilities were only discovered after the war by the Allied troops when they liberated the camp prisoners. As we were standing on that platform, waiting for others to descend from the cattle wagons, my father, who was standing next to me, had a premonition that something awful was about to happen to us, and he wanted to give me some advice concerning what I should do in case we were separated from each other.

He said, "My child, my dear daughter, remember to follow the path of love, forgiveness, and tolerance no matter what happens. Let the candle of hope burn in your heart at all times. Take care of your mother, look for her, find her, and cherish her. I hope that she will survive. Hang on to the three strong pillars of life: faith, hope, and love. Follow the broad, countless streets of knowledge and beware of the dark, narrow alleys of ignorance. Don't forget me in case something tragic should happen to me and I will never be able to come back to you."

My uncle also gave me advice before we were separated. He said, "Remember what I always told you. Pain increases our endurance. We have to tolerate pain in order to survive and to maintain our emotional strength and not fall apart under any adverse situations which we may encounter." He also reminded me to maintain my physical fitness even if he was not around anymore.

"I promise that as long as I live I will always remember you both and respect your wishes." I have lived my life committed to living up to that promise.

What followed as we stood on that platform was a truly gruesome, living nightmare. It was hard to comprehend that it was not a frightening dream, but reality itself.

First, the SS officers ordered us to form two columns with rows of five, men on one side, and women and children on the other side. This was the painful beginning of the separation of the families.

The second phase was very shocking and agonizing. I will never forget it. Our two columns were facing the SS officers' selection team. Dr. Josef Mengele was the head of the team. Another chief selector was Dr. Fritz Klein.

I saw Dr. Josef Mengele in person as chief selector and high-ranking SS officer. He made a point of looking us over personally and making instant decisions concerning our fate. He directed some people to the left, others to the right, indicating the directions with quick, jerky motions of his cane. We didn't realize at that time that "left" meant death in the gas chambers of Birkenau and "right" signified life. Mengele was a tall, well-built, good-looking man with dark hair and dark, bushy eyebrows. He was clad in an impeccably neat uniform and wore highly polished boots. The cold, callous, and composed expression of his face and the sharp, piercing look in his eyes while he hand-picked his victims horrified us. He sent many of my family members to the left. I was directed to the right, escaping for the time being, the terrible fate of my family members and fellow prisoners.

Dr. Mengele and his SS physicians' team selected for the gas chambers all the infants, the children up to fourteen years of age, the old people, the sick ones, the invalids, the pregnant women, the mentally disturbed, etc. because they were considered useless and unable to work. "*Arbeit mach frei*" was their motto: "Work gives you freedom."

I was fortunate to be eighteen years old, healthy, and strong at that time, so I was saved for work. We were "good enough" as we figured out later to be assigned to the gruesome task of dragging corpses of the innocent victims, to dig the death pits where the bodies were thrown in like garbage and incinerated, to erect pyramids of Jewish flesh and blood in order to burn the last remains of guiltless human beings, to be slave laborers in the nearby armament factories, to be selected for criminal medical experiments at the laboratories of Dr. Josef Mengele, and to be subjected to other various and humiliating purposes.

Those Jewish prisoners who were pointed to the left also had to form a long column in rows of five. They were accompanied by the SS officers and guards. They crossed the railroad tracks and headed in the direction of the killing facilities where they were gassed and cremated. How could something so barbaric happen in the 20th century in a civilized country like Germany?

We were kept in the dark. We didn't know at that time about the existence of the killing facilities nor about the horrible fate of our family members who were considered "not useful." How could one ever imagine that the monsters of history would execute such madness? How could Hitler acquire such power and carry through such diabolical acts? Where were those who could have stopped it all from happening?

The separation of families at the selections was a heartrending sight: Men and women being separated from their loved ones, the horrified children, crying in desperation while being taken away from their mothers. The Germans lied to us and told us that the children and old people would get good care and the assistance they needed. Red Cross ambulances came to pick up the sick people, the old people, and others who were too weak to walk. We were told that they would be given appropriate assistance. What cruel demonic lies they were! We learned later on that the ambulances took all those people to the killing facilities so they could be exterminated. The purpose of all those lies was to lead the people to the extermination places willingly, since they were not suspecting the awful truth. Their fate was sealed at our arrival at Birkenau but nobody knew it. They were taken to their death chambers with little protest or rebellion. The SS officers shot anyone who protested.

At the selection, many people tried to run after their family members, to join them on their way to wherever they would be taken. The SS officers became brutal, beating the people with their clubs. There were shots resounding in the air, there were agonizing screams of suffering. It was all a horrible nightmare. I felt numb and dazed. I can't describe the great grief I felt. I was so shocked I couldn't even cry. I had a feeling that it simply could not be real. Maybe these were only insane visions.

The selections were made quickly and within a short time, I was separated from all my family members. I saw my father and my Uncle Eugene being pointed to the right, marching with the column of men. It was my last look at them. I never saw them again. I found out at the end of the war that they were taken first to the concentration camp of Buchenwald and then to Dachau where they both perished. Those of us lined up in the column of women, who were pointed to the right, were accompanied by the SS guards. We marched on the so-called Lagerstrasse, the camp's main street, which led to the actual camp of Auschwitz to which we were assigned.

The main camp of Auschwitz was located at a relatively short distance from the extermination camp of Birkenau where the prisoners not considered useful were taken for their extermination. What a horrible arrangement. Organized mass killings were taking place on a daily basis. Sometimes I wonder how I survived, being locked into such a place where death was following me constantly.

We marched on the Lagerstrasse for a while. Finally we arrived at the main camp of Auschwitz. I could see a huge camp surrounded by concrete pillars and barbed wire. The pillars stood four yards apart, were fifteen inches thick, and about ten to twelve feet high. They were connected with a system of double reinforced barbed-wire fence charged with high-intensity electrical current. An electric lamp was attached to the top of each pillar and projected its strong light inwards towards the inmates behind the fences, looking like a glowing eye watching the prisoners at all times.

I could also see highly-elevated watchtowers with guards inside them, equipped with machine guns.

I saw that inside the fence there were primitive wooden buildings and women dressed in pathetic, ragged clothing. Their hair was completely shaven and they were begging for food. To me, the place looked like a mental asylum. I couldn't imagine that shortly I would find myself among them.

Part Two

Chapter 8

All of us Jewish women from the Hungarian transport who were selected for life marched in rows of five accompanied by the male SS guards to our unknown destination. We were frightened and terrified, reflecting on the cruel treatment we encountered upon our arrival in Auschwitz-Birkenau. We were all, I'm sure, wondering what shocking and painful miseries we would experience next.

Our guards led us to a large building. We had to wait for awhile in front of its main door. Then the big door opened and we were brutally pushed inside. Some of our guards came in with us. After we entered, the door was closed behind us.

We were forcefully driven by the SS guards into a very large room. It had white painted walls and was strongly illuminated by bright lights.

There were a number of SS officers inside. There were so many of us in the room that we could hardly move. A translator was also present who translated in all languages the orders of one of the SS officers:

"Everybody must undress! Drop your clothing and your shoes on the floor in front of you, including all your valuables if you have any! No identity papers or photos can be kept either!"

We looked at each other in amazement. We couldn't believe that we were going to be humiliated to such an extent that we must expose ourselves before all the men in the room. Naturally there were protests among us, but anyone who objected was beaten and forced to comply.

So finally all of us undressed, as we had no other choice, and we stood stark naked in front of all the officers and guards. They laughed at us, mocked, and ridiculed us.

The ultimate humiliation came to those who happened to have their menstrual periods at that particular time, for they had to discard even their menstrual pads. I felt lucky that I had had my period earlier in the month and at least was not exposed to that additional humiliating experience.

Other women came into the room clad in striped prison clothing. They were Polish women prisoners who had been deported to Auschwitz earlier than we had. They were ordered to remove all our clothing, our shoes, and other belongings from the floor. They did their job silently. We found out later that those women carried all our discarded belongings into the stockroom where they sorted everything. From there everything was taken to the Canada warehouses where all the belongings confiscated from all the prisoners were stored and gradually shipped to the different German cities for use by the German population.

That represented the ultimate robbery of us Jewish people: taking away from us everything including our identities by robbing us of our personal papers and meaningful memories.

Then we were brutally pushed by the guards into the next room which was the shaving room. There were SS women inside who directed and ordered Polish men and Slovakian women prisoners, who had been in Auschwitz for quite awhile, to shave our hair from our heads. None of them were professional barbers nor beauticians, but that was not important as long as they performed the crude and cruel job of depriving us of our feminine pride.

When we came in, the room was already partly filled with the hair cut from a previous group of deportees. Other women prisoners were collecting the piles of hair of different texture, color, and length that littered the floor, and were placing them into large sacks. Even our hair was stolen from us! We found out later that it was used for wigs, pillowcases, and mattresses for the German population.

Some of the SS women inside the shaving room were being courted by SS officers, who again were laughing and jeering, making fun of our nakedness.

As soon as we came into the room, we were grabbed by the prisoners who were waiting for us with their shears, scissors, and clippers. They were urged and harassed by the SS women to do their job fast so that other deportees who were waiting outside the door could be subjected to the same indignity.

I stood there naked in front of the SS men and those doing the haircutting. I felt terribly ashamed. I placed my hands over my breasts trying to hide as much as I could of my naked body.

My hair was long, down to my knees. I had two long braids twisted around my head and fastened to my scalp with bobby pins. One of the SS women spotted me when I came in and seemed to derive special pleasure from cutting my hair. She grabbed the shears from one of the prisoners and got hold of me. She smiled in anticipation of her enjoyment in cutting off all my hair and witnessing my pain and desperation. She knew how it would hurt me to lose my crown of especially beautiful chestnut-brown, thick, shiny hair.

I was horrified when I realized what she intended to do. She grabbed me, and without even taking the trouble of removing my braids first, or at least loosening them from my scalp, she placed the shears at the base of my neck and started shaving me, moving the shears up and down, back and forth, painfully pulling on my hair, while I begged her in German: "*Bitte, Bitte, lassen sie mir ein bischen haare*", ("Please, please, leave me some hair"). She was laughing and so was the SS officer who was courting her. They made fun of me, totally ignoring my feelings.

Finally my whole crown of hair dropped to the ground. I was in shock, speechless. I couldn't even cry. It was hard for me to accept the experience as real. Perhaps it was only a nightmare from which I would wake up soon.

But as I looked around I could see how every one of us was clipped and sheared, and the ground was filled with hair which was constantly collected in sacks by the women prisoners.

Neither my pubic hair, nor the hair under my arms was shaved. It seemed that the SS woman derived enough satisfaction seeing me suffer the loss of my hair from my head. Perhaps it was beneath her dignity to shave my private parts. At least she spared me from that further humiliation.

Suddenly I felt a sharp pain on my back. The SS guards were equipped with short rubber clubs. One of them hit me because I lingered a few seconds in the room after my hair was taken. They drove us out of the shaving room, pushing, hitting, and kicking us to get out fast—fast. They were yelling at us, "*Heraus, heraus, schnell, schnell,*" meaning "Out, out, fast, fast," to the adjacent bathroom for taking showers. I touched my head and I felt some small tufts of hair here and there on my scalp.

Many of us were pushed at once into the tiled bathroom where it was impossible to take a real shower because of the tremendous crowding. Cold water sprinkled upon our bodies. The guards again harassed and persecuted us, yelling "*Schnell, schnell, heraus, heraus.*" Their harsh commands resounded in the room. We received no soap nor towels to dry ourselves. We were hurried out of the room while we were dripping wet and chilled. We entered the next room where they applied some liquid disinfectant on our bare scalps, which was very irritating and painful.

Then we were thrown into another room to get our prison outfits. Here another surprise awaited us. The

clothing which was distributed to us was selected randomly and consisted of all sorts of worn, old, shabby, ridicu-
lously ugly dresses. Size, length, style didn't count. Some
women among us got shabby evening dresses with low-cut
décolleté in the front and back; others got short skirts
which didn't even cover their knees; others got baggy
clothes and blouses with holes in them. We were deliber-
ately made fun of and looked pathetic, ridiculous, unattractive, and repulsive. Slender women got large-size
dresses. Hefty women got dresses which were tight-fitting
and uncomfortable. We received no underwear at all.

In other words we were clad in disgusting, dirty, shabby,
ragged clothes, another insult to our femininity.

I got a dark blue, long dress with long sleeves. The dress
reached down to my ankles and was way too big for my slender body.

Then the shoes were distributed randomly, not according
to the sizes of our feet. Some of them were wooden Dutch
shoes. I received a pair of high boot-like shoes with laces.
They also had built-in orthopedic plates, presumably needed by the previous owner. It was painful for me to walk in
them—the plates bothered me but I couldn't do anything
about it. You couldn't complain or request a more comfortable pair. You couldn't protest. You had to take whatever
they gave you.

At least the shoes were a size bigger than my feet. Others
scored worse than I by getting shoes which were tight on
their feet, or yet others who were unlucky and got the wood-
en Dutch shoes which were unstable, stiff, and rubbed the

skin of the feet, producing painful blisters and lacerations which, in the course of time, got infected. Of course, there wasn't any kind of treatment offered to us prisoners.

Having infections could become life-threatening in the sense that any condition which affected a person's ability to work would make that person not useful. Whoever fell into that category would be eliminated in the gas chambers.

Clad in bizarre humiliating attire, we were taken to the paint room where a stripe of red paint about two-inches wide was brushed on the back of our clothing, extending from the base of the neck down approximately two-feet long, or more.

After that last procedure, we were led by the guards from that building which was labeled, "Disinfection and Bath."

Once outside we had to again form rows of five. A strange thing happened after we looked at each other. Some among us started laughing because we looked so strange and comical without our hair and dressed in weird attire. Others were crying. We were transformed within a short period of time into pathetic, ridiculous, tragic clowns.

We marched again with our guards on the *Lagerstrasse*, the camp's main avenue. As we went along we could see endless rows of primitive barracks behind barbed-wire fences charged with high-intensity electrical current, punctuated by elevated watchtowers with guards equipped with machine guns. There was no vegetation anywhere, no grass or trees. We marched on a dirt road across a terrain of clay towards the barracks to which we were assigned.

Finally we reached the many rows of primitively constructed barracks of the Hungarian Jewish women's camp:

BIIC complex. We found out later that it consisted of 34 huts designated for 32,000 women.

We were led to a big gate which was firmly secured by an unusually large padlock. There was a guardhouse before the gate. One of the guards came and opened the gate and we were pushed inside by our escorts.

After we entered, the gate was locked and we suddenly became *häflinges* (prisoners) whose every move was monitored. From then on we were trapped. We lost all our freedom and had no control whatsoever of our lives.

My first impressions of our camp was that it looked like a true prison. I could see many rows of primitively constructed barracks looking more like woodsheds separated by narrow streets. Wherever I looked, there were reinforced gates, electrical wire fences, and guard-posts. The SS guards were stationed on elevated platforms and equipped with machine guns. The camp was separated by electric fences from other camps located nearby.

Once we were inside the camp, the guards broke our long columns of women into smaller groups, taking each group to a different barrack. All the barracks were already occupied by many women prisoners taken from previous Hungarian transports. The women already in the barracks did not welcome the new prisoners since there were already too many prisoners in each barrack.

But that was not taken into consideration by the Germans. They didn't care. We were not considered human beings anymore. In their eyes and minds we were the inferior

Jewish race, the vermin of society. Therefore we could be humiliated, brutalized, and killed. Our feelings were totally ignored.

I was led with one of the groups to a most primitive barrack. We were pushed in by the guards. The women inside were yelling, "There is no more room here," but their complaint met deaf ears. We were driven inside forcefully by the SS guards. We were so crowded that we could hardly move.

Our barrack was constructed from inferior wood. Its walls had large cracks in them. Its roof was littered with big holes and it didn't have any electric lights. It was dark inside because it had only two small windows. There was a dividing wall in the middle of it and there were two separate entrances.

It was completely bare. There were no bunks inside, no place to sleep except the hard wooden floor. In one corner there were a few blankets scattered on the floor. In another corner there were two big pails stinking of urine. Those were placed evidently as our bathroom facilities.

By the time all of us were inside, the overcrowding was unbelievable. We were 500 prisoners inside a barrack which didn't have the capacity to accommodate half our number.

There was lots of noise inside—screaming and protests. But the SS guards' rubber clubs were used on the protesters and proved to be effective weapons to establish silence and a forced acceptance of the painful situation.

The guards who led us to the camp departed, but there were others ever present all around us, occupying the elevated platforms with their machine guns.

A woman came in who actually was a prisoner, a barrack chief selected by the Germans to be the superintendent of the barrack. She seemed to be no better than the SS guards—she had a whip in her hand and she was brutal and mean, her voice harsh and unfriendly.

She yelled at us, "Nobody can leave the barrack. At night the guards have the right to shoot anyone who tries. The latrines outside can be used only in the daytime. At night you have to use the pails in the corner!"

I wondered how a fellow prisoner could treat us with so much hatred and brutality.

We learned from the other women prisoners who had arrived previously that she was the *blocova*—our barrack chief, selected by the SS officials from among us inmates, just like the *kapos*—the supervisors of the work detachments called *kommandos*. We were told that we would meet them later and that they were as cruel and ruthless as the *blocovas*. Some of these inmates volunteered for their jobs in order to earn privileges from the SS officials. We learned that they had barracks with private rooms furnished decently, access to good food, decent clothes, and adequate grooming facilities, while we were kept in filth, starved, and showered with blows. They used their power fully and even enjoyed ruling over us and persecuting us.

They sold their souls to the Nazis and became like them. In order to maintain their positions, they behaved like our SS guards towards us. Otherwise they would be demoted and replaced by other prisoners who would be willing to use the inhuman practices of the Nazis. It was sad to find out that we had such evil people among us Jewish women prisoners, willing to betray and hurt their fellow comrades.

The Germans knew that there always would be those among us who would volunteer for those jobs in order to assure themselves a better life.

After awhile the *blocova* left and darkness descended upon us—so, at nightfall we were all trapped in our barracks with no light, no food, no drinks. The only light came from the big reflectors outside on the top of the fence pillars and from the big flames belching from distant chimneys. Our nostrils were filled with the sweetish, nauseating odor of burning flesh and smoke which seeped through the cracks of our barracks's walls. We didn't realize at that time that the flames and the smoke came from the crematories of Auschwitz-Birkenau.

At nightfall we had to lie down and sleep on the hard wooden floor of the barrack, pressed together like sardines due to lack of space. There was not enough room for us inside to extend our legs, so we had to pull them in and lie on our sides in a crouched position pressed tightly to each other. We had no pillows or blankets to cover ourselves. We slept in the same clothing we had received at the bath house.

Some women took off their shoes and placed them under their heads, using them as pillows.

There was so much discontent, frustration, and anger among us. If we wanted to turn on our sides, we woke up the others lying next to us. That gave rise to conflicts and fights. Our stress level was remarkably high due to all the traumatic experiences within such a short period of time. This led to irritability, impatience, and intolerance. We also were thirsty, hungry, uncomfortable, and distressed. It was hard for me to fall asleep under those circumstances and all kind of thoughts passed through my mind. One of my recurring obsessive thoughts was: *Why didn't we get away from our native city of Kolozsvár with our families before the Jewish discrimination reached its peak? Maybe we should have gone a long time ago, leaving everything behind that we owned and fleeing to a country where Hitler couldn't reach us.* But I realized that it was senseless to think about it. We were locked up in Auschwitz and we couldn't change our situation.

Then I began wondering where all my family members had been taken. *Will I ever see them again?* I was also afraid of the unknown, wondering, *What will happen to us next?*

I was concerned about our barrack's bathroom facilities. What would I do if for some reason I couldn't use the pails at night? I was hoping that I wouldn't have to urinate. But what if I had to and couldn't hold my urge? How would I ever be able to get to the pails with the darkness and the crowding?

Fortunately all of us newcomers were extremely dehydrated because we hadn't had any water whatsoever, and due to that, we didn't need to empty our bladders. I felt such sadness, desperation, and helplessness.

After awhile I felt so exhausted that at some point I fell asleep.

It was bliss to sleep and disconnect myself from the nightmarish reality. In my dream I was not in Auschwitz but at our home in Kolozsvár with my family.

I was in front of our mirror in the bathroom combing my long hair.

I was a free person surrounded by love and harmony, with my parents nearby.

Chapter 9

I was suddenly awakened from my soothing and comforting dream to the nightmare that was my reality. The door of our barrack opened and the SS guards burst in with their rubber clubs, yelling at us as they came in. *"Heraus, heraus, schnell, schnell."* They started using their truncheons (clubs) all over our bodies. We were expected to get up almost instantly and to be ready to do anything, no matter how painful, unfair, cruel, or unreasonable their commands were. It was still dark outside, but the glare of the reflectors illuminated the faces of my confused fellow inmates. It was not easy to get up fast from our awkward positions; the crowding and the hard surfaces on which we slept made us stiff and achy. Being so violently interrupted in our sleep was a shocking experience. We had no idea what time it was because we had no watches. Later on we found out that it was 4:00 a.m. We were all scared, wondering what they intended to do to us at such an early hour.

Finally we were hauled out to stand in front of our barrack. The *blocova* appeared with some of her helpers and we

Photo 16 - Roll call at Auschwitz, Magda can be seen close-up in Photo 17.

were ordered to form rows of five. The *zåhlappel* (roll call) began.

It was chilly outside and we were inadequately clothed. At least I had a long dress of heavy cotton with long sleeves that provided some warmth. Some of the prisoners who got skimpy and ragged evening attire, very short skirts, or dresses made out of thin, delicate materials suffered from the cold, especially because we had not been given any underwear.

We waited, lined up for hours. The prisoners from other barracks were also lined up in the same fashion. We were told that the roll call was conducted in all the camps of Auschwitz-Birkenau.

We had to line up long before the counting took place and stand upright, each row well-aligned. Gradually it became daylight. The blocova was in charge of the counting, but her helpers were there, too. Some of them were the kapos—women prisoners themselves, officials in charge of the kommandos (work detachments)—just as ruthless as the blocova. They made sure that we didn't deviate from our lines.

The *blocova* counted and recounted us to make sure no one was missing. We were waiting for the high German SS officials of the camp. They also wanted to be sure that every prisoner was present. Even the sick inmates had to stand for the roll call. Anyone who died in the barracks had to be taken out and placed on a blanket in the front row in order to be counted.

The roll call sometimes lasted for five or six hours. Through all that time we had to maintain orderly positions:

straight, aligned, silent, and motionless. We were not allowed to converse with each other. If we deviated from our lines we were punished—if only one person in a row changed her position even slightly, the whole row where she was standing was punished. We had to kneel, lift our hands above our heads, and keep that position as long as required by the dignitaries of the camp. Anyone who dropped her hands was beaten up by the *blocova* and the *kapos*.

Photo 17 - Magda is centered

As we stood at roll call we could see the red flames of the crematories, and we inhaled the air filled with smoke and the sickening smell of burning flesh.

Finally the chief SS officials of the Auschwitz-Birkenau camps arrived to check the correct number of prisoners in the camps.

It seemed that everyone was in awe and fear as the dignitaries arrived. Even the *blocova* and her assistants, the *kapos*, were visibly anxious and tense.

The high officials—the SS men and women—were dressed in impeccable uniforms and well-polished boots. They looked well-nourished and cheerful. We found out later on from other inmates the names, ranks, and personality traits of our inspectors:

Joseph Kramer, who was the commander in chief of Auschwitz-Birkenau, was a heavyset man of short stature. He had short-brown hair and black callous-looking eyes. There was something frightening about them. We heard that he was very cruel. He also determined the rate of exterminations in the camp, taking orders from Berlin. He was known to beat up the inmates in a most violent and brutal way. Therefore, they called him the Beast of Auschwitz.

Dr. Joseph Mengele was chief SS physician of the camp and chief selector of the deportees in Auschwitz-Birkenau. I recognized him as he was the one who, with a small motion of his cane, decided between life and death for the arriving deportees. He seemed to be in good humor, humming to himself.

Dr. Fritz Klein, whom I also had seen at the selection platform when we arrived, was another of our chief selectors. He was shorter in stature and not so good-looking nor as well-built as Dr. Mengele, but cruelty and ruthlessness were their common traits. In that sense they were very much alike.

An unusually beautiful young woman with sky blue eyes and an angelic-looking face walked among them. We later learned her name was Irma Griese. We were also told that she was the highest-ranking SS woman in the camp of Auschwitz-Birkenau. She had a great figure and her military uniform fit her perfectly. She looked like she enjoyed her position and power. She carried a silver pistol in her holster at her side and a whip in her hand. The whip handle was ornamented with precious-looking stones. It seemed that it was a prized object to her and that she intended to use it often. We heard from the other prisoners that, although she had that angelic look, she was one of the most cruel and vicious SS women. She was called the Blonde Angel of Death.

The other SS woman in the group was named Hasse. She was heavyset, mean-looking, and unattractive. She didn't match the look of Irma Griese, but they were similar in viciousness as we later learned. Other SS women of less importance also accompanied the chieftains.

We heard from our fellow inmates that they were also very vicious. Some of them even outdid the SS male guards in cruelty.

We were frightened, tired, hungry, thirsty, and brutally mistreated. We didn't know what to expect next. During all the long hours of roll call we were not allowed to go to the latrines, which was a torture in itself. When some among us couldn't withhold their urges and urinated, or even worse, defecated on the spot, they were punished by having to clean up their mess with their bare hands. In addition, they were beaten up by the *blocova* and the *kapos*, who, in order to retain their positions and the special privileges that went with them, were just as ruthless as the SS women. They betrayed us and seemed to even enjoy their power over us.

All of us were praying not to suffer that humiliation. We tried to exert as much control as was possible over our natural urges.

Joseph Kramer approached the *blocova*, asking her, "*Wie viele scheisse stücke sind am diesen platz?*" meaning, "How many pieces of shit are in this place?" He believed that we were only disgusting, filthy pieces of excrement. We were not considered human beings with feelings. Therefore, we could just be discarded and annihilated upon whim.

The officials were counting us again. Irma Griese was looking for a victim among us in order to satisfy her sadistic desires. She picked one of us, a woman in her thirties who, according to Griese, wasn't standing as straight as she should and wasn't well enough aligned in her row. The woman looked weakened by dehydration and wasn't feeling well, or maybe was coming down with an illness.

Irma Griese pulled her out and whipped her real hard and then kicked her back to her row, smiling and enjoying the poor woman's suffering. She had the right to do with us whatever she wanted, and we had to watch her violent act in silence. We each wondered who she would choose at our next roll call.

At last the counting and recounting ended and to our relief, the roll call was over. Only then were we allowed to use the latrines, which consisted of wooden boards with holes, placed over deep ditches. They were our outdoor bathroom facilities where we had absolutely no privacy whatsoever. We were sitting very close to each other, and we also had to wait in line to use them.

We had no paper to wipe ourselves. We had no peace even there. We were supervised by SS women guards, timing us. We were allowed only a short time to satisfy our needs and when the allotted period was over, we were chased back to our barracks. Whoever lingered longer at the latrines risked being beaten. While we were there, we were not allowed to talk much. Anyone who didn't comply with that rule was whipped. The SS women guards in charge of the women's camp were brutal and vicious. They derived pleasure from kicking, slapping, and whipping us.

They drove us back to our barracks, where we sat down on the hard floor feeling uncomfortable in our soiled clothing. There was no water, so we couldn't clean our hands or bodies. We were filthy and stinky.

But what disturbed us most was our almost unbearable thirst. There was no drinking water. Our mouths were extremely dry and our lips were parched. We craved water.

Finally we were led outside by the SS women guards because the so-called breakfast had arrived. We were impatiently waiting for it, but it turned out to be a big disappointment for all of us.

The so-called coffee, our only nourishment for the morning, consisted of a brown-colored, disgusting-looking liquid which also had an offensive smell. It was brought in from the kitchen of the camp in very large kettles with two handles. Each of those extremely heavy containers was carried into the camp by two women prisoners. It would have been difficult even for strong men to carry those backbreaking loads.

Other prisoners explained to us that the SS women at the kitchen who were in charge of the organization, supervision, and transportation of our food, also determined the number of the inmates assigned to the transportation of each kettle of coffee. They allotted only two women food carriers for each of those heavy kettles. That was part of their mad game and sadistic pleasure. They enjoyed looking at the hard struggle, the pain and suffering experienced by those women prisoners, who in their weakened physical condition, due to their inhuman treatment by their captors were forced to lift, to carry, and to walk with those heavy weights and deliver their contents to the different barracks. It was a great torture for them to do that.

We also found out later, that those women inmates, the food carriers, were selected for that job by the *blocova*. They were part of the work detachment called *Ess Kommando* (food carriers).

I hoped that I would never have the misfortune to be chosen for that assignment. As the kettles were full of boiling hot liquid, some of the contents spilled on the bodies of the carriers during transportation, causing serious burns.

Each of us was supposed to receive one cup of coffee. The distribution of the coffee was done by the *blocova's* helpers, called *stubendiensts*, who were selected by her from the inmates and charged with the servicing of the barrack. She chose the most ruthless and mean women for that job. They were also equipped with clubs and whips.

Nothing went smoothly. Some people got totally out of control at the sight of the coffee. It didn't matter how miserable it looked or tasted. It was the vital fluid they had waited for so long. Due to their unbearable dehydration, they rushed to the kettles, attacking the carriers, trying to get there first, which resulted in the spilling of the hot liquid, which in turn, caused injuries to those inmates who stood nearby. The attackers were mercilessly beaten by the *stubendiensts*, who also acted like policewomen at the distribution of our food.

At last we managed to swallow some liquid, no matter how disagreeable it tasted. It was soothing to our throats and dry mouths and moistened our cracked lips.

After the distribution of the morning coffee, the food carriers took the empty kettles back to the kitchen and then returned to our camp. The poor women were totally exhausted, hungry, and in pain due to lifting and carrying the huge coffee kettles.

After we drank our cup of coffee, which was by far not enough fluid since we had nothing to drink for a long time, we were again allowed to use the latrines. We wondered when we would be able to wash ourselves, but we found out that there was no water for that purpose. There wasn't even any drinking water.

In the so-called washrooms which were extremely primitive, the pipes were rusted and we heard from the other prisoners that there was seldom any water flowing from the discolored and worn faucets. Once in a long while when some water dribbled from them, it was much too little to be useful. It was also contaminated, having an unusual yellowish color and bad smell. Yet some of the inmates would fight to swallow a few drops of it. Then they would get sick with dysentery, which in turn would lead to a lot of suffering and, in some cases, to death.

If you couldn't control the urge to drink anything no matter how harmful it was, you ended up dead. If you got sick, you faced the danger of being considered not useful and ended up in the gas chamber.

All of us were terribly dehydrated. It isn't easy to assert self control in a situation like that, but it was life-threatening to all of us to lose control over ourselves and give in to despair—to not use some wisdom in our judgments and actions. There were no showers around, so we couldn't clean ourselves at all. We couldn't even wash our hands coming from the latrines, where no paper existed.

The SS women were aware of that and, therefore, they chased us back directly to our barracks from the latrines. They didn't care about our discomfort and suffering. They had no compassion for us. They were clean and neat, dressed well, looked well-nourished, their hair nicely coiffured. In their eyes we were dirty, filthy, Jewish women, the vermin of society, the inferior race which had to be tortured and ultimately exterminated.

We were harassed and persecuted from all sides. We also found out gradually that our movements in the camp were restricted. There was a boundary set for us and the male SS guards at the guard-posts were instructed to shoot us if we ever crossed it. So we couldn't even walk around freely in the camp. We could circulate only in a very limited, designated area and most of the time we were confined to our barracks.

After we returned to our barracks from the latrine, all of us newcomers were assembled outside, in the front of our barracks, by the SS women guards. They distributed to us prison tags consisting of small, flat, rectangular metal tags with six-digit numbers etched on them, hanging on chains like pieces of jewelry. We had to wear those tags around our necks all the time, and we even had to sleep with them. From then on we became insignificant six-digit numbers, women without names nor identities, one more way we ceased to be considered human beings.

Fortunately no one in our transport was tattooed after our arrival at the camp. At least our numbers were not etched painfully into our skins. It seemed that the Germans no longer felt motivated to implement their tattooing process on us, figuring that we would not last there for long anyway under those terrible circumstances. They also knew that sooner or later they would exterminate all of us.

Shortly after the distribution of the tags, the second roll call was announced. Again we had to form rows of five standing at arm-length distances from each other in upright positions, motionless, speechless, and perfectly aligned for many hours in front of our barracks. We were wondering if there would be any other incidents like the ones we witnessed at the morning roll call.

We were concerned that we might face again the punishments of kneeling or being beaten up by the *kapos* and we were terrified of Irma Griese and her viciousness. We wondered who would be her next victim.

We were also afraid that we would not be able to control our natural urges and we would end up forced to clean up our mess with our bare hands and also be beaten by the *kapos*. What if that happened when the SS high officials were present? Irma Griese could beat us to death for that offense—taking it personally and interpreting that we did it intentionally to show disrespect for her.

We dreaded the roll call. It turned out to be a repetition of the first one. The difference was that Joseph Kramer, the camp commander, was not present among the high SS officials supervising the roll call. One other difference was that instead of the morning chill, we had the hot sun beating upon our bare skulls. By now we were so awfully dehydrated that some people fainted and were carried away. The sad part was that we never saw them again—we had to wonder what had happened to them.

So we were not even allowed to faint because that would mean that we had to be punished for not maintaining our upright positions. I think that the whole purpose of all those countings was to torture and to demoralize us to the extent that we would lose our desire to stay alive under such conditions. They really didn't care whether we were dead or alive, so why did they continuously keep track of us?

Finally, the second roll call was over. We were again allowed to go to the latrines. Our clothing became more and more soiled and we were again chased by the SS women guards from the latrines to our barracks.

When we returned they distributed blankets to us—one blanket for five people. Because of this scarcity the women were constantly fighting with each other, attempting to attain the blankets for themselves.

After the distribution of the blankets, which were supposed to be kept in one of the corners of the barrack, the arrival of our dinner was announced. We were assembled outside. The *blocova* supervised the distribution of the food. Her helpers, the *stubendiensts*, were the ones to divide the food among us.

First they distributed to each of us a small metal bowl with two handles which hung on a firm, coarse string. We had to tie those containers to our waistlines, wearing them at our sides at all times, throughout the day and also during the night. We were warned to take good care of them because we would not get another if we lost them.

We eagerly waited to be served. We were very hungry because we hadn't had any food for several days, since before our deportation in the cattle railway cars to Auschwitz-Birkenau.

Then the so-called soup came. It was carried again in large kettles with two handles. To each kettle, two women prisoners were assigned by SS women guards, just as with the kettles of coffee in the morning. The reactions of some of our fellow inmates were the same. They rushed forward trying to be the first ones. They almost overturned the kettles. Some of the miserable soup for which we were waiting with great anticipation was spilled. Some people standing close by were hurt. The *stubendiensts* were such brutal women, using their whips again, chasing away the people who got absolutely wild and uncontrolled at the sight of the food. Hunger and thirst can turn people into animals and they lose all their inhibitions, humanity, and dignity. Finally order was established by the *stubendiensts* and by some of the SS women who also used their clubs.

Each of us got a small bowl of the most disgusting and nauseating concoction that you can imagine. The soup had hardly anything in it. It had an awful smell and dirty appearance. A few rutabagas were floating in it along with some kind of strange impurities. It tasted awful, but it was the only food after days of hunger and thirst. We had to drink it from our containers. The only way to drink it without vomiting was to close our eyes and squeeze our nostrils, so we couldn't smell its nauseating odor. Shutting our eyes and not looking at it helped us to swallow it. The rutabagas in it were not washed prior to the cooking and we could feel the sand between our teeth.

The second course of our dinner consisted of a six-and-a-half-ounce piece of stale, black bread which tasted like sawdust. To that was added a very small piece of margarine. The miserable coffee, the soup, the stale bread, and the small piece of margarine constituted our daily ration of food.

Naturally all that so-called food didn't appease our hunger or our thirst. We rapidly consumed our disgusting soup. We took our bread and margarine to our barracks in order to savor it slowly—taking small bites so it would last longer. I had to decide whether I should save a small piece for the next day, but most of the time it was wiser to consume it entirely and not leave anything behind.

Some among us decided to reserve some portions of their bread for the next day, placing the small pieces under their heads and sleeping with them. But it was risky to do that because most of the time the bread was stolen during the night and eaten by their fellow inmates who were sleeping next to them. Hunger can turn people into thieves and beasts. The fight for survival among us was very fierce.

I savored my hard bread. Although it had a bad taste, it was the first solid food given to us and, therefore, it became the most important item we eagerly waited for at the end of each day.

Gradually I looked around, hoping to find some familiar faces among the women. Unfortunately I couldn't see any members of my family. But suddenly to my great joy I spotted Pere, the fiancée of my Uncle Eugene, and her sister Jackie. They were also happy to see me and we decided to stick closely to each other. They came over to my side so that we could sleep next to each other. It was so comforting to be together with them. Pere was thirty-nine years old and Jackie was forty-one. Both of them were close to my mother's age.

I recognized two girls, Lily and Ilona, whom I had known before. They had been classmates in elementary school, although they were older than I. We rejoiced at our encounter. At least I found some friends among the inmates.

I also realized that I was one of the youngest among the women.

It was getting dark at late evening in our barrack and the SS guards ordered us to be silent. They were yelling at us, *"Lager ruhe. Lager ruhe,"* which meant "Camp silence. Camp silence." Their harsh commands echoed in the air. We couldn't converse any more with each other. We had to lie down on the hard floor, pressed together in awkward positions, using one blanket for five of us to cover ourselves. It was getting cold in the barrack at night. The blanket was pulled constantly back and forth by the people next to us.

The black night gradually descended upon us, but through the small windows and the big cracks in the wooden walls of our barrack, the constant flames of the crematories were visible and the highly offensive smell and smoke seeped through. The bright lights of the reflectors also crept in. Finally I fell asleep.

I found myself again in a different dimension. In my dream I was coming home from school. As I entered our home, I enjoyed the wonderful smell of my mother's cooking. I knew unmistakably that she had prepared stuffed cabbage for us for lunch—my favorite dish. The table was set in the kitchen. I could see the fresh, soft homemade bread in the center of the table. I felt so hungry I even broke off a piece of bread and put it in my mouth. It tasted so delicious. I was looking forward to our meal.

I was having a wonderful lunch with my parents. The stuffed cabbage was exquisite, the best that I could ever remember and there was also a big water can filled with crystal-clear water on the table.

My mother asked me, "Why are you more hungry than you ever were? Didn't you have your snack in school?" I said, "Mother, there was no food there whatsoever."

As I tasted all those delicacies, suddenly I woke up. It was 4:00 a.m. The guards came as usual to assemble us for the morning roll call. Another day began but we had nothing good to look forward to. Our torture had started again on the third day in Auschwitz.

Chapter 10

*E*ach day started the same way—first with the roll call when once again we stood motionless for hours, getting cold, being beaten due to minor offenses like not standing upright or being unable to control our bladders and bowels. We tolerated the insane whims and the sadistic urges of Irma Griese, the cruelty and unkind treatment of the *blocova* and her helpers. We were forced to drag the sick people out from our barracks, to place the dead on the blanket in the front row, and to witness the fate of those who fainted.

Each day we faced the primitive latrines, getting more and more filthy and stinky, unable to wash ourselves. We were kept on a starvation diet, deprived of drinking water, and knew not what frightening new surprises awaited us.

Our life seemed to consist of a series of tortures. The inmates who had arrived earlier were in an even worse situation because they had been exposed for a longer period to the torments of the camp.

They told us about the selections which took place every week at the roll calls and which were conducted by Dr. Mengele, Irma Griese, SS woman Hasse, and Dr. Fritz Klein. They selected people for all kinds of purposes. The inmates also told us that there were all kinds of rumors in the camp that some women in weakened condition were taken away in Red Cross trucks to an unknown destination—and they never returned.

Others were taken to work in nearby ammunition factories. Everyone wondered about the constant flames belching from the chimneys and the peculiar smell of burning flesh. We were living in constant fear of the unknown.

On our third day things got worse. The miserable coffee arrived as always; but this day one of the coffee kettles was overturned by some of our inmates who rushed wildly and forcefully towards it.

The whole contents of the kettle spilled on the ground and it was pathetic to watch some of the women lose all their pride and dignity and lick like dogs the spilled coffee from the ground even while receiving harsh blows from the *blocova* and her helpers.

Watching this pitiful scene, I felt that the Nazis had succeeded in dehumanizing us through their cruel and inhumane treatment. There were others among us who refused to sink to such an animalistic state regardless of circumstances. I couldn't allow myself to sink so low as to abandon all the values and principles I had grown up with. I had to assert self-control and maintain my true identity. I couldn't let anybody take that away from me. My thirst was not quenched and I wondered, *When will I be released from my dehydration?*

After that unfortunate incident we were deprived of some of that awful-tasting, so-called coffee which, although it had no nutritional value whatsoever, was our only warm, life-saving fluid which we needed so badly for survival.

The desperation and loss of control of some of our fellow inmates were detrimental to all of us. However it was hard to be too critical of their behavior. It was extremely painful and agonizing to tolerate our camp life and the suffering and humiliations to which we were subjected. The dire adversities which we had to endure gave rise to emotional disturbances and abnormalities among some women.

After we drank our coffee, a very strange and bizarre event took place. Some SS women came to our barrack and distributed postcards, telling us to write letters to our relatives, if we had any, wherever they were located, or to some friends or acquaintances in our native country wherever they might be residing, or we could even correspond with members of our families located in distant countries. We must be careful not to use Auschwitz-Birkenau as the return address on our cards; we should put "Anne Walsee" instead. Also, we were instructed what to write. They told us to write that we were well-treated, that we were having a nice time, and that our food and living quarters were good. In other words, we were supposed to fool everybody. We were upset and disgusted that something so evil was requested of us. But we were afraid of being singled out and gravely punished if we didn't comply with their requests. Surely we would be severely punished if we returned our cards blank.

I wrote a card to my relatives who were living at that time in Palestine, the present state of Israel, which was then under British mandate. It was not established yet as a Jewish state. A cousin of my mother was living there with her family. I thought that it was far enough away that Hitler couldn't harm any Jewish people there. I also had relatives in Bucharest, Romania, but I didn't dare to write to them for fear I would place them in jeopardy.

All of the inmates wondered why the Germans were asking us to do this. What other devilish plans did they have in mind?

We found out much later that the locality of Anne Walsee, which they wanted us to use as the return address, was a resort town close to the Swiss border. So we drew the conclusion that this German scheme had a dual purpose.

First of all, perhaps they acquired some information this way about other Jewish people who might have been in hiding and could be deported. Secondly, it was a way of giving the impression to the public that the rumors of the existence of Auschwitz-Birkenau were unsubstantiated. According to the contents of the cards it would seem to the world that we Jewish people were wonderfully treated by the Germans, interned in a resort town with good food and lodgings. What a horrible lie to feed to the public.

While writing my card, I felt sad about being forced to lie and not being able to express my true feelings. I also felt that we prisoners were again humiliated, ridiculed, and taken advantage of by the SS, so that they could continue their inhuman treatment towards us, and the world would not know what was really happening in the camp. Perhaps that was one of the many sadistic pleasures of the SS officials.

After all our cards were completed, the SS women guards collected them along with the pens which had been distributed. They warned us that we would be gravely punished if any of the pens were missing.

After that we were allowed to go to the latrines. There were some among the women who were suffering from dysentery. They couldn't control themselves and emptied their bowels in front of the barrack. They were beaten because they were not supposed to dirty the ground. It wasn't their fault, but that didn't count. They had to clean up their mess. I was afraid that maybe one day that could happen to me, too.

I felt sorry for them and started to cry. I wiped my tears with my fingers because I had nothing else to use. We were tired, thirsty, and hungry, but we had to line up again for roll call. The high SS officials appeared as usual, counting and recounting us time and time again. It started raining slightly. The few drops of water were welcome. At least some moisture reached our dry lips.

At some point we heard the loud, shrill sound of sirens, which in turn created commotion and agitation. We could see SS guards with their guns running in all directions, with German shepherd and Doberman dogs at their sides. We also heard some shots in the air. But despite all of that, the roll call continued.

We wondered what was happening. We found out later that one of the male prisoners in the camp tried to escape and the guards were hunting him down. We also learned from others that from time to time there were escape attempts going on in the camp, but all of the fugitives were apprehended and executed. Some were shot, others tortured, and then they were hanged in public in order to show everyone what happened to prisoners who tried to escape. It seemed that nobody had a chance to escape from Auschwitz.

I began to think that maybe the only way to survive was to tolerate the suffering and have the hope that somehow things would change one day and we would be liberated. But it was hard and painful to tolerate our life in the camp, and so it was difficult to fight for our survival.

After awhile things quieted down. I wondered what happened to the prisoner who tried to escape. Finally the second roll call ended and we could use the latrines for which we had to wait for so long—and from where we were chased again as usual by the SS women guards back to our barrack.

We waited again for our miserable dinner. As soon as the big kettles were brought in by the food carriers, the mad rush of some of the prisoners to the kettle was repeated. It reached a point where the kettle of soup was almost overturned. Our dark, stale bread for which we eagerly waited was distributed. The small piece of margarine which we normally received was replaced with an equally small portion of some kind of fruit jam.

After that we retreated again into our barrack. I felt so hungry that I was happy to have even that small piece of bread regardless of how bad it tasted. Pere and Jackie were sitting next to me consuming their bread and small jam rations. They noticed that I was silent and withdrawn and were concerned about my sad state of mind.

Pere asked me, "Are you feeling alright? Maybe tomorrow we will have a better day." They tried to cheer me up. It was very comforting to have them around. They really cared about me. Jackie even managed to get a blanket for us for the night.

But I still felt so lonely. I missed my parents. I wondered what had happened to them. I didn't feel like talking too much, although at that early evening hour we were allowed to talk to each other until the *lager ruhe* (camp silence) was announced by the SS guards.

There were so many things happening during my three days in Auschwitz. The many shocking incidents which we experienced gave rise to depressing thoughts and feelings within me, prompting me to silence. I had to face and accept the nightmarish reality into which I had been thrown. I had to find a way to tolerate my joyless and seemingly senseless life.

Pere and Jackie were also depressed although they tried to be very protective of me. I felt their anxiety and desperation. None of us in our barrack was exempt from those emotions.

There was a physician among us in our barrack who was pointed out to me by one of the other women; they told me her name was Ida. She was an older woman, in her late thirties. I wanted to meet her but perhaps at a later date. I was not in the mood now to talk to anyone. I was told that she was persecuted and disliked by the *blocova* probably because she was an educated, successful professional person, while the *blocova* was a rough, uneducated woman who liked to assert her power over us, especially over the more intellectual people in our barrack.

Then there was a younger, twenty-five-year-old woman who was interested in conversing with me. She even came to me and introduced herself. She was also from Kolozsvár. I listened to her but I didn't feel like having any company. I just wanted to withdraw into myself. It's sad, but I don't even remember her name.

Another woman came and talked to Pere and Jackie. I listened to their conversations. She said that her name was Ilus. She was from my native city. She was a married woman, and she wondered what had happened to her husband, where he had been taken after the selection platform of Auschwitz-Birkenau.

Gradually it got dark in the barrack and we laid down again on the wooden floor for the night. There was fighting for more space and for the blankets, twisting and turning. I couldn't sleep. I wished I could be at home with my parents, surrounded by love and gentility. Finally I fell asleep. In my dream I was coming home from my piano lesson. On my way I stopped at one of the best pastry shops in our city. As I entered, I smelled the aroma of freshly baked goodies. I ordered a hot chocolate and my favorite coffee cake. Everything was so delicious. I left the shop feeling happy and filled with energy. At first I walked fast, then I was running, enjoying my freedom. My two long, thick braids, which had bows at their ends, were flipping back and forth. My dream was rudely interrupted by the loud voices of the guards—"*Heraus, heraus, schnell, schnell.*" It was time for *zåhlappel* (roll call). It was 4:00 a.m. and it was the beginning of our fourth day in Auschwitz.

The roll call started in the usual way except that our *blocova* was not present. Another inmate appeared instead of her, also equipped with a whip, and she looked just as mean as our *blocova*. We found out that she was the *vertreterin*, the *blocova's* representative. Another inmate came along with her. We learned that she was the *schreiberin*, the *blocova's* secretary, who was in charge of editing the report of the roll call.

For awhile we assumed that perhaps our *blocova* had been demoted by the SS officials who probably wanted to replace her with an even crueler and more wicked person, someone who would be even more merciless and violent towards us. All of us inmates felt that our *blocova* was bad enough. She played perfectly her role of betrayal and callousness by fully adopting and executing the inhumane policies of the SS officials. We were afraid of what would happen to us if someone else was chosen who would treat us even worse than the original *blocova*.

But our concerns were unsubstantiated when our *blocova* showed up later. We saw that she had other people in her entourage besides the *stubendiensts* who were chosen to terrorize us along with the *kapos*. She even had her personal servant called the *califactorka*. She exerted a great deal of power over us *håflinges* (prisoners) and over her staff.

Our fellow inmates told us later that all those privileged women prisoners had a much better life than the rest of us. They lived in better constructed barracks which were unlike our dilapidated ones. Their living quarters were provided with beds, pillows, blankets, and attractive furniture pieces. They also had access to better food, better clothing, bathing facilities, and toilets which looked very different from our filthy and stinky latrines.

All these privileges were given to them by the SS officials in return for their services to them. They surely sold their souls to the SS in order to receive advantages for themselves. They became just as brutal and heartless to their own comrades as the SS guards.

I was very sad to see that. I had thought that only persons who lacked conscience and were devoid of any principles, compassion, and decency could engage in that kind of evil behavior. It taught me that our camp life and struggle for survival could turn some people into beasts. But there was no guarantee of staying alive even for beasts.

There was always the possibility that those women inmates who served the SS could be demoted and replaced by other ones after awhile, if they tired of them. If that were to happen, then those prisoners who betrayed us would have to face their fellow inmates whom they had victimized and bear the grave consequences of their acts.

Being preoccupied with all these thoughts, gradually I became very depressed and asked myself whether my life had any meaning anymore. I also wondered how long I would be able to tolerate an existence of continuous emotional and physical suffering, living in an environment where love and caring didn't exist, where hatred and violence ruled.

After we stood for long hours in the same uncomfortable, motionless position, the roll call finally ended—and as usual we ran to the latrines to relieve ourselves. I noticed that there were some women among us who tried to tear off a small piece from the length of their dresses in order to wipe themselves. I was advised by one woman, who had been in the camp longer than I, not to do that because that was considered by the SS to be a show of disrespect for the Reich's property and brought severe punishment. I was thinking that the Germans didn't have any respect for our properties which were taken away from us without our consent. They robbed us of all our good clothing, piled them up in their warehouses, and gave us old, ragged, discarded clothes while they kept ours for the use of the German population. But their dishonesty had to be accepted. We had no right to express our feelings about it.

Several days had passed since our arrival at the camp and through all that time we couldn't wash ourselves. The dried pieces of our own feces on our clothing were disgusting and had a bad smell. There was no way of taking off and changing our soiled clothes. We wore them at roll calls and all day long. We also slept in them. They never left our bodies. We also had to inhale nauseating body smells throughout the night because we were pressed so closely to each other.

After our so-called coffee break, the second roll call of the day began. The expected SS high officials appeared again like always, but another woman came along with them whom we had not seen before. She was a good-looking and well-built woman in her early thirties. Her wavy, short, blonde hair was nicely combed and brushed. She emanated a strong fragrance of perfume which was common of the SS women officials. She was dressed in a clean blue suit made of a heavy cotton-type material, tailored close to her body, attracting attention to her shapely figure. She was wearing a pair of oxford-style closed shoes with laces and she carried a whip in her hand. She looked self-confident and relaxed, giving the impression that she tremendously enjoyed her power over us. We wondered who she was. Evidently she was not an SS woman because she didn't have an SS uniform.

We found out that she was the *lagerälteste*, selected by the SS officials from among the inmates who had been in the camp the longest. She had been entrusted with the highest authority among all the deportees. She was like a queen who reigned over all the 32,000 women in our camp. She had the greatest freedom among all of the prisoners and could circulate freely all over our camp. She was not responsible to anyone except to the SS officials. Her only restriction was that she could not leave the boundaries of our camp.

We also heard that she had private quarters, well furnished. She had good food, nice clothes, and had access to other so-called luxuries in contrast to our total lack of even the minimal primitive necessities.

We wondered what kind of indecent means she might have resorted to in order to be singled out by the SS from among all the inmates in the camp for the most beneficial and powerful position. She had the highest rank among us, having almost as much power delegated to her as to the SS women officials. In return for these advantages, she naturally had to become heartless and cruel to us. She had to behave like an SS woman.

We also noticed that she was surrounded by other inmates who seemed better dressed and in much better condition than the rest of us. Our comrades informed us later that those people at her side were the members of her staff. One of them right next to her was the *lagerkapo* who was her representative, the associate chief of the camp. The others in her entourage included: the *arbeitdienst*, the service chief who selected and organized the different work groups and assigned a number of prisoners for each, the *rapportschreiberin*, secretary and office chief of the *lageralteste*.

All these dignitaries had their private quarters which could not be compared to our filthy and stinky barracks. They had the best life among all of us in the camp. So, we learned that we had a hierarchy in our camp, with special treatment granted to a very few among us.

The rest of us were kept in misery, having absolutely no way to change our fate. It was questionable if we could survive under the terrible conditions to which we were subjected in the camp.

Each day we became more and more dehydrated and hungry on our starvation diet which, in turn, had a weakening and demoralizing effect on us. There were some among us standing at roll call who got their menstrual periods. As the SS officials didn't provide any pads, tampons, or underwear, the blood flowed freely down their legs and the SS men and women who were assisting in the roll call yelled at them, calling them dirty, stinky Jewish vermin.

There was no end to the humiliations.

As I stood speechless and motionless during the second roll call of the day, witnessing all that, a great sadness and helplessness descended upon me. Tears flowed rapidly down my face, and being deeply involved in my thoughts, I didn't notice that one of the SS women was coming my way. I was taken by surprise when she stood in front of me and suddenly delivered a hard slap on my face. She punished me because I was not supposed to cry during roll call. It was disrespectful to do that. I felt my face swelling up. I never had received corporal punishment from my parents. I grew up with gentility. That slap was the first one I ever experienced. I didn't even have the freedom to cry and express my feelings. I had to accept in silence an undeserved and brutal act of violence.

At the end of the roll call all of us were exhausted and depressed. Again we headed to the latrines where more and more dirt piled up on our clothing. We waited more impatiently than ever for our disgusting soup and stale bread. Our miniature ration of fruit jam from the night before was replaced with a razor-thin slice of sausage of dubious origin. As I was biting into my stale bread I looked around our barrack and it seemed to me that after being there for only a few days in captivity, we already were showing strong signs of physical and mental deterioration.

I still didn't feel like talking too much to any of my comrades, even including Pere and Jackie. I watched Ida, the lady physician dressed in a flimsy and dirty short dress. She seemed to be cold. I saw her tearing off a piece of the blanket which she shared with others, placing it against her breasts under her dress in order to get some warmth, although her sleeping partners were objecting and getting very upset about it. They warned her not to do that considering how the Germans felt about any damage to the property of the Reich, although hundreds of blankets were stolen from the deportees and stored in the huge, so-called Canada warehouses in Auschwitz-Birkenau. But we had no access to them. We had to sleep on the cold and hard wooden floor of the barrack through the night, poorly covered, chilled, simply bearing the cold. Everyone of us was in a bad and somber mood. Another night began—a dream world in which we found some peace. We knew that we had nothing good to look forward to on our fifth day in Auschwitz.

Chapter 11

*T*he fifth day started as usual with the roll call at 4:00 a.m. It was still dark and cold outside, but the glaring lights of the reflectors atop the concrete stanchions of the electric, barbed-wire fences had a blinding effect on us. We were cold, sleepy, and bone-tired.

I wondered whether we would be able to maintain our sanity under the extremely stressful and awful lifestyle imposed upon us. We had no peace at any time and we lived with total lack of freedom. Our lives were controlled by the SS officials who kept us on a starvation diet and robbed us of our identities. To them we were only numbers which could be wiped out any time. Our life had no purpose anymore. We were only objects to be tortured and gradually driven to our deaths.

The camp inmate dignitaries and the SS officials arrived. They looked rested, well-fed, well-groomed, and cheerful. Irma Griese, the camp directress, was parading in her spotless uniform, carrying her elaborate whip ready to be used on some of us for her own pleasure. There was a German shepherd dog at her side on a leash. We wondered what other evil acts she planned to carry out on us. We heard that the dogs in the camp were vicious. They were trained to attack at command and to track down fugitives. They could tear people apart. It dawned on me that Irma Griese had another sadistic whim; perhaps she intended to let loose her dog and command the animal to attack some of us.

She would enjoy seeing our blood running from wounds inflicted by the dog's attack. But that was not happening so I concluded that she wanted us to be terrified of what could happen to us if she would let her dog loose. She managed to create fear and anxiety among us. Maybe that was another aspect of her sadistic fun. She enjoyed using her power, which she probably hadn't possessed in her normal everyday life outside the camp before she became the feared SS woman.

I looked around at my fellow inmates trying to spot Ida from my barrack. I located her easily. She was ahead of me in her row of five. I worried about her. She didn't look well. Then I noticed that the behavior of the SS women was somewhat different. They examined us more carefully than usual, placing their attention on our miserable clothing.

Sure enough they discovered the pieces of material missing from the clothing of the inmates who had torn off pieces of their attire at the latrines in order to wipe themselves. They were pulled out of line and received solid beatings for committing the offense of ruining their ragged dresses which were considered to be the property of the Reich. I was grateful to the person who had warned me at the latrine not to rip off any part of my soiled and stinky dress.

And then one of the SS women approached Ida. She noticed the padding under the doctor's dress. She pulled out the piece of blanket and began violently slapping her face time and time again, until it turned bright red and swollen. Finally it seemed that the doctor could not stand being humiliated and beaten any more. She couldn't control her rage and anger and she started beating the SS woman. She was instantly subdued by the SS guards and taken away by them. We never saw her again. We were sure that she was shot. For attacking an SS woman, the punishment was death.

The SS officials were enraged and all the other people in her row, including the people standing in the rows behind her and the ones standing in the rows in front of her were punished. Our row was included. We were forced to kneel on the hard ground with our arms lifted above our heads as long as the SS officials wanted—which turned out to be about one hour. Whoever lowered her arms was beaten up. It was the first big torture I experienced.

I tried to put myself into a trance and keep my arms upright in order to avoid the painful slashes of the whips and the other kinds of beatings. I can't explain or understand how I got this unearthly power to do that. I placed myself in the hands of God, asking His assistance, and He performed a miracle on me. I was one of the few who was not beaten.

So our roll call had a very bad start. I was very sad that I would never again have the opportunity to see Ida, whom I respected for her courage in doing what she did. I would have liked to know her better and maybe develop a friendship with her over time.

From that incident I also learned what would happen to any inmate who could not control her emotions when humiliated and tried to rebel against injustice. If we wanted to stay alive in the camp, we could not afford to lose control no matter how difficult it was under those conditions. We had to swallow our pride and repress the anger we felt in order to survive. It was very hard to do that but it turned out to be the most reasonable conduct.

After that unfortunate incident another new event took place at our roll call. The *arbeitdienst*, the *lageralteste's* service chief, came forward to select a number of inmates for a work group in charge of cleaning the latrines. That squad was called the *sheisskommando*, the shit group.

It was the duty of the inmates selected for that job to carry out the night pails filled with urine and feces from the corner of our barrack and to empty them into the latrine. Then they were given pails in order to scoop up the fecal material from the filled up ditches of the latrine and empty them into a four wheeled wagon. They had to pull the loaded wagon to the fields where they spread out its contents over the ground to be used as fertilizer.

The women were supervised by the SS male guards who were very cruel. They yelled at them to work harder and faster. They used their rifle butts to beat them. Some of the women ended up with permanent injuries from those blows.

I was very relieved not to be included in that group.

On our sixth day in Auschwitz, the selections for the various work detachments took place at the roll call.

The *arbeitdienst*, the service chief who organized the different work groups, selected inmates for the garbage collector's group, assigned to haul the garbage from our camp. He chose others for the group of camp policewomen, whose job was to patrol the barbed-wire fences and keep an eye on any prisoners who got too close to the wire and tried to make conversation with women inmates enclosed on the other side of the fences. Members of this group were given blue prison uniforms.

Also, selections were conducted for the kitchen staff of the camp. Very few women were chosen for that particular privileged assignment.

We found out later that a total of 400 women were working in the camp kitchen. They were selected from the other barracks of our women's camp as well as ours. We heard that they received better accommodations than the rest of us and they had more access to food. Some of them had the opportunity to steal some food, although the kitchen staff was supervised by the SS women. If they were caught stealing, the punishment was grave; they were either severely beaten or executed. The risk was great but the temptation to do it was even greater. Acquiring more food meant the extension of one's life. At the same time it was also a death threat.

The high SS officials were also conducting different kinds of selections on that day. A special announcement was made:

"We need volunteers for the work in the quarries. Whoever volunteers for that assignment will get more food. We need women with nice strong legs for that. So, all of you volunteers come forward and lift up your dresses so that we can assess your legs."

When I heard that, I told Pere who stood next to me that I wanted to join that group because it would mean more food for me.

Pere got a strong hold of me and said: "I will not let you do that. You never know what the SS has in mind. You can't trust them. Maybe they just want to lure you in, promising more food, and then will subject you to very humiliating purposes. You are a naive young girl, but I am older and I have more insight into the special degrading purposes which they might have in mind."

Later on I was very grateful to Pere for preventing me from volunteering, because we eventually learned that those young women who volunteered for the quarry work were placed in brothels for the use of the SS men. They lived in special barracks and wore a black triangle on their clothing above the heart placed on a piece of white cloth, which represented their identification mark. We also found out that some of the young girls whose hair was not cropped at the disinfection and bath house were also selected for the same purpose. I remembered one very beautiful girl whom I saw in the shaving room. She had long black hair. One of the SS officers pulled her out from there and her hair was not shaved. At that time I was jealous of her and thought that she was luckier than I. But after Pere explained things to me, I realized that I would rather be bald and unattractive than be used for such humiliating purposes.

Some of the women were selected to be slave laborers. We found out later that they were assigned to work at some of the factories located near Auschwitz like D.A.W. Deutches Aufrustungswerk, Siemens-Werke, and Krupp. All these factories were involved in the production of armaments.

Other inmates were taken, as we learned later, to Monowitz Arbeitslager near Auschwitz, which was actually part of Auschwitz-Birkenau, to work in a factory belonging to Buna Werke and controlled by IG Farben AG, which produced a synthetic oil and a special rubber called Buna. The camp itself was also called Buna.

There were rumors in our camp that the prisoners working there were treated very badly by the guards—and many of them died. Most of them were Jews.

On each day in the camp we experienced unexpected, painful, and shocking surprises at roll calls. On our seventh day in Auschwitz the dreaded "special selections" took place. We heard from our other comrades that it would be a frightening and potentially fatal weekly event.

All of us, the 32,000 inmates of the Hungarian Jewish Women's Camp, were lined up as usual in front of our barracks at the big open area called *Zählappel Platz* (roll call place) waiting for the chieftains of the special selection committee.

The feared selections were conducted by Dr. Joseph Mengele, chief SS physician, medical director of the camp of Auschwitz and head of the special selection committee, and Dr. Fritz Klein, medical director of the women's camp in Auschwitz. He was originally a Hungarian physician from the city of Brasov in Transylvania, and was a fierce, ardent, and fully dedicated supporter of the Final Solution. He was deeply involved in the annihilation process. Also on the committee were Irma Griese, chief directress of the camp and supervisor of the concentration camps, and the vicious SS woman Hasse, who was also a camp directress.

After being in Auschwitz for only a week, we newcomers already showed serious signs of weakness due to our starvation diet and the unhealthy, unhygienic conditions of camp life. But the ones who had come several weeks before were in worse shape than we, having lived for a longer period under the terribly adverse circumstances. The physical and emotional suffering had taken a huge toll on them.

Depression also became rampant among us due to our seemingly hopeless situation. Some among us were suffering from dysentery, a life-threatening disease if not treated. It involves the inflammation of the large intestine accompanied by sharp pain, the constant urge to evacuate the bowels, and the discharge of mucus and blood. Others were stricken with pneumonia and scurvy due to the extreme vitamin deficiencies that resulted from poor nutrition.

Many among us were afflicted with trench mouth due to the lack of drinking water which resulted in extreme forms of dehydration. The illness consisted of the inflammation of the oral mucosa and in many cases it caused the swelling of the cheeks, lips, and tongue, also involving the gums and the floor of the mouth. Due to all those symptoms, it became difficult to chew or to swallow the hard, stale bread given to us. We were tortured in many ways. Some people lost their teeth. As we had no toothbrushes nor toothpaste, there was no way to maintain any oral hygiene.

Finally, the members of the Committee arrived. We had to completely undress before them so they could assess whether we looked well enough to be considered useful for work or would be declared inept and useless.

Dr. Mengele looked at each of us and made quick decisions on our destiny, selecting the weaker and sick ones among us while he softy hummed some arias from his favorite operas. He pointed with his finger at the ones he considered not useful and they were pulled out of their lines and taken away by the SS guards. They were brutally hauled into the trucks parked at the camp's main avenue, the *Lagerstrasse*. The trucks were marked SB (*sonderbehandlung*), meaning special handling. Some time later we learned that *sonderbehandlung* meant extermination in the gas chambers. The inmates who were selected in this way met the same fate as all the people who were pointed to the left by Dr. Mengele at the selection platform upon our arrival at Auschwitz Birkenau.

Once we learned this, we were terrified, not knowing who would be selected next. It frightened me to think that I could be among the next ones condemned to death if my health were to fail, as there was no medical help nor any medications available for us in the camp.

After the elimination of the sick and feeble from our ranks by Dr. Mengele, the grand selector, who was also called the Dark Angel of Death, the selections for the various work detachments or *kommandos* began.

The *arbeitdienst* appeared and he was instructed by the *lagerälteste*, the most powerful inmate of our camp, to select a number of women for the various work detachments.

Some among us were chosen to work in the quarries, others to clear the litter near the selection platform at the railway station where convoys of deportees were constantly arriving. Yet others were assigned to the so-called *unterkunft*, the place where all the loot collected from the deportees was sorted. Others were to work at the Canada warehouses in Auschwitz where the belongings which were taken away from the convoys were stored. Some among us were selected for the hard labor of road construction and for draining the marshlands of Auschwitz. I was chosen with a group of other young women to be part of the ditch-digging kommando.

After we drank our morning coffee, all of us who were selected for digging ditches were guided by the SS guards to our place of work. We passed through the main gate of the camp and marched on the *Lagerstrasse*.

We encountered on our way a group of men prisoners who wore striped prison garb and were engaged in repairing the roads of the *Lagerstrasse*, filling the potholes along it. SS guards were supervising them. As we passed by I noticed that there was a men's camp located on the opposite side of the *Lagerstrasse*, facing our women's camp, separated by an electric wire fence.

I found out later that it was the Camp BIID complex where 20,000 male inmates lived. We heard that some of them were Polish men who had been deported to Auschwitz long before us. I wondered how they could have survived being in Auschwitz for a longer period of time. Some of them looked to be in somewhat better condition than we. That gave me hope that perhaps the men were treated better than the women, although their barracks were as poorly constructed as ours.

In my work group there were also women who had been selected for our detachment from some of the other barracks of our camp. They were accompanied by their respective SS guards. None of the SS guards were kind to us. They used their clubs on us if we didn't march fast enough. We were constantly threatened and harassed.

We walked for a distance of about 500 yards from our camp on the yellowish clay ground and suddenly, to our surprise, we passed by a grove of young birch and pine trees. In the midst of them, partly hidden, was a long, one-story building which had a big, square, tall, brick chimney spewing great tongues of flames. A sweetish, nauseating smell of burned flesh, scorched hair, and smoke filled our throats and nostrils. The smell was even stronger and more disturbing than the one we experienced back in camp. It emanated directly from that building which was before us. The guards were guiding us in that direction.

We entered a sort of a clearing and stopped there. We didn't know at that time that the building we were looking at was Crematory No. 3, the so-called killing facility, equipped with a gas chamber and crematory ovens. We found that out much later. We also detected another similar building, more deeply hidden in the birch and pine forest. We found out later that it was the Crematory No. 4 killing facility, likewise equipped with a gas chamber, crematory ovens, and a towering chimney. The sky was clouded by the smoke and at the same time illuminated by the raging fire rising from those chimneys. Before we learned about the existence of the killing facilities, we had wondered what was burning in those buildings. We thought they were some kind of factories, but we wondered what kind of materials were produced there that required the use of such tremendous heat, creating such an unbelievably offensive odor. It seemed that we were trapped in a hell.

On the barren ground of that big clearing were many shovels which the guards distributed to us. We were ordered to start digging. They told us to dig a series of very deep, wide, and long ditches. We wondered why and for what. We learned much later the sinister reason they wanted the ditches dug.

Digging ditches in sticky clay ground is a backbreaking job, even for men. On top of that we were told to work fast. The eyes of the cruel SS guards were constantly focused on us, pushing us to continuously work faster and faster. They used their truncheons freely whenever they decided that our work was too slow.

We were digging and sweating for hours without getting any fluids or food while they had their lunch period, eating their sandwiches and enjoying their drinks.

We were not even allowed to talk to each other. But in the very short recesses—only a few minutes—we managed to exchange some information with our fellow inmates from the other barracks. We found out that their living conditions were also awful and there was a lot of sickness going around which was untreated.

We were concerned about the women among us who seemed to be on the verge of collapse. We tried to help them as much as we could. While I was digging and in pain from the effort, I thought of Uncle Eugene's words to me at the time of our separation at the selection platform. *Pain increases your endurance. You have to tolerate pain in order to survive in life*. I suddenly fully understood the meaning of his words.

It seemed to me that we would have to tolerate the pain of digging for quite awhile in order to accomplish the orders of the SS. There would be a lot of digging to make such extensive trenches.

Finally the day passed. It was late in the afternoon when we returned to the camp. We felt exhausted, hungry, and extremely dehydrated. We could hardly wait for the miserable soup and stale bread, the only food we got throughout the whole day. But before we received our poor nutrition, we had to bear the roll call once again.

Finally the night descended upon us and for a few hours we were relieved of suffering, and we could find some peace and normalcy in our dreams. It was the end of another day in Auschwitz.

Chapter 12

The first day of our second week in Auschwitz began with the same rituals. None of us looked forward to that, nor to the slave labor to which we were assigned. We wondered how long we would last under the almost unbearable circumstances of our daily life in the camp.

The work of digging deep ditches, for which I was chosen, was exhausting and painful. As on the previous day, after breakfast we left the camp with our guards marching again towards the clearing next to those low buildings in the trees to continue digging.

While we worked, we could hear screams coming from the direction of those buildings. We didn't realize that those were the wails of the people who were being brutally forced into the gas chambers. We learned later from other prisoners who had been in the camps for a longer time that those were the last agonized cries of the victims.

We had a terrible day. The lack of drinking water was torture. We were also starved and yet we had to withstand our misery and have control over our emotions if we wanted to stay alive. It is amazing how much strength we can evoke when our lives are threatened. The life force within us can uncover more strength and endurance than we ever imagined. We knew that we had to last through the day so that we would be declared useful. Otherwise we would be executed.

On our way back, a light rain started to fall. At first we welcomed it because it provided us some moisture. We tried to swallow the few drops of rain in order to appease our thirst. But then the rain intensified. We were pleased about that because perhaps our bodies and clothes could be cleaned in some small way. Our clothing became wet. We had been heated up and were sweating profusely from our work, so the rain water was soothing and cooled us down.

But our small comfort was short-lived because the clay ground on which we were marching became muddy and sticky and our poor-quality shoes were sinking and sticking to the mud. It became difficult for us to walk on that slimy surface which slowed us down too much. The guards were wearing their nice, solid, black boots and did not experience our problem. They had absolutely no sympathy for our predicament. Indiscriminately they used their clubs on us, commanding us to walk faster than was humanly possible under those circumstances.

Finally we reached our camp. Regardless of how tired we were from our ordeal, we had to tolerate the torture of the evening roll call. Our fellow inmates who returned from their respective work *kommandos* were in the same fix. Our clothing was wet, our shoes covered with mud. We suffered from the cold during the night. We were uncomfortable, irritable, more intolerant of our comrades. There was more bickering, quarreling, and fighting for space and blankets.

At last, silence was established and despite everything, finally we fell asleep. I wondered if I wanted to ever wake up again. There was a death wish building up in my heart, mind, and soul. I am sure this was true for most of my comrades as well. But at 4:00 a.m. we were brutally awakened as usual by the guards and another day in Auschwitz began.

During the following days more inmates from the other barracks of our camp were selected for our ditch-digging *kommandos* at roll calls. By the fourth day of our second week in Auschwitz, our number had increased to 400 women.

The SS guards forced us to dig frantically for many hours with only a few short intermissions in between. Gradually the deep and wide ditches were formed.

As we got deeper and deeper into the clearing, we detected two additional, much larger, two-story buildings located a short distance from Crematories No. 3 and No. 4. Their massive, square-shaped, brick chimneys were enormous and extended high up towards the sky. Tremendous flames were belching from them, and their smoke was clouding the firmament. The nauseating odor of burning flesh emanating from them was so intense that it affected our breathing. Then, to our horror, we heard deafening screams resounding from those buildings—the sharp, shrill cries of the terrified victims entering the gas chambers. It is beyond words to describe how we felt working in such a monstrous and demonic environment.

We couldn't believe that there were even much bigger crematories than the first two. We learned in the course of time that those were the No. 1 and No. 2 killing facilities, where mass murders were continually taking place throughout the day and also during the night. This was hard for us to believe, even though we were so close to them and had seen them daily. We literally couldn't accept that what our senses were telling us was really true. It took us some time to face the truth.

The hard labor began to further affect our health and our emotional state. We became very depressed, and the thought that one day we, too, would become the fuel of those ovens horrified us. Each day we got weaker. We were losing weight and illnesses loomed. At roll calls we could see that many among us had started looking emaciated, had fallen into deep depression, and were most likely harboring suicidal thoughts.

The end of the second week was approaching when the grand "special selection" was again scheduled. By then many of us were in bad condition.

At the roll call of the fifth day of the second week in Auschwitz, Dr. Mengele selected 15 women among us for SB (*sonderbehandlung*), and 150 inmates from the various other barracks of our camp, a total of 165 women selected for extermination. On the same day other selections were conducted for different work *kommandos*. For instance, felling trees in the forests around Auschwitz, a dangerous assignment and extremely hard work, especially for women. Then selections were made by the *arbeitdienst* for the corpse gatherers kommando. Being so young and not yet looking too weak, I was chosen, along with a good number of other women from the various barracks of our camp.

On that day I was transferred from the ditch-digging kommando. I heard later that some of the women from my former kommando unfortunately perished. They were shot by the guards when they collapsed at work.

So on the fifth day in our second week at Auschwitz, I became one of the corpse gatherers. Our job was the gruesome task of collecting the corpses from all parts of the camp and hoisting them up on four-wheeled wagons under the supervision of the SS guards.

First of all, there were corpses to be gathered along the electrical barbed-wire fences—the bodies of the women who chose to end their lives by running into the fences. After a short convulsion they met their death, their savior from suffering. They considered their lives senseless and decided to end it in their own way—the only freedom available to them was to commit suicide.

The patrolling policewomen dressed in blue who were supposed to prevent anyone getting close to the electrical wire could not prevent the suicides. The wish and determination to die could not be stopped by anyone. It was a strong and powerful force.

It was a shocking, horrifying experience to look at the yellow, lifeless faces of the victims, their wide open eyes, their rigid open jaws, their stiff emaciated bodies covered only with their ragged, stinky clothes. I felt a great sadness and sorrow seeing my poor, dead, fellow prisoners who chose death in order to find peace and dignity. I felt that perhaps all of us were destined to be killed one way or another by being tortured and slowly driven to insanity.

The four-wheeled wagons were stationed at a central place near the fences. We had to drag the corpses to the wagons. First we got hold of both of their hands, then we bent our backs, and dragged them to the wagons. It was a hard and trying job. It was also a horrible feeling to touch the icy cold, rigid hands of the dead. In order to hoist them onto the wagons, each of us needed the help of another person. One of us had to get hold of both hands of the corpse and the second person had to grab both feet, and with one single move, the cadaver was swung into the wagon.

After we collected all the corpses from the wire and threw them into the wagons, the guards ordered us to haul the wagons out of the camp into the *Lagerstrasse*. From there, we pushed the wagons into the clearing next to the crematories, where the deep, wide ditches had been dug by the ditch-digging kommando to which I had been assigned during the previous four days.

Those wagons were heavy and it required lots of effort on our part to push them. A number of us were assigned for the transportation of each wagon. Once we managed to get the wagon there, we had to dump the corpses into a particular ditch which was deep enough to qualify for a death pit. Then we returned with the wagons to the camp in order to gather the dead bodies from the barracks. It was very important to do that because if somebody died in the barrack, the dead person had to be pulled out by her fellow live inmates for roll call, because everyone in the barrack had to be accounted for.

The corpse had to be placed in the front row on a blanket, stretched out beside the living in order to be counted. Or even worse, in some of the barracks the requirement was that the dead body be carried out and placed in a standing position by two live inmates in order to be counted.

Until the body was taken away by the corpse gatherers kommando, the dead had to be present at each roll call. If by any chance the corpse gatherers couldn't pick up the body for several days due to their heavy loads and being overworked, the dead body had to be present until it was taken away.

The barracks in our camp were in deplorable condition. Many of them were rat-infested. That is why it was important to carry the dead out. It was terrible to live with dead bodies in the barracks. After awhile the inmates would place them outside behind the barracks. Having corpses out in the open attracted rats. Of course, all the filth and the terribly unsanitary conditions to which we were exposed brought along illnesses, rats, and lice.

Even the birds didn't like our environment. We saw mainly crows flying around. There was no way that we could remove during our work period all the corpses from the thirty-four barracks. There were too many of them. The death rate was staggering. Some of the barracks were inhabited by women who had lived in the camp for many months. Most of them looked emaciated, and were extremely depressed to the point where they were manifesting mental disturbances. Some inmates called these poor women the *mussulmens*, the living dead. They were walking around as though in a daze, with a vacant look in their eyes as though they were living in another dimension, completely disconnecting themselves from our hellish reality. Later I found out more about them. Deep depression drove them into a stage of insanity. It was very sad because I knew that if they did not get hold of themselves, they would be on the list of *sonderbehandlung*.

Some of the corpses we pulled out of the barracks were partly deteriorated. But the most terrible ones to look at and handle were the ones which had been placed behind the barracks and were partly eaten by rats. There were some among them who were almost entirely eaten by rats. Because we could not handle them anymore, we left those in place so they could be consumed in their entirety.

Some of the interiors of the barracks were different from our barrack but the conditions in them were just as bad. Some buildings had rows of narrow wooden shelves along the inner walls, one above the other, extending from the floor almost to the ceiling. They were divided at short intervals by vertical wooden planks and looked like cages. Many people had to sleep in each of those cage-like compartments. The crowding was tremendous. There was lots of filth in them and they smelled horrible.

Other barracks had rows of bunks stuck on the top of each other from floor to ceiling. The bunks were very narrow and the inmates slept on the bare boards. Many people shared each of those bunks.

We dragged corpses, throwing them on the wagons and pushing them to the death pits, back and forth for many hours. During all that time we had no food nor drink. We became terribly dehydrated.

Towards the latter part of the afternoon we returned to our camp. We were exhausted and very depressed after seeing so much death and tragedy. We also were concerned because after handling so many corpses, we couldn't clean ourselves at all. It was a shocking, unhealthy, painful, disgusting, backbreaking, and gruesome job to which we were subjected all day long. We also had to tolerate the cruelty of the guards who used their clubs on us, forcing us to work faster.

In addition to all that, we heard that our camp was infested with grave and contagious illnesses like pneumonia, diphtheria, dysentery, scurvy, typhus, scarlet fever, infectious skin eruptions, etc. No treatment, no medication, or hospital facilities were available to us. Getting any of those diseases was life-threatening.

Because we got no information about the health conditions or the illnesses of the inmates whose bodies we handled, we were very concerned that we might have contracted some of their fatal diseases.

Being sick in the camp presented a great danger because it meant that one was not considered to be useful anymore and therefore had to be eliminated.

We lived constantly with fear and terror.

When we got back to the camp we had no water to even wash our hands. We spit on our hands using our saliva to somehow clean them before touching our small ration of black stale bread given to us each evening.

On those nights I had great difficulty falling asleep. I thought of all my dead comrades whose lifeless bodies I had been dragging. I grieved for them. I couldn't blot out the death pits from my mind.

I was afraid that death was following me, too, and would catch me sooner or later. The dark shadow of despair and hopelessness descended upon my spirit and weakened my desire to fight for my life. I recognized the signs of depression and I knew that I needed God's help to give me back my courage and hope in order to be able to survive, and to assist all of us in our fight for our lives.

I began to pray to the Almighty Creator for myself and for all of the inmates. My thoughts and feelings were expressed in the following prayer, written down much later, as a survivor of the Holocaust.

Prayer

Oh, God, upon you I call.
Please listen to my cry,
in the silent chambers of my soul,
and don't let us die!
Almighty Ruler of the Universe,
don't turn away from us!

Don't let us fall,
give us strength to bear
all this humiliation
and degradation.
Let your people survive
the trials of torture
and extermination.
I pray for myself, for my family,
and for my fellow prisoners.
Oh, Lord, send us hope and courage.
Don't let us stagger.
Don't let death
thrust into our hearts
its poisoned dagger.
Send us courage to control our fears,
and hope, to wipe our tears.
Grant us faith to fight
and ignore the pain.
Almighty God, guide us well.
Don't let us sink
into sorrow's deep hell.

Towards the end of my second week in Auschwitz I witnessed a tragic and heartrending incident. One of my coworkers in the corpse-gatherers kommando recognized the body of her mother among the corpses of the women who committed suicide by the electric wire.

She was one of the fortunate ones whose mother was selected for life by Dr. Joseph Mengele at the selection platform upon our arrival at Auschwitz-Birkenau, and they remained together. Although the mother was an older woman, she looked vigorous and younger than her age. Therefore, she was considered good enough for work together with her daughter. But their joy didn't last for long, because when they entered our women's camp, they were separated. The mother was assigned by the SS guards to another group of women to be taken into a different barrack. It was hard to tell which one of the thirty-four barracks in our camp the mother had been taken to, but our comrade had been hoping to find her and be reunited with her parent one day.

My co-worker was very depressed all along, having great difficulty accepting the horrible existence in our camp life. She constantly worried about her mother and was determined to look for her, to find her, to be with her, and to help her stay alive.

Her strong quest and desire to fulfill her wish gave meaning to her life and became one of the strong motives for her own survival. But seeing her mother dead, she felt that she had lost everything, including her desire to exist. She totally broke down emotionally and was unable to cope with the pain of her loss and her feelings of utter hopelessness. She touched the electric wire and dropped dead.

I was ordered by the SS guard to drag her body away from the wire and to hoist it up into the wagon with the help of another inmate. All of us were deeply affected and we became very depressed over the death of one of our comrades.

We were horrified by the thought that what we had seen could happen to us, too.

Would we also discover one day the bodies of our loved ones by the wire, or inside a barrack, or behind one? Would we likewise be driven to nervous breakdowns and to killing ourselves? After that awful incident I wondered whether those among us who ended their own lives were not better off than the rest of us who were destined to be exterminated. But in the meanwhile, before that, we had to be subjected to a great deal of suffering, torture, and extreme humiliation.

After we returned from our work on that day, I became preoccupied with all kinds of sinister thoughts. I questioned whether it was worthwhile to fight for the seemingly sense- less life we were having in the camp. On that particular night, the soup tasted worse than ever and my small piece of stale bread was harder than ever.

Pere and Jackie noticed my depressed state of mind and tried to cheer me up—unsuccessfully. They were wonderful to me. I noticed that some of my fellow prisoners in the barrack didn't look well anymore. We were gradually deteriorating.

I had difficulty falling asleep. Even when I finally dropped into a deep sleep I had no peace, because a horrible and frightening nightmare shook up my whole being.

I had the following dream. I wrote it down in 1983 in the form of a poem.

Delusion

I am lying in my bed,
feeling a dullness in my head.
Somebody cries,
I open my eyes,
I feel a sharp pain
in my chest.
A stranger is boring a hole
in my breast,
reaching for my heart
to tear it apart,
leaving in its place
an empty space.
With horror, I realize
that my hands and feet are tied
and all my movements are denied.
I try to shout for help
but no sound leaves my throat,
my vocal cords are caught
and squeezed by terror.
Fresh blood is staining
the pure color
of my sheet.
Then, I see a white hand
wiping everything clean,
and there is no trace of me
or of the place
where once I have been.

Could this be real
or is it a fake?
Am I dreaming
or am I awake?

For awhile, through all my ordeals in the camp, I tried to hang on to hope, courage, and positive attitudes, remembering the message of my father at the selection platform before we were separated from each other at Auschwitz-Birkenau.

"No matter what happens to you, hang on to the strong pillars of life, faith, hope, and love, and don't let hatred enter your heart."

I also tried very hard not to follow those of my fellow prisoners who committed suicide. Those of us who, despite the horrors in the camp, still carried the strong force of life within us, fighting to stay alive, tried to prevent our fellow inmates from reaching that final stage of depression when they killed themselves. Sometimes we were able to do that, other times we failed in our efforts. In the course of time depression and suicides became rampant in the camp.

It wasn't easy for me either to keep up positive thoughts in such a negative, evil, and hateful environment. By the end of my second week in Auschwitz, I was gradually sinking deeper into depression.

The first sign of it was my refusal to eat our disgusting and stinky food. Pere and Jackie urged me to eat. They were concerned about my state of mind and tried to help me by telling me, "Swallow this disgusting food as though it were a medicine to assure your survival."

Then, another symptom of depression manifested itself: my desire to withdraw from others and be preoccupied with somber thoughts and feelings of helplessness. I closed my ears with my hands in order not to hear the conversations of my fellow prisoners in our barrack, trying to blot out the existence of my horror-filled environment. At that point I got scared because I recognized the more advanced symptoms of the mussulmens in the camp—the prisoners who reached the stage of confusion and emaciation when they touched the wire or were selected for the gas chambers. Sometimes they were beaten to death or shot by the guards. They became lost souls. I didn't want to end up like them. What scared me the most was that I began to have suicidal thoughts. I felt that I couldn't take any more dealing with corpses day after day. I was tired of my life. *What kind of existence do I have as a corpse gatherer? Probably one day I will not be able to drag the corpses, hoist them on the wagons, and push the wagons to the death pits. What will happen to me then? For how long will I last doing that gruesome hard labor, considering our starvation diet and the illnesses to which I am exposed daily? Why not put a stop to my suffering and end my life when I want to?*

One night I couldn't stand it anymore. I got up and headed to the entrance door of our barrack. It wasn't easy to do that because I woke up many who were sleeping very close to each other. Finally, I reached the door. I got out and I was looking at the wire fence which was charged with high-intensity electrical current. I wondered if those who touched it and died instantly weren't better off than myself. For them, the agony was over and they found peace in death. On that night, I was courting death and I had the ominous thought of getting up the courage to end my life. And yet there still was deep down within me the desire to live. It wasn't easy to part with my life. Suddenly I felt a hand touching my shoulder. I was terrified. To my surprise it was my fellow prisoner Lily—my schoolmate in elementary school.

She said, "Aren't you ashamed of yourself? What are you trying to do? How can you be so selfish? You are only thinking of yourself! Don't you care about your loved ones, your family? Don't you want to see them again? What if at the end of the war they are waiting for you? Do you want them to suffer until the end of their lives by losing you? Come back with me now and promise me that you will never do this foolish thing again."

That was like a miracle. I came to realize that she was right. I decided to get hold of myself before it was too late. She was my savior. It was very strange and wonderful that she followed me, saving me from killing myself.

Lily and her sister Ilona were from a very poor family. They were always poorly dressed and they also had low grade-point averages in their studies. They were often ridiculed by some of the children in our class and I always felt sorry for them. I also noticed that while all of the children brought food from home which we consumed at our ten o'clock recess, the two poor girls never brought any food from their home. I decided to give my sandwich to them everyday for a while. One day my mother asked me: "Are you eating the snacks which I prepare daily for you to take along to school? I noticed that lately you are unusually hungry when you come home." Finally, I confessed to my mother what I did with the food she gave me. My mother was a charitable and compassionate person. She said to me, "Why didn't you tell me that earlier?" From that time on, every day when I left for school, she sent a separate food package for the girls and some money to buy milk for them. She did that throughout all of the four years during which I attended the elementary school.

Lily and Ilona never forgot my kindness in bringing them food everyday which they very much needed. It is remarkable that years later my mother's good deed was most generously rewarded, when in the camps at that critical point in my life help came to me from one of the girls who cared enough for me to save me. After that incident, Lily and I became close friends.

In the days following, Lily gave me lots of support and tried to improve my depressed mood by telling me that things might change, maybe unexpectedly for the better. We just had to keep up our hope and fighting spirits.

My friend helped me a great deal. She pointed out to me that I had to bring back the light of hope into my heart and that I had to convince myself that if I could keep up my motivation to fight for my life and endure all my suffering, then I would somehow survive in a miraculous way. I had to live one day at a time. At the end of each day I thanked God for helping me to survive. I had to believe that no matter how remote it seemed, there was still a chance for an unforeseeable change for the better.

I also had to find meaning in my life which would give me the strength to fight for my life. I told myself that I had to keep on living for the sake of my family so that I could see them again, and be together with my loved ones. That gave meaning and a purpose to my life. It was very crucial to bring some positivity into my situation. I needed my energy so I would be able to work, which in turn assured my survival to a certain degree.

Chapter 13

*T*ragic events constantly occurred in our camp. At one of the morning roll calls in my third week in Auschwitz, there was the following announcement made by the SS officials: "All pregnant women please step forward. From now on you will receive larger portions of soup and bigger rations of bread and also you will be sent to hospitals at the time of your deliveries."

Some of the women believed them and came forward from the different barracks of our camp. The offer of more food was very tempting and important for their survival, especially in their condition. They didn't realize that they were being tricked by the SS.

We could see them being taken away in the black Red Cross ambulances, the same ones into which the sick and the old and disabled people were hauled away from the selection platform at our arrival to Auschwitz-Birkenau. We knew that they were being sent to the gas chambers.

There was one pregnant woman in our barrack. We warned her not to volunteer because the SS could not be trusted. They resorted to all kinds of schemes and lies in order to carry out their demonic acts.

Fortunately she followed our advice and thus we saved her from death. From then on we tried to protect her in any way we could. But we were very concerned about her safety. We wondered what would happen to her when the more prominent stages of pregnancy manifested themselves. The greatest danger to her life would arise during the grand selections when she would have to bare herself before Dr. Mengele.

Meanwhile, there were other horrible things happening beside the railway station platform at Auschwitz-Birkenau. Some of our fellow inmates worked there carrying the luggage and other belongings left behind by the deportees. They loaded it into the trucks parked there for transportation to the Canada warehouses and then cleaned up the litter left on the tracks. They told us about the constant arrival of six trains daily with cattle cars packed with deportees. They were Jewish deportees from Hungary and from the other European countries which were under German occupation. They also told us about the continuous selection of thousands of people for the gas chambers. They reported to us that huge quantities of possessions of all kinds were taken away from the deportees. There was a constant need for more and more workers to carry and load the trucks with all those possessions.

Even though more workers were added gradually to that job, huge piles of belongings were laying on the ground for several days before they could be collected and transported to the Canada warehouses, which were a system of thirty huts located near the crematories. All of them were packed to the roofs with all the materials stolen by the Nazis, although constant trainloads were transported to Germany where the goods were distributed to the Reich's population.

Our fellow inmates who worked at the Canada warehouses sorted the goods taken there. Much of it had to be sorted on the ground beside the huts because there was no space inside. The suitcases so carefully packed by the deportees were opened and their contents dumped on the ground in big heaps, in front of the huts which were located close to the birch grove beyond the crematories, encircled by a high fence. Looking through the fence, the women could see people who had been selected to be gassed waiting in the birch grove—women, children, old people, and others being taken to killing facility No. 3 nearby. They had no idea what they were waiting for. Sometimes they waited for one or two days until their turn came for extermination because the killing facility was overtaxed. The women working at the Canada warehouses were in better condition than the rest of us because they had access to some of the goods themselves. Any stealing of the so-called Reich's property was highly punishable, even by death, but nevertheless many women took that risk. Some of them got away with it; others did not and lost their lives.

Our work load in the corpse-gatherer's *kommando* also increased a great deal as the conditions in our camp deteriorated. Demoralization, depression, and illnesses were widespread, and as no assistance was given to the sick people, many of them were dying. Due to all that, more suicides took place. More corpses were lying around to be picked up, and more and more death pits were filled with corpses. Additional ones were dug by the ditch-digging *kommandos*. The corpses were incinerated in those open pits by pouring flammable fluid over them and placing firewood to provide more fuel on top and between them. The stench became almost unbearable. Camouflage fences were built so the death pits would be hidden from view, but the horrible smell and smoke around them could not be ignored.

Some prisoners were getting weaker and it became harder for them to drag the bodies and to push the wagons. They were severely beaten by our SS guards and some of them lost their lives during those beatings. As we were incarcerated in a world of madness, there were more mental breakdowns among us.

As the exterminations in Auschwitz-Birkenau took giant proportions, even the four crematories working full-time could not burn all the bodies of the people who were constantly gassed day and night. So additional buildings had to be used as gas chambers. In addition to collecting corpses from our barracks and from the wire, we were also assigned to pull the corpses from the older, more primitive gas chambers located near our camp and load them on wagons and big trucks, which dumped the corpses into the death pits. As the rate of extermination escalated, many of the gassed bodies were also pulled out of the killing facilities. The crematory ovens were highly overtaxed and couldn't burn them.

Those corpses were also loaded on the trucks and delivered to the pits.

We also heard that thousands of people of all ages were shot daily by the SS guards at the outskirts of the crematories and thrown into giant ditches (about 50 yards long, 6 yards wide, and 3 yards deep) which were dug by a team of male prisoners. The corpses were then incinerated.

High fences camouflaged those pyres and the trees of the nearby birch grove also hid the crime scenes. But the smoke and the wildly raging fires rising from those huge pits could not be hidden from view.

Towards the end of my third week in Auschwitz, I was again entering into a very pessimistic and somber state of mind. I felt that I couldn't stand my suffering any longer. Witnessing the constant destruction of our lives, dragging and loading corpses day after day, inhaling the foul smell around us, and looking at the raging flames rising from the death pits and crematories was becoming unbearable. I was afraid that it would drive me to insanity. So, by my fourth week in Auschwitz I was gradually sinking deeper into depression and hopelessness.

What made things even worse was that my menstrual period was approaching and I dreaded it. I always had painful cramps and heavy bleeding during my periods. In the camp we had no protective pads. I didn't even have any underwear. The blue dress was already stinky and badly soiled. It hadn't left my body since my arrival at Auschwitz. I wondered what would happen to me if during the time of my menses it became more difficult to work. Would I end up being beaten to death by our SS guards like some of the others?

I realized that I had to do something to extricate myself from my desperate situation. Otherwise, I would end up killing myself. There was always the possibility of touching the electrical wire. It offered instant death. But I was only eighteen years old and deep down in my heart and soul, I still wanted to live and fight for my survival. I turned to God and asked for His assistance to give me strength, courage, and motivation to go on living. There was nobody who could help me and I felt that it was too difficult for me to help myself. I opened my heart to the Almighty with the following prayer which I wrote in the form of a poem later on in my life when I was a free person.

In the silence of the night,
my heart is filled
with sorrow and fright.
In the hands of the SS monsters
lies my fate.
Oh, Lord, give me strength
to bear the strain.
Don't let me disintegrate.
Help me to restore
the broken pieces
of my shattered life.
Cure my sores,
ease my pain,

liberate me
from the Devil's domain.
I feel so weary, so strange.
King of the Universe,
only You can change
my destiny.
Please listen to my laments,
hear my cry,
and don't let me die.

It seemed that my prayers were heard and acknowledged by the Creator because some positive ideas entered my mind. I came to the conclusion that I had to alter the pattern of my negative thoughts and that it was crucial for my survival to somehow shock myself out of depression. There was no way I could get any professional help to pull me out of the dangerous predicament in which I found myself trapped. I came to the realization that I needed to take action.

At first, in order to ease my intolerable suffering, I came up with the thought that the only way I could cope with the horrible conditions in the concentration camp was to build an invisible, imaginary, emotional shield around myself that nothing could penetrate. In this way, I could anesthetize my feelings and tell myself that I didn't feel the physical pain when an SS guard hit me, nor the emotional suffering of being continuously subjected to such inhumane treatment. That is what I did. Many of my fellow prisoners also resorted to this system for the sake of their survival.

The danger in this way of thinking, however, is that once one solidifies this shield in one's mind and keeps it there long enough, one will not only not care about the pain one experiences everyday, but in the course of time, one tends to lose interest in preserving one's own life. This way of thinking made us feel like living dead people, falling into the deepest pit of depression without even realizing it.

Later on a better idea came to my mind. Because I had developed immunity to the blows given me by the SS guards through autosuggestion, I knew that I had to resort to some method whereby I could reawaken myself from that morbid condition. I had to put myself back in touch with reality and make myself aware of my surroundings again. I needed the return of my sensations, even if pain would be involved. I knew that the only reasonable way for me to do that would be to inflict some pain upon myself. This way I felt that I would react to pain, and that this action would enable me to break the invisible shield that I had created before it permanently closed me off from reality.

As we didn't have any way of cutting our fingernails because we were not provided with scissors, our nails became extremely long. The only way to trim our nails was to bite them off. I had even lost my desire to do that in the frame of mind that I was in. But when I dug my long, sharp fingernails deep into the flesh of my arm until blood ran out of the wounds, I suddenly felt pain. Then I told myself while looking at my arm, "You are alive! This is your vital blood you are looking at! What do you want to do? You have to make a decision right now before it's too late. Do you want to live or die, to be or not to be?"

I had to figure out which way to turn. Should I choose life or death? First, I asked myself if there was any meaning to my life under the circumstances in which I was trapped. I tried to justify the reason for choosing life. These were the following favorable points which could determine that choice:

1. Regardless of the awful conditions I was facing, I wanted to live because I wanted to see my family again, even though I didn't know if they would survive the Holocaust. But if they survived, they would be waiting for me. I couldn't let them down because I loved them and couldn't bear the thought of making them suffer at my loss.

2. I wanted to do so many things in my life and I was eighteen years old, too young to die.

3. I wanted to experience liberation from my captivity, to be a free person again.

4. I wanted to return from the camps and talk about my experiences so that the world would be informed about the great injustice done to the Jewish people.

5. I didn't want to die, fall into oblivion, and be thrown into a mass grave.

After I chose life, I made a sacred promise to the Almighty, my Creator, that I would fight fiercely to stay alive and I asked God to give me strength and the courage to overcome my doubts and fears, to be strong enough to continue to bear my suffering and keep on fighting for my life. Strangely, after my resolve to choose life, a peaceful feeling descended upon me, and although my situation didn't change at that time, my faith in God gave me hope.

Indeed, I was still locked up in a terrible prison, but I felt that somehow I would find a solution to my situation. It occurred to me that I could start planning to escape. I visualized that perhaps with the metal container which we received for our soup, I could hit the guard in the head at the gate while he slept. I would then remove his clothing and his gun. I spoke the German language, so that would help me somehow to succeed in my escape. Very deep in my heart I knew that all of these plans would most likely not happen, because there were also elevated watchtowers in the camp which were occupied all the time by guards armed with machine guns. But I had to bring some positivism into my thoughts in order to enable myself to go on. I had to use the tools of deflection; in other words, to divert my thoughts from myself and focus them on finding a way out from my self-preoccupation and introduce hope back into my life to help me cope with my depression during my captivity.

In my imagination I heard the voice of hope addressing me. I wrote its message in the form of poetry later on in my life after my liberation from the camps.

Hope Introducing Itself

I am hope,
the best friend of life,
your constant guide.
I am always at your side.
My vigilance will never end.
You can rely on my helping hand,
no matter how bleak
the scene of life may be.
My bright streak of light
will always be in sight
to brighten your destiny.

Hope's message helped to overcome difficult and trying situations in my life many times. It was lifesaving during my captivity in the concentration camps.

During my fourth week in Auschwitz, a strange thing happened. I didn't get my menstrual period and none of my fellow inmates had theirs either. All of us in our women's camp completely lost our periods throughout our captivity in the camp.

There were rumors circulating among us that the SS women at the camp kitchen who were in charge of the preparation and distribution of our food poured some kind of white powder into our soup which suppressed our menstruation.

Although we were very concerned about what kind of chemical substance we might have been subjected to and about the adverse side effects it might create, we were relieved that we didn't have to deal with our menstruations which created big problems under the adverse conditions of our camp life.

At the beginning of our fifth week, torrential rains pounded in full force the camps of Auschwitz-Birkenau, lasting for two days and nights. We got drenched standing at roll call in the morning. Regardless of the bad weather, we still had to wait for the SS officials to count us, but they never showed up. It was very disturbing and unpleasant to be totally soaked. Our wet clothing clung tightly to our bodies. But despite all of our discomfort, we benefited from the rain. After several weeks having no water whatsoever available for us for washing ourselves and our clothes, our bodies and our soiled, smelly clothing were cleaned at least partially by the rain. During all that time we received no drinking water either, and we were constantly extremely dehydrated. The rain provided us with the very vital, much-needed fluid. We filled our metal bowls with rainwater and quenched our thirst and soothed our dry, parched lips.

We derived another major benefit from the rainy days. Due to the fact that the roads in the camp became very muddy and sticky from the constant downpour, we didn't go to work. That was a blessing and a much-needed break from our strenuous and extremely stressful work assignments.

But the rain also caused some serious problems for us. We had no replacements for our wet clothing. We had to wear it as it was and tolerate the unpleasant wetness until eventually it dried on our bodies. We had to sleep on the barren, damp floor of our barrack, poorly covered. We suffered from cold throughout the night, and we were also chilled during the day.

The adverse weather conditions also caused an unfortunate incident in our barrack which later on took a tragic turn. I will never forget it. This incident demonstrated how a traumatic experience can trigger a psychosis in a person who acted normally before the shocking occurrence. It involved one of our fellow prisoners, a kind and gentle twenty-five-year-old woman.

Because our barrack was poorly constructed and the roof was filled with big holes, the rain started pouring into our living quarters and the water level gradually became several inches deep. We were given pails to remove the stagnant water from our barren wooden floor. That stressful situation created mass hysteria and lots of agitation among the prisoners.

There were 500 women in our barrack and it was terribly overcrowded, which by itself was a disturbing and agitating factor. In the middle of the barrack there was a dividing wall with a connecting door separating the 500 of us into two sections of 250 prisoners living on each side of the dividing wall. Each section of the barrack had a separate entrance door. The prisoners on both sides of the connecting door were in the same situation; the water was pouring constantly into our spaces. But the prisoners on the other side of the wall had the false illusion that we were much better off on our side, so they decided to invade our place. They broke down the connecting door with full force. You can imagine what it was like when 250 women came in screaming. It was a mad, awful, dangerous stampede, which created a tremendous commotion. Unfortunately, our twenty-five-year-old fellow prisoner was close to the door and she began screaming. She defended herself by trying to strangle the people who came in next to her. She seemed totally out of her mind.

Due to all that noise and screaming, the *blockälteste* (senior barrack supervisor) came in with her whip and the SS guards came with their clubs to restore order. We got well beaten up. Finally everything quieted down and the 250 invaders retreated to the other side. But it happened that throughout the entire week there were more inundating rains. Each time it happened, we faced the same problems: the rain was pouring into our barrack and we used the pails to remove the water. But unlike the first time, we had to accept and live with the discomfort. We realized that our mass hysteria would only result in beatings and more suffering for us. At least we didn't have the invasion of the people from the other side like on that first day.

Nevertheless, our twenty-five-year-old fellow prisoner had a hysterical psychotic attack every time the heavy rains were pouring into our barrack. She became totally confused. She would scream, become aggressive, and attack and try to strangle some of the other prisoners. She was beside herself, in a delirium, reliving in her mind the initial frightening and shocking experience she had had. We tried to help her by holding her down. We worried about what would happen to her, because her psychotic spells were getting worse each time. After her spell subsided, she couldn't remember what she had done. We knew that those prisoners who had mental breakdowns like hers were executed because they weren't considered useful anymore. So it was very important that her condition not be discovered. We had to protect her as much as we could.

Then the horrible event took place. We had an unusually bad thunderstorm, accompanied by strong gusts of wind, and gushing water flooded our camp. Again the water poured into our barrack. We accepted our fate and were removing the water, as usual. Our poor psychotic fellow prisoner was having the worst spell when suddenly, because of the severe weather, the *blockälteste* came in, accompanied by SS guards to review the situation. When they came in, our fellow inmate was screaming, heading toward the *blockälteste*, trying to strangle her. It was her final spell. She was taken away and shot by the guards. We felt sorry about the death of our fellow inmate who under normal circumstances would have had a different fate. That showed us how crucial it was for our survival to control to the best of our abilities our mental attitudes and our reactions to extreme stress and suffering. But naturally, each person has a different psychological makeup and therefore the adaptation ability, the stress tolerance, and the reaction to unforeseen, shocking experiences varies from person to person.

Chapter 14

At the beginning of my sixth week in Auschwitz, the dreaded special selection again took place. By that time, more and more people were picked from our camp by Dr. Mengele for the gas chambers.

We heard that the grand selector also had experimental laboratories set up in Auschwitz-Birkenau which were located near the crematories. That terrified us because we faced the danger of being selected by him for criminal medical experiments, being used as human guinea pigs.

We were told that other SS physicians in the camp were collaborating with him in those macabre projects. One of them was Dr. Carl Klauberg, a gynecologist who sterilized some of the young women prisoners by injecting them with a certain chemical substance that burned their wombs. Women inmates were also exposed to harmful radiation in those laboratories in order to study the effect on humans. Others were injected with sex hormones. There were also those selected for all kinds of horrible experimental surgeries.

We were also told about Dr. Mengele's pet projects. He conducted terrible experiments on male twins and dwarfs by castrating them, and attempting to change the color of their eyes by injecting into them certain dyes that eventually caused blindness. He was also killing them by injecting chloroform into their hearts and dissecting them afterwards. He administered blood transfusions using incorrect blood types. He also performed all kinds of experimental methods of sterilization and other criminal medical experiments on female dwarfs and twins.

Other ghastly stories circulated in the camp about the Dark Angel of Death's horrifying experimental surgeries conducted on the inmates, like grafting of bones and muscles, limb amputations, all kinds of mutilations, and organ removals without anesthesia or antiseptic care. Some prisoners were inoculated with disease germs like cancer, tuberculosis, etc. Thousands of inmates died as a result of those experiments. Those who were terribly mutilated were thrown into the killing facilities.

Hearing all that, we were even more terrified not knowing what would happen to us at the special selections when Dr. Mengele would point his finger at some among us. We wondered to what other unbearable tortures we would be exposed. I was grateful that so far his finger had not pointed in my direction. But what would happen to my other comrades who were selected by him?

We never had peace. We lived in constant turmoil, fear, and terror of the unknown. We were totally helpless and our destiny was controlled by the SS demons.

We were always concerned about the fate of the pregnant women among us. Besides the one in our barrack whom we managed to save momentarily from death at one of the previous selections by preventing her from volunteering to reveal her condition to the SS officials, there were others in their early stages of pregnancy who were unaware of being pregnant at their arrival at camp and discovered their condition only later on.

We had to protect them the best we could, so their pregnancy would remain hidden from the SS guards and high officials. If their pregnant states were revealed, they would be taken to the gas chambers. The SS officials did not need pregnant women. They were considered not useful and, therefore, had to be eliminated. We heard that in one of the barracks in our camp a very primitive kind of infirmary had been established, conducted by a few inmates, physicians, and nurses who were fiercely determined to offer help to the pregnant women in order to save them from the gas chambers.

We were told that this camp infirmary acquired a drug which was administered by injection to the pregnant women, causing abortion of the fetus. In the more advanced stages of pregnancy, it brought forth premature births.

We also learned that in those cases when a woman actually gave birth to her baby, a lethal dose of a certain toxic substance was given to the newborn. That way at least the mother could be saved. The procedure was not revealed to her. She was told that her child was stillborn. That was a more acceptable situation to her. Otherwise, the mother and her baby would be killed in the gas chamber.

All that was a desperate effort on the part of the infirmary personnel to save the lives of the pregnant women. It was extremely difficult and agonizing for them to resort to such cruel and horrible methods.

It was the last day of my sixth week in Auschwitz-Birkenau. The dark, ominous clouds of depression again descended in full force upon me. I was living in a world of madness, where mass killings were daily events. Being in such close contact with so many corpses, I felt that a part of me also was dying and utter sadness fell upon my sick and suffering soul.

I was tired of living and yet I knew that I couldn't allow myself to succumb to desperation and hopelessness, because I would end up dead like so many of my comrades. I had to get hold of myself.

When we left for work on that particular morning, I noticed that there was a group of male prisoners working in our camp clad in striped prison clothing and wearing striped prison berets on their heads. They were repairing the big holes on the roofs of some of the barracks. A number of SS guards were watching over them. I hoped that they also would repair the sizable gaps in the roof of our barrack and plug up the numerous big cracks in the walls of our primitive living quarters. It would have been helpful to us because it would prevent the flooding of our barrack during the many rainy days which we had at that time in Auschwitz-Birkenau.

The heavily overcast day intensified my depressed mood. More and more corpses had to be cleared on that day. The tremendous flames and smoke rising from the chimneys of the crematories and the sickening smell emanating from them were driving many among us to insanity, giving rise to more suicides. The prolonged fluid deprivation and lack of solid food had a devastating effect on our health, causing the development of serious infectious diseases and other grave illnesses. Due to that, the death toll among us was steadily rising and reaching staggering proportions.

At the end of our work day in the late afternoon we were dragging ourselves, exhausted, hungry, and thirsty. We craved our miserable soup and stale bread—no matter how distasteful it was. Finally we returned to our barrack for the evening roll call. Being ravenous, I rapidly consumed the smelly soup. Afterwards I ran into our barrack before the distribution of our bread in order to grab a blanket for the night for our group of five women. Later on, when everyone came in, there was always a big rush and fierce fight for the blankets.

It was getting dark inside at that early evening hour. Not too much light could come in anyway through the two small windows we had. I was heading in semi-darkness to the corner of the room where all the blankets were placed. Suddenly I came face to face with a man prisoner who evidently was hiding there.

I was taken by surprise. I was shocked and frightened by that strange encounter. I froze in place. I was wondering how the man got there, who he was, and what he wanted Although I felt a great apprehension and amazement, I didn't run away. My curiosity overrode my fear. He noticed how frightened I was of him. He looked at me silently for awhile and then he handed me a piece of bread. I was hesitant to accept it. I wondered if what was happening to me was real or an illusion.

Then abruptly he broke the silence and asked me, "*Sprechen sie Deutsch?*" meaning, "Do you speak German?" I said, "*Ja.*" Then I questioned him, "*Wer sind sie and warum haben sie mir diesen stück brot gegeben?*" ("Who are you and why did you give me this piece of bread?") He seemed very pleased that I spoke the German language. He answered my questions. "I am a twenty-five-year-old Polish Jew. I was deported to Auschwitz much earlier than you Jewish people who were brought here from Hungary. My family members were gassed. I am living in the men's camp, Block B11D, on the opposite side of the *Lagerstrasse*, across from your women's camp. I gave you this bread because I wanted to help you."

I said, "I don't want to deprive you of your bread ration, so I can't accept it." But he insisted that I should take it, claiming that it was an extra piece he had.

"But how did you get into our barrack without being observed by the guards?"

He said, "I will explain it to you tomorrow. I will be here again to see you and bring you more bread. Don't mention our encounter to anyone." He left, using the back entrance of our barrack. After he left I was in a hurry to eat the bread given to me. It was so wonderful to have that small extra nourishment. I thought since I had that additional food that perhaps I could set aside a small portion of my daily ration of bread for the following day.

I ran out fast from the barrack to be present at the distribution of my daily ration of stale bread—and I kept silent about my strange encounter.

The following day turned out to be a very miserable one. At first it was just cloudy but later on a light rain was falling. The road became moist and slightly sticky. We had the same problem as on any rainy day—it was harder to walk, more difficult to work, the corpses became more slippery, we were getting more soiled, the guards were yelling and threatening us, more beatings occurred. It seemed that the flames of the crematories were also more intense. The smoke was considerably more irritating to our throats and eyes. I wondered whether we would be able to tolerate our torture much longer. Some of the inmates in our group were on the verge of collapsing.

I thought that maybe the only good thing amidst all that misery and suffering was meeting the Polish prisoner. I was looking forward to seeing him again, but I was not sure if he really meant what he said or if it would be possible for him to show up. On that evening I did the same thing as on the previous one. I didn't wait for the distribution of the bread, but instead ran into our barrack and headed to the same corner of the room—and there he was. The Polish man was waiting for me and had brought me another piece of bread.

At that time I was determined to find out more about him and about the things going on in our camps. I also wanted to know how he came to have extra food to give away.

We could only talk for a few minutes before the other inmates came in. During that brief period of time he told me that he was working at the selection platform at Auschwitz-Birkenau. He was part of the Canada Brigade, a work detachment assigned to clear the cattle cars of deportee belongings and load them into trucks to be transported to the Canada warehouses near the crematories. He told me that he also worked inside the Canada warehouses with a work *kommando* selected from the inmates by the German officials. Their job was to check the seams and linings of the clothing taken from the deportees and look for built-in pockets and secret compartments where they might have managed to hide jewelry, money, or other valuables. The Germans were very eager not to miss any goods brought along by the deportees. There were close to 2,000 women prisoners and over 1,500 male inmates delegated for that particular job and they were guarded by the SS.

He informed me that there were 20,000 inmates living in his camp, mostly Polish men, but also Hungarians, and there were others like him working at the Canada warehouses. He told me that their barracks were terribly crowded and in awful condition just like ours.

It was time for him to go. He left our barrack like before through the back entrance. I had to eat my piece of bread in a hurry because if my comrades had seen it they would have asked me how I acquired it, and maybe even suspected me of stealing it.

The Polish man appeared on the next evening at the same time, bringing me another piece of bread which was lifesaving considering our starvation diet. I got more information from him about what was going on in the camps.

He told me that there were many inmates in the Canada Brigade assigned to sort the goods taken from the deportees. In the stolen suitcases they found food items packed among their clothing like canned foods, wine bottles, cheese, and other products, including medicines, cigarettes, and other items. Therefore, whoever worked there had access to food and clothing. Stealing was common among the inmates although it was a risky business and life-threatening if they were caught in the act.

He said that the cigarettes and the alcohol were very important items. Some of the guards could be bribed by presenting them with those items. He explained to me that working in the Canada Brigade, he had access to food and to the above mentioned items, and he had become skilled at stealing.

Fortunately he had not been caught so far. I figured that he probably bribed some guards with cigarettes in order to get into our barrack. As I looked at him, I noticed that he didn't appear emaciated and he was quite handsome in his two-piece, striped prison garb and his striped beret.

Each day I looked forward to seeing him. I considered him a good friend, a nice and compassionate person who was helping and trusting me. When we met the fifth time he behaved somewhat differently. Instead of sharing information, he was telling me how pretty and attractive I was. I became suspicious of his intentions. Despite my young age and naiveté, I couldn't be fooled. How pretty could I look with my shaved head, my tired and dirty appearance, and my stinky dress, unwashed for several weeks? Then my suspicions were justified when he came close to me, put his arms around my waist, and tried to caress my body all over. I was shocked and disappointed, realizing that he had an ulterior motive in his mind, giving me the bread and trying to get close to me. I felt humiliated and disrespected.

I pushed him aside and told him, "I thought that giving me the bread was an act of kindness and caring on your part. But now I see that you expected me to prostitute myself in return for your gift. If that was your intention all along, then don't bring me any more bread and don't ever come back. But if I am wrong in my assumption, you can prove that bringing me food was an act of good will on your part by not expecting anything except friendship in return. Think about it. Today I refuse your bread. You can give it to someone else because you have humiliated me."

I wondered if he would show up again but he never did. I figured that my intuition was correct. It was so sad experiencing deceit and abandonment. I came to the conclusion that maybe true and pure friendship didn't exist in an environment where there was such a fearsome fight for survival, where a piece of bread became a cheap commodity for buying and using a person.

At the beginning of my eighth week in Auschwitz, there were special selections again. At that time, many inmates among us were either sick or in very weakened condition. They were considered not useful anymore and therefore were condemned to death. At the same time, there were also selections for work detachments for the others. I was selected with 500 other young women (300 Hungarian and 200 Polish women) from the various barracks of our camp for a new assignment. We wondered what would happen to us next.

In the morning we were given our evening portions of bread, which was very unusual. Then the male SS guards led us out of our camp to the railway station. We were placed into locked cattle cars and we left Auschwitz for an unknown destination.

During my previous seven weeks in Auschwitz I learned a lot about what was happening there. I had seen all the horrors, the terrible crimes committed, and the crematories working day and night. I knew that crematories No. 1 and No. 2 were the largest organized killing centers and crematories No. 3 and No. 4 were smaller but just as efficient in their functioning.

During my stay in Auschwitz-Birkenau there were all kinds of gruesome rumors circulating in our camp about what was taking place inside the killing centers, but only much later did I find out the correct information.

I learned that each of the largest two-story killing facilities (No. 1 and No. 2) was equipped with a huge underground dressing room and an enormous gas chamber, having the capacity to kill 3,000 people all at once. On the ground level was a very large incinerating room equipped with 15 ovens.

On the second floor were the living quarters of the *Sonderkommando,* the special work detachment of several hundred Jewish inmates selected by the German officials who were assigned to the gruesome task of handling the corpses of the gassed victims and servicing the crematories.

The smaller, one-story killing facilities (No. 3 and No. 4) had the same arrangements except that everything was contained on one level and their gas chambers had the capacity of killing 2,000 people all at once.

What happened to the people who were driven to those facilities?

Those deportees who were selected by Mengele to be gassed upon their arrival at Auschwitz-Birkenau were totally unaware of their terrible fate. They were accompanied by the SS guards and by professional classical musician inmates selected by the German officials to play for them. Could these people have imagined that it was their funeral march?

What happened to them after they entered the gates of the killing facilities?

At first 3,000 of them were led into a giant underground dressing room marked "Bath and Disinfection," where men, women, and children of all ages were forced to undress in front of each other. Whoever protested was beaten. They had to dispose of all their valuables, too. They were told to do that in order to take a bath. Then all the 3,000 people were pushed into a well-lit, enormous gas chamber located at the end of the dressing room. Once they were inside, the big swinging doors of the gas chamber were locked, air-tight, the lights were switched off, and a lethal gas called Zyklon B (with a base of hydrate of cyanide) was administered from outside through a system of underground pipes connected to the square, porous, sheet-iron pipes inside the gas chamber.

The gas seeped through the perforations and within five minutes, all the 3,000 deportees inside were dead. Some of the pregnant women gave birth in their last agonizing minutes of their lives.

After death the bodies of the victims were piled up in huge heaps. They were covered with blood, scratches, and feces because they injured each other in their struggle for air during those last five, horrible minutes of their lives. They also involuntarily defecated in that process.

After everything was over, the doors of the gas chamber were opened and the men of the *Sonderkommando* went in, wearing gas masks, to clear the chamber of the corpses. They hosed them and dragged them into the elevators which carried the bodies to the incinerating room. But before they were shoved into the ovens, their hair was shaved, so it could be cleaned and used for wigs, and pillow and mattress stuffing's. Their artificial limbs were removed, and their gold teeth extracted.

They stripped the dead of everything. The ashes from the crematories were used as fertilizer on the surrounding fields and gardens, and enormous quantities of the ash was dumped into the nearby Vistula River. All the clothing and other belongings left behind by the victims in the underground dressing room were loaded into trucks and taken to the Canada II warehouses.

The *Sonderkommando* men who had their living quarters on the second floor above the incinerating room were Polish,

Greek, French, and Hungarian inmates. They were provided with good food, decent lodgings, and comfortable bathing facilities. But their good life lasted only a short time. After four months of service they were killed, cremated, and replaced by others, so that the secret of what was going on there could not be revealed to us prisoners, to the German population, nor to the other countries of the world. That way the Germans could go on with their constant mass killings of all the Jewish people and fulfill Hitler's dream of exterminating all the Jews of Europe, who lived in the countries occupied by Germany.

Hitler also considered Gypsies an inferior race along with the Jews. They also were deported to Auschwitz-Birkenau and Dr. Mengele used many of them as guinea pigs in his infamous laboratories, conducting horrible experiments on them. Many Gypsy twins were castrated and mutilated.

There were also nuns and priests incarcerated and even executed in Auschwitz-Birkenau as Hitler forbade religious practices. They also were victims of the Holocaust along with the Jewish people, the Gypsies, and all the others who were considered the enemies of the Reich. Other victims were the political prisoners of all kinds of nationalities, although they were better treated than the Jews and Gypsies. The common criminals in Auschwitz got the best treatment.

But during June and July of 1944, when I was a captive in Auschwitz-Birkenau, the main focus of the Germans was concentrated on the Final Solution. It was considered their priority project.

During all that time the railroad cattle cars were carrying Jewish people in great masses from the various Hungarian ghettos to their execution in the killing factories of Auschwitz-Birkenau. Statistics showed later that during that short period more than half a million Jews from Hungary were killed in the gas chambers of the killing facilities.

I also learned later that in October, 1944, two-and-a-half months after I was taken out of Auschwitz-Birkenau, our Hungarian Jewish women's camp was liquidated and among the 32,000 women, only a few thousand survived. The others were in terrible condition and they were gassed and cremated. The survival rate in Auschwitz was minimal.

In the same month, on October 7, 1944, the twelfth group of *Sonderkommando* men rebelled. They blew up the No. 3 killing facility with dynamite and badly damaged No. 4. They were helped by the resistance group which was operating outside of Auschwitz-Birkenau. Seventy-seven SS officers lost their lives, but unfortunately all the *Sonderkommando* men of the four killing facilities were killed and cremated. Even the following thirteenth *Sonderkommando* group of men serving the killing facilities were gassed and cremated after that.

However, a very few *Sonderkommando* men still managed to escape and survived. Their testimonials revealed all the crimes committed there. Even some of those who were killed left behind their testimonials enclosed in bottles and canisters which were found buried in the ground of the courtyards of the killing facilities after the war.

The terrible crimes committed in Auschwitz-Birkenau could not be concealed because of those of us who survived the Holocaust. We were eyewitnesses to those criminal, cruel, and barbaric acts which cannot ever be denied.

Part Three

Chapter 15

We once again found ourselves cramped in locked railway cattle cars. Fifty of us were pushed into each wagon by the SS guards. The Polish prisoners were separated from us and were placed in other cars.

Finally the train started moving. Its steam locomotive huffed and puffed. We were leaving Auschwitz and all its horrors behind. I thought of all my dead companions and of my family members who had been killed in the gas chambers. I also wondered what would happen to our fellow inmates there after our departure.

The cattle cars were filthy. We had to sit on the smelly, wooden floors. It evoked the painful memories of our deportation to Auschwitz-Birkenau.

We were scared, hungry, and thirsty. We were given a single pail for our bathroom necessities and we were deprived of fluids. Fortunately, Pere and Jackie were also selected for our group and we were together in the same cattle car. Lily and Ilona were also with us. That gave me some comfort. At least I had some friends along. Ilus, the older, married woman from our barrack, was among us, too. I found her to be a compassionate person.

We traveled for two days under very stressful conditions. At night it got cold in our cattle car and we had no covers of any kind. We only had our ragged, dirty clothes and still no underwear.

Our conversations in the wagon centered on food, water, and fear and anxiety about our fate. We couldn't see much through the small openings of the primitive wooden boards that made up our compartment.

In the afternoon of the second day of our journey, the train stopped. The bolts were opened and we found out that we had arrived at Bremen, the second largest port city in Germany, located approximately 500 miles from Auschwitz-Birkenau.

Bremen is situated in the northern part of Germany on the banks of the Weser River, about forty-three miles from the North Sea and also about sixty miles from Hamburg, the largest port city of Germany, which is located on the Elbe River.

After we descended from the cattle cars, we were divided into two groups. Our group consisted of 300 Hungarian inmates, the other contained the 200 Polish prisoners. Each group had to form rows of five and we were led by the SS guards to trucks which were waiting to take us to our camp at the outskirts of the city.

As we rode in the trucks, we were horrified to see the city of Bremen in ruins. It looked like a graveyard with only parts of the buildings left standing, sticking out like tombstones. We realized that we had been taken to a war zone. We thought that Bremen must have been bombed day and night by the Allied Forces in order to look like that. We learned that we had been taken to Bremen to clear the ruins and perhaps also to remove the corpses of the aerial bombing victims from the streets.

German business contractors hired us as slave labor. They paid the German officials for our work, from which we got no benefit except harsh treatment. We also were considered expendable—we could be easily replaced by other prisoners from Auschwitz after they had drained all of our strength. We wondered what would happen to us, how long the war would last, and whether or not we would survive the bombings and the hard labor to which we would be assigned.

As we passed through the devastated city, we could see caravans of people moving away, carrying their possessions, seeking refuge somewhere else where it was safer to be. All of us were in a somber mood, feeling helpless and fearful of what our life would be like in that sinister-looking place.

Finally, the trucks arrived at the gates of the camp. There was a guard post in front of the highly-secured gate. One of the guards came out and opened the gate for us. The prison camp was surrounded by a high, heavy, intertwining barbed-wire fence, but it was not charged with a high-intensity electrical current like the ones in Auschwitz-Birkenau. We were pleased to see that.

In the enclosure behind the fence were rows of wooden barracks which were better constructed then the ones in

Auschwitz-Birkenau. Each barrack had a chimney. There also were guard posts occupied by armed SS guards beside the barbed-wire fence.

After we got out of the trucks, we again formed rows of five and the SS guards took us into our barracks. A number of the buildings were assigned to the Hungarian inmates and the others located across the way were for the Polish prisoners. We were divided into groups of sixty to seventy persons per barrack.

The barrack where I was taken with my group of people was a fairly large-sized room. It had electrical lights. Along its walls there were rows of three-tiered bunk beds. In the middle of the room there was a heating stove fueled by wood. The bunk beds in the barrack had two-inch-thick mattresses on them filled with straw. There was a blanket spread out on each of them but there were no pillows around. Each bunk bed was assigned to a single person. That seemed like a big improvement compared to what it was like in our barrack in Auschwitz, where the crowding was so terrible and we had to sleep on the bare floor pressed together like sardines.

In one corner of the room there were two pails for our bathroom necessities at night. At least we could stretch out normally during the night and not experience the cramped positions we had to endure in our barrack in Auschwitz. Any small improvement in camp life was of utmost importance to us.

Our supervisors at the Bremen camp were the SS men and women guards, but there were also some Wehrmacht soldiers (soldiers from the regular German army, not part of the SS troups) watching over us.

Finally we settled into our room. Pere, Jackie, and I tried to hang on closely to each other. We occupied one of the bunk beds with three tiers. Being the youngest, I climbed up on the third tier of the bunk bed. Pere settled on the second tier and Jackie on the lowest one.

Ilus, Lily, and Ilona settled on the adjacent bunk bed next to us. Ilus occupied the lowest tier of the bed, and Lily and Ilona settled on the two tiers above her. It was a good feeling to have my friends close by. We cheered each other the best we could.

We were looking forward to getting some food and something to drink. Our thirst was almost unbearable. Lo and behold, after awhile soup and bread was served to us and it tasted better than the disgusting, smelly soup and the miserable bread we received in Auschwitz-Birkenau. There were at least some potato slices and a few vegetables in the soup. Those were items of significance to us, considering our former watery soup at Auschwitz-Birkenau. The portions of food were also somewhat bigger than the ones in Auschwitz. The distribution of it was done by the SS women guards. There were no *blocovas* among us. We drank our soup from our metal bowls which we had carried along with us from Auschwitz.

After we ate the so-called dinner, we were allowed to go to the outdoor latrines which were also very primitive, similar to the ones at Auschwitz. The only difference was that they had a fence around them so that they were somewhat more private. There were also fewer of us so it was a little easier to get to them.

We didn't have the harassment we had endured in Auschwitz where we were only allowed a short time to satisfy our needs and risked beatings if we took too long. But just like in Auschwitz, we had no paper to wipe ourselves. Before we reentered our barrack, we noticed that there was a water faucet attached to the outside wall of our barrack and clear water was flowing out of it. That was a wonderful experience. Finally, we had access to some water and we could at least wash our hands, coming from the latrines. That was another very big improvement in our camp life in Bremen.

It was the end of our first day in Bremen. We were tired and exhausted, but more hopeful. The dark night enveloped our barracks. It was wartime when bombardments were frequent, so we had to have darkness inside our barracks. The guards outside were all around us, stationed at their guard posts.

It was a big relief to us that there were no killing facilities at Bremen, and we didn't have to face the big flames of the crematories nor inhale the smoke and the terrible odor coming from them.

Our barracks had somewhat bigger windows, no cracks in their walls, and no holes in their roofs.

At last all of us lay down on our bunk beds. Our clothes and our bodies were still dirty but it was such a relief to have individual bunks and a blanket for each of us.

We wondered what our next day would be like …

◆　◆　◆

Early in the morning we were awakened by the SS guards who came into our barrack, chasing us out of there. We again heard the familiar yelling, *"Schnell, schnell, heraus, heraus!"* The guards were armed and also had rubber clubs. The whole scene looked familiar to us, reminding us of Auschwitz-Birkenau. All of us in our camp were assembled outside in front of our barracks, but to our surprise, there was no roll call. Instead the so-called morning coffee of very poor quality was distributed to us by the SS women guards.

After we drank our coffee from our metal bowls, we had to form rows of five and we marched for a few minutes with our SS guards to the open trucks which took us into the center of the city. Once we got there we were assigned to different streets to clear the rubble left after the bombardments. We were supposed to look for whole bricks, stones, and metal pipes which might have remained intact after the bombings and could be reused for construction purposes.

We had to enter all kinds of spaces between the ruins of the bombed houses along the particular streets where we were working. There were incendiary bombs in some of those places which would suddenly explode when stepped on. The SS guards didn't mind exposing us to such dangerous assignments because our lives were not important to them. It didn't matter if some of us were blown up because we were easily replaceable.

We realized that although there were no killing facilities in Bremen, there were other life-threatening dangers looming. Our work involved lots of lifting which was a backbreaking job by itself. On top of that, we were in a place where there were constant heavy bombardments. We had no gloves while we worked and handling the rough materials was painful and scratched our skin.

In addition to our guards, there was also a foreman there from the construction company which had hired us as slave laborers from the German authorities. He was unkind to us and constantly watched over us, urging us to work faster.

The houses in Bremen were mostly constructed of bricks and their basements were built of stones. Therefore there were lots of brick and stone ruins to be cleared. The materials which could be reused had to be hauled into trucks. We carried heavy metal pipes, bricks, stones, and other parts of the destroyed houses to load them on trucks. It was very heavy work for us women.

It was sad to look at some of the streets where all the houses had been leveled by the bombs. War is a terrible curse for everybody.

We could see civilians walking on the streets to their places of work, carrying small suitcases filled with some of their belongings. It was a precaution they took so they would not lose everything they possessed in case their homes were hit by the bombs. They wanted to save at least a few small assets. I felt sorry for them, too. They also were the victims of the war. Regardless of the cruel and hateful environment into which I was locked, my compassion and humaneness could not be killed.

During all our work hours we didn't get any food or drink. Again we suffered terribly of dehydration, especially considering that we were sweating a great deal during our heavy labor.

Occasionally we pulled out bodies of victims which had been buried under the rubble of some houses. We saw the ugly and cruel face of the war and its human sacrifices. We prayed for peace and harmony.

We had been working for several hours when suddenly we heard the sound of the sirens. The Allied bombers were coming. We had to interrupt our work and seek shelter in a hurry.

The civilians in Bremen were prepared for that at all times. There were shelters all around the city. Most of them were solid underground bunkers. Yet there were also those which were ten stories above ground, very massively built, having the capacity to accommodate big crowds. We heard that those were safer and gave more protection during the bombardments than the underground ones. Even if they were directly hit by a bomb, several of their stories remained intact.

The prisoners were never allowed to enter any of them. We were always taken to the smaller underground bunkers.

The underground bunker we were taken to by our guards had a massive steel and concrete door and extremely thick and heavy-looking concrete walls. It had electrical lights and wooden benches to sit on.

When we got in, there were already a number of civilians inside. Shortly after we settled, we heard the loud roaring of the war planes and then the whistling sounds of the bombs as they came down, big explosions one after the other.

We were scared and prayed that our bunker wouldn't be hit by the bombs. We had to sit silently and hope for the best. It was the first time in my life that I experienced a bombardment. All of us inside the bunker were terrified. We felt that at any moment we could be next to explode.

We were surprised at how calm and composed the people of Bremen were. They were accustomed to daily and nightly bombardments, and they were disciplined. It was amazing to see how they had gotten used to their miserable lives during the war. Some of them had nowhere else to go, so they accepted and lived with the constant threat to their lives. Hitler did a lot of harm to his own people, too.

The bombardment lasted for quite some time. Finally the sirens sounded again, indicating the end of bombing, and we gradually left our bunker. The scene we faced when we got outside was very depressing.

Houses were burning and there was heavy smoke in the air. Fragments from the shattered buildings were scattered on the streets. Many people were in despair, finding their homes leveled. There was confusion and chaos. The transportation vehicles in the city were affected. Some people were hurt because they were unable to reach shelter in time. They needed assistance. Being stuck on the streets of Bremen during bombardments could turn into tragedy. Some people lost their lives. The bodies of the aerial bombing victims had to be collected and there was lots of rubble to be hauled away. We were facing a horrific nightmare. I had never seen anything like it. I felt great compassion for all the suffering people. War was an evil force, bringing along only destruction, death, and disaster.

Our SS guards were eager to get back to our camp. Fortunately our trucks were not damaged and finally we could leave the streets of Bremen and return to our barracks. Because of all the commotion in the city, it took us longer to get back to our living quarters.

When we entered the gate of our camp, every one of us was checked by the SS women guards. It was highly punishable to be found with anything taken from the bombed houses or any food items that we might have had the opportunity to find and take along with us.

At last, we were taken to our barracks and we received our soup and bread which we had been anticipating throughout the day. It was so soothing and comforting to have some warm food.

After that, we retired to our bunk beds for the night, finally getting some rest after our trying, exhausting, and shocking experiences on the streets of Bremen.

Although I was tired, I couldn't fall asleep. I couldn't wipe out of my mind the horrible scenes of the tragic events which took place on my second day in that doomed city. I wondered whether I would survive the hard labor to which I was subjected and I was afraid of the bombardments. I didn't want to die. I felt that I had yet many things to accomplish in my life. I wanted to live, regardless of all the extreme hardships and suffering.

Eventually, I fell asleep and had a strange dream in which my fear of death was reflected. In my dream I was walking in a cemetery and I could hear the voices of the dead people coming out of their graves. They were telling me, "The bombs hit us! We hope that you will be saved from destruction and not end up here below, among us. But no one can tell what might happen to you!"

My nightmare was abruptly interrupted by the loud voices of SS guards: "*Heraus! Heraus! Schnell! Schnell!*" It was the early morning of my third day in Bremen.

We were again taken to the streets of Bremen in order to continue the clearing of the ruins left from the intense bombardment of the city we had witnessed on the previous day.

We were assigned to work at the site of one of the houses which had been totally leveled at that time. When we got to that place, there was a frail, feeble-looking old lady standing there with a small shovel in her hand, trying to dig a hole in the bare ground where her house had been just a day before. I felt great compassion and pity for her. She looked so distressed and pathetic. I could never forget her. She lost everything she owned and there was no way that at her age she could replace her assets. She had become destitute in one day.

I wrote of our encounter and our exchange of thoughts many years after my liberation from the camps.

Futility

A frail and feeble old woman
was digging a hole,
poor soul!

Her face was wrinkled,
her skin looked shriveled,
her spine was bent.
Her hair had lost its color and shine,
it was as white as snow
at Christmas time.
She wore a pair of old brown shoes.
A shabby grey coat
covered her thin body.
A wornout black velvet hat
trimmed with purple lilies
rested on her head,
reminding me
of a faded funeral bouquet.
Her knotty fingers
were grasping firmly
a small shovel,
plunging it continuously
into the hard ground.
She kept on working frantically,
gasping for air
now and then
in despair.
As I watched her,
my heart was filled
with compassion and pity.
I asked her kindly,
"Dear lady,
what are you looking for?

Please save your energy,
don't work so hard anymore."
She straightened, and looked at me.
Her eyes were dull and sad.
Tears ran down her pale cheeks,
and pointing to the piles of crumbled ruins,
she said,
"This is what's left
of my house.
There is buried my family.
I am looking for my silver box
containing my golden jewelry.
I could sell it,
and get some money
so I could eat
a few warm meals occasionally,
and I could have a bed
to rest my aching bones.
To hell with wars!"
she shouted.
And she grabbed again her instrument,
thrusting it deeper and deeper
into the earth,
hunting for her lost treasure,
and hoping to find the small remains
of a lifetime.
But the hole was empty and hollow.
Lost was her past, her present,
and her tomorrow.

I turned to her and exclaimed,
"Please tell me your name.
You and I
share a common destiny.
We both are caught
in war's ugly, cruel,
and bloody game."

There was no way that I could deter that poor, old lady from continuing to dig and search for something valuable hidden in the earth on which her house had been built. I even offered to help her dig but she refused my offer. Maybe she didn't trust me and worried that I would want to share part of the treasure. She needed all of it for her survival.

After a while the siren was heard, alerting us that again the Allied war planes were approaching and we hurried to look for shelter. Although we were scared of the bombs, we welcomed the bombers because at least we could have a break from our exhausting work, sitting on the benches of the bunkers. But it was a false alarm. However, it took awhile until the "all clear" siren was heard and we had to leave our bunkers and start working again.

We were hungry and thirsty. We had backaches from the heavy weights we were carrying and loading onto the trucks. Later in the afternoon we returned to our camp. We were checked upon entering as usual. Our dinner was served. Finally, we retired for the night. Another day had passed by in Bremen.

♦　♦　♦

On our fourth day in Bremen we were accompanied to our workplace by the most vicious SS guards. Two of them were exceptionally cruel. One was a short and stocky young man who took pleasure in kicking us without any reason as we walked to the open trucks in the morning. The other one was a tall, well-built, good-looking man. He reminded me of the infamous Dr. Mengele. He enjoyed doing the same thing as his comrade.

We knew that we would have a miserable day. Our intuitions were right.

On that day we were taken to a bombed-out metal pipe factory. Among the ruins there were buried heavy, thick metal pipes which we had to dig out. One of them was especially heavy. We were supposed to lift it and throw it on the trucks where all the others were loaded. Only a small number of us inmates were assigned to lift it. It was way too difficult for us to do without getting more people to help.

I spoke the German language well. I decided to talk to the good-looking SS guard, hoping that maybe he would have enough decency to realize that we needed more helpers. I explained to him that we had difficulty lifting and carrying the pipe. I asked him to allow us more helpers. He asked me, "So, you need more help? I am going to give it to you." He came over to assess the situation. I believed him. He looked at us and said, "I will help you by counting to three, and if you are unable to lift this piece of metal, I will shoot all of you." We realized that he meant what he said. It was very strange that when our lives were threatened, we did the seemingly impossible: we lifted and carried the pipe and threw it on the truck. The life force within us created a miracle. Afterward all of us suffered severe back pain. We thought that we were badly injured. It turned out that we were fortunate, ending up only with strained muscles. We couldn't understand how that was possible. It just showed that if we had to, we could tolerate more pain and suffering than we could imagine.

We were hoping that the bombers would come so we could interrupt our work. Our wishes came true. We heard the roar of the bombers and we could even see the silver-colored Allied war planes in the distance, heading our way. The sirens were wailing and to our relief, we again entered the bunkers where we could rest. The bombardment lasted for about one hour, off and on, during which time we sat silently on the benches inside the bunkers. Even the whistling sounds of the bombs coming down and hitting targets, causing big explosions, didn't bother us anymore. The most important thing was that we were inside, away from the streets of Bremen.

When the bombardment was over, the scene on the streets was again the same as after each bombing: houses burning, smoke in the air, ruins, injured people, casualties. We were assigned to clear the ruins, to drag the bodies of the victims to be loaded into ambulances. It was hard to get back to our barracks following the bombardments. It took us a fairly long time to get to our camp. Another day passed by and we were happy that we were still alive.

Chapter 16

*T*he big surprise on the fifth day in Bremen was that for the first time, Wehrmacht soldiers from the regular German army accompanied us to our place of work. That was an unusual occurrence. We were aware from the beginning that their behavior towards us was very different from the SS guards. They didn't treat us with cruelty. They were more humane. They didn't kick or slap us while we were walking to our open trucks, and they didn't use harsh words against us. We were very pleased about it, although we were still suspicious of them. We thought that maybe they were up to something and intended to trick us in some way. We were not accustomed to having any kindness expressed by our guards.

But our Wehrmacht soldier guards proved themselves trustworthy. On that particular day, we were taken to clear some different streets of piles of stones and bricks. There was a foreman there from one of the construction companies that hired us from the Germans. While he was there we had a hard time because he was watching over us, harassing us, pushing us to work faster. Our guards didn't do that. One of our Wehrmacht guards was kind to us and when the foremen disappeared temporarily, he said to us, "Take it easy, relax a little, I will make a sign to you when he shows up." We were amazed: that was the first kindness and human understanding that had been directed towards us.

We were always preoccupied with the idea of finding some food buried underground at our places of work on the streets. Sometimes the discarded food in a garbage can was also a source of some nourishment, considering our starvation diet.

On that day, our Wehrmacht guards allowed us to explore a garbage can if one was available. It was one of our best days. Among the ruins of one of the houses we found some rags which helped us a great deal, because we could wrap them around our hands, protecting them somewhat from the rough edges of the partially destroyed building materials which we had to handle. The guards left us in peace and allowed us to take them. One particular Wehrmacht guard continued to be exceptionally kind and compassionate towards us.

There were some false alarms of bombing raids on that day but nothing much happened. The fifth day slowly passed by and we were again in our barracks stretched out on our bunk beds, looking forward to rest and sleep before we faced the morning of our sixth day in Bremen.

♦ ♦ ♦

That sixth day in Bremen was a lucky one. First of all, again the Wehrmacht soldiers were our guards who took us to our work place in Bremen. That by itself was a good omen for us. We anticipated a better day and better treatment.

On that day our work assignment was to clear the ruins of a bombed cheese factory. My friend Ilus found some big round blocks of cheese buried among the ruins. At first it was not clear what they were because their top layers were burnt and they looked black and hard. But Ilus was a resourceful and imaginative person. She was determined to remove the hard crust by using a sharp fragment of a brick. Underneath the top layers of the burned surface of the cheese, there were the soft, white, edible parts of the cores, which tasted delicious. All of us had a feast on that day.

It was lucky for us that we had our Wehrmacht guards with us and not the SS ones. They allowed us to dig out, clean, and distribute the blocks of cheese among us. It was a wonderful experience. The SS guards would have beaten us for even trying to dig out the blocks of cheese. They were very cruel and sadistic. I truly believe that some of them were psychopaths. In the camps they enjoyed beating us and depriving us of anything which would help us to survive.

At some point, Ilus, who also spoke German, asked our guards if they would like to have one cleaned block of cheese for themselves. To our surprise, they accepted her offer. They didn't have that much food themselves. There were hard times in Germany during the war. Everything was rationed. We couldn't believe our eyes seeing our guards eating the cheese offered to them from a Jewish inmate. It was a unique and wonderful experience, sharing our food with our guards. We wished that they would come with us every day, but we knew that it would not happen. Our work day ended. It was our best day so far.

It was Sunday, my seventh day in Bremen. On that day we didn't go to work. It was our day of rest which was very much needed considering the hard and stressful labor which we faced daily on the streets of Bremen. On that day we could take time to groom ourselves in a minimal way.

In the morning, after we drank our coffee, we were allowed to go outside to the water tap attached to the side of our barrack to wash our hands and faces. Then we filled a few pails that had been given to us with water and carried them into our barrack. Finally, we removed our filthy clothes which hadn't left our bodies for over two months. We rubbed some water with our hands over our bodies in order to clean them to a small degree. We didn't have anything to dry ourselves. Then we wiped some of the dirt from our clothing by wetting the small pieces of rags which we had found among the rubble of the bombed homes, the rags that the Wehrmacht guards had allowed us to keep. We brushed off some of the accumulated, dried, disgusting filth. As there were no showers in our camp, that was the only way that we could clean ourselves in some small way. Then we lay down naked on our bunk beds and covered ourselves with our thin blankets for a short time. It felt good to air our bodies and our clothes.

On Sunday, we received our soup and bread at noon. We didn't have the freedom to walk around freely in our camp because we were surrounded by armed SS guards along the barbed-wire fence of our camp. Our movements were monitored. In many ways we were confined to our barracks although we were free to go to the latrines.

We spent our free day mostly resting on our bunk beds and talking among ourselves. We reminisced about our good times when we were with our families, our loved ones, and we had freedom and a normal lifestyle. There were endless discussions about food, citing different recipes for cakes and dinner preparations.

Then we expressed our fears about our future, wondering if we would survive and visualizing what our liberation would be like and what would happen after our liberation from the camp, upon our return to our families. Whom would we find? Would any of our loved ones be alive? The thought of losing them terrified us. Because we were a much smaller group in our barrack compared to the big numbers in Auschwitz, and because we had individual bunk beds which gave us more comfort than the hard wooden floor of our barrack in Auschwitz where we had been pressed together like sardines, we got along much better with each other.

I managed to talk to other young women who were somewhat closer to my age. Among them were two sisters who also were former residents of my native city of Cluj. One of the women was a student at the medical school of the University of Cluj. She was about twenty-two years old. Her sister was about twenty years old. They were talking about the young men who had been courting them. Some of the older women in our barrack who were in their mid-thirties and early-forties talked a great deal about their husbands, their married lives, and their children whom they probably would never see again. They expressed their grief and pain. Pere was talking about her love for my Uncle Eugene, and Jackie was thinking about her husband.

I liked Ilus who was forty-one and a very caring person. She was helpful to me, very protective and motherly. She was worried about her husband. Lily and Ilona were closest to my age. We talked about our years in the elementary school when we were in the same class.

On that Sunday, the guards left us in peace. They probably figured that they had to do that in order to ensure we could work throughout the following week. It seemed that from then on, we would be exempt from work every Sunday. That was wonderful news for us. At least we would have some freedom and rest one day a week.

During the following weeks, the bombings of the City of Bremen continued almost daily. There also were many false alarms. Frequently we spent time in the bunkers. But we enjoyed that situation more and more despite its life-threatening implications, because it gave us some respite from our trying work assignments. The hard labor of clearing the streets of Bremen went on day after day. The Allied war planes also dropped their bombs during the nights, creating fear, destruction, and terror. We were caught in the middle of all that. But as time went on, somehow we got used to that perilous environment. We realized that we had to accept it because we had no other choice. The most important thing for us was to stay alive. It was inevitable to feel depressed under the grueling circumstances we experienced, but nevertheless, unlike in Auschwitz, suicides were less prevalent among us in Bremen.

The desire to survive was stronger in us than the wish to die.

The month of August came to its end. The season of autumn was on its way. The weather changed. It was getting colder in Bremen. In September, there were more cool, rainy, and humid days. It was getting colder in our barracks and we still had only our poor, deteriorating clothing which we had received upon our arrival at Auschwitz. It was inadequate for the cold fall weather. Our thin blankets did not give us enough warmth at night anymore.

Towards the middle of September, we were taken to work in the vicinity of the Weser River, at the site of a bombed brick factory. There were big piles of whole bricks lined up for us to haul and load on a big truck. They evidently were saved and assembled after the bombings. I will never forget that particular day. The weather was miserable. There was a slow, constant drizzle, along with a cold wind. We had vicious SS guards with us and a nasty foreman from one of the construction companies that hired us from the Germans. He also persecuted us, pushing us to work faster. We had a day of torture.

We had to form a long chain of people. One of us was assigned to stand at one end by the piles of bricks. She had to pick up one whole brick at a time and throw it to the next person in line. And in that fashion, the bricks were thrown piece by piece from one person to the next in line. The last person standing at the other end of the line was stationed by the big truck. She was the one to throw the incoming bricks into the truck. We didn't have any gloves while we were doing that. Nobody cared how we felt when the cold and rough bricks hit our hands time and time again, creating scratches and abrasions on our skin.

We were also hungry, thirsty, and cold. I was very sad, and tears were running down my face. I was thinking that if my parents could see my suffering, it would break their hearts. They probably wouldn't even recognize me: shaved and dressed like a clown with my long, blue, spotted, dirty dress, hanging like a sack on me. They would cry to see my palms bleeding, due to the merciless, constant impact of the rough bricks on them. The SS guards took pleasure from our suffering. We were the "dirty, Jewish, valueless prisoners" who were not to be spared from cruelty nor pain.

My thought at the time was: *Life without liberty is plain agony.*

Nobody provided us with any food or drink during all of our working hours. On that day all of us felt such sadness, hopelessness, and distress. We asked ourselves how much more suffering we could tolerate.

We hoped that the Allied war planes would come soon to save us temporarily from our torture. We always could count on them. And sure enough, they did come to our rescue. Fortunately, nothing much happened. It was only a false alarm, but we could find relief in the bunker.

After we returned to our barrack, we rinsed our hands at the water tap as well as we could and hoped that they would somehow heal by themselves as there was no treatment available for us for our wounds. There was no disinfectant around. We didn't even have any soap. We wondered what the following days would be like and what other misfortunes we would encounter.

It was the end of the third week of September, the time of the onset of our biggest Jewish holiday, the Day of Atonement, Yom Kippur, which represents the Day of Judgment. We believe that on that day God is going to register us in the book of Life or Death.

It was early in the evening on the day before the actual holiday. After returning from our work on that day, I had a pretty severe sore throat. It was hard for me to even swallow the soup and it was too painful to eat my hard, stale bread. So I traded my portion of bread with one of my fellow prisoners in exchange for her bowl of soup the next day. Bread was a very important item, being our only solid food. Therefore, I had no problem making a deal with my comrade.

I felt awful, and I lay down on my bunk to rest. My sore throat worsened and I knew that I had fever because I was getting very cold and somewhat dizzy. I realized to my horror that I was coming down with a strep-throat infection. I used to have this same infection often in my teenage years. I became very worried and restless. I realized that I needed help. I got down with difficulty from the third tier of my bunk bed. I was so dizzy that I was hanging on to the wall and heading to the infirmary which we had in Bremen, in order to ask for a painkiller, something to alleviate my discomfort. We could come up from the barracks and walk directly through a hall to the infirmary. I fought my way through and entered it for the first time. For a while I hadn't even known of its existence. There were two or three nurses there, wearing white robes.

The infirmary was very primitive, consisting of one large room which had two parts. One part had some drugs, mainly a very limited number of painkillers, like aspirin. In the other part, there were fifteen or twenty regular beds with mattresses which could accommodate the very sick people. When I saw that, I wished I could stay there and sleep on one of the regular beds throughout the night, or maybe also during the next day, and be taken care of by the nurses and exempt from work until I felt better. Some of the beds were occupied by sick people. But the German nurses who worked there were not very compassionate towards us prisoners. I asked one of them for an aspirin, but she told me to get out because I wasn't sick enough and I didn't get anything.

We had to be very sick in order to be accepted there. A strep throat in their opinion was a minor illness. But if one had the misfortune of getting a serious disease, it was life-threatening to stay there any length of time, because one really didn't receive much treatment. Also one would be considered not useful for work anymore and would end up being taken away from there to be exterminated, perhaps in the

257

gas chambers of Auschwitz. They didn't need sick people who couldn't work in Bremen.

In my opinion, the whole infirmary was just the antechamber of Death. Even if we had scratches or abrasions on our hands from work, we had to live with them because we couldn't get any disinfectants or bandages. Maybe the only ones who got help in that infirmary were the SS personnel.

As a prisoner in Bremen, your only chance of surviving was being able to work. After I was thrown out of the infirmary, I realized that I couldn't count on any real help from there whatever my problem was.

I returned to my barrack feeling very sick. I could barely climb up to the third tier of my bunk bed. I had fever and an extremely painful sore throat. After an agonizing night, I felt weak and exhausted. I dreaded the morning, knowing that I would have to perform the hard, backbreaking slave labor of clearing the ruins and the bodies of the bombing victims on the streets of Bremen, exposed to the cold weather.

In the morning, I begged one of the guards to let me stay in the barrack, but he said that I couldn't because I wasn't sick enough for that, even though my sickly condition was obvious to everyone. I figured that it would be my end if I had to work on the streets in cold weather with high fever. I prayed to God that the Allied war planes should come so that we could go to the shelter where I could sit down and be out of the cold wind. The only good thing was that we had some Wehrmacht guards with us who were more considerate than our SS guards.

It was the Day of Atonement. Our guards took us to work at the site of a bombed jelly factory. My friend, Ilus, found an old raincoat in the rubble, which was a welcome miracle because I was shivering all over my body due to my fever. Ilus gave it to me, seeing my sickly condition. It felt so good to have that coat on my body. I warmed my freezing hands in the pockets of that coat. The Wehrmacht guard who was standing next to me, supervising our work, allowed me to keep the coat. He felt sorry for me. He was our most humane guard. It was my luck that he was with us on that morning.

Another miracle happened to me on that day. As I was digging, I found two small jars of jelly in the rubble. I hid them in the pockets of my coat and I hoped they would not be discovered by the guards. I wanted to take them along with me to our camp, although it was very risky to do that. If the jars were found when I was checked at our return, I would be severely punished by being beaten, or placed in the punishment cell. But I was desperate to have them because I figured that their sweet contents would be soothing to my throat.

We had been working for about two hours when the sirens went on. The bombers were coming, and we interrupted our hard labor, going to the nearby underground bunker in a hurry. It was such a relief for me to get away from the streets and the cold and rest on the wooden bench in the bunker. On that day on our holiday of the Day of Judgment, the biggest bombardment of the city of Bremen took place. It lasted for about forty-five minutes, on and off. We could hear the whistling of the bombs hitting their targets, followed by huge explosions. At one point, there was a tremendous detonation and we knew that the explosion happened close by, because the electrical lights in the bunker went off and our whole bunker was shaking back and forth. Its heavy steel and concrete door was pushed open under the horrendous pressure of the nearby impact. I was terrified and I prayed, "Oh, God, don't let me be a cripple and die in the gas chambers. Better to let me die on the spot and register me in the Book of Death on this Day of Atonement." But the shaking of our bunker stopped. No bombs hit us.

Shortly after that, the "all clear" siren signaled that the bombing was over and the war planes had left.

When we finally got out of the bunker, we faced a horrifying scene: the bunker next to ours had been hit and all the Russian prisoners and others in that bunker died.

The Wehrmacht guards who were with us in the bunker believed that all of us Jewish women were protected by God and that it was the Judgment Day for the others. They were pleased that they were with us and that they had survived.

When we had entered the bunker, there had been a car nearby. After the bombardment it looked like a compressed piece of metal. Homes were burning. People were caught by the flames and were running out of their houses. The loud, shrill sirens of the ambulances were heard. Some of the people were wounded. There were casualties all around. Many people died on that day.

The memory of that day was imprinted in my mind forever. Only later on, many years after my liberation from the camps, I wrote the following poetic narrative describing what I witnessed on that Day of Atonement in the city of Bremen.

The Doomed City

The dark clouds of tragedy
were hanging over the forsaken city.
I felt sorry for humanity.
The earth was shaking,
bombs were exploding.
Funnels of black smoke
were twisting in the air,
poisoning the atmosphere.
I remember a young girl
caught by the fire,
fleeing from her burning home.
Her slender body was trembling
from fear and pain.
She was crying desperately,
"Please save my family!
They are trapped inside."
But all efforts of rescue
were in vain.
Encircled by the raging flames,
her house was rapidly collapsing
to the ground.
Her parents were never found.
She wasn't the only victim of the war.

I have seen so many more
during my captivity,
in the second-largest port city
of Germany.

Seeing all that devastation, our guards were worried that another round of bombardment might occur, and they were anxious to get back to our camp as soon as possible. They were concerned about the difficulties in transportation, as many vehicles had been crushed during the bombardment. But fortunately our trucks were intact. We left Bremen in a hurry, while so many people needed help. Although I was feeling very sick and going away from the stricken city and not being on the streets was beneficial to me, I felt that it was not fair to abandon the poor people who were hurt and not give them any assistance. We would have liked to comfort them and help them, but our guards did not allow us to do that. Their main concern was their own safety and nothing else mattered to them.

When we returned to our camp, we found only rubble. Our barracks had been bombed and they were leveled. The infirmary also was hit. Had I been inside it or in our barrack, I would have died. We were taken to another camp further away, located in the far suburbs of Bremen. Due to the chaos and all the excitement, we were not checked, so I could smuggle in my two little jars of jelly. I was lucky because probably I would have been severely beaten by the SS guards if they had found them. Bringing in any food items, even a rotten potato which we might have found in a garbage can, was highly punishable. The German officials' purpose was not to keep us alive, so any extra food meant help for our survival. Finally we got into our new living quarters which had similar arrangements to those in our previous camp.

Later on, the soup and bread was distributed. Due to my severe sore throat, I had difficulty in even swallowing my soup, and again, I gave away my bread to my comrade, making another agreement with her that in exchange, she would give me her soup on the following day.

I was cold and miserable. I was suffering so much. Chills were running down my spine. When everything was quiet and everyone was asleep, I opened my two little jars and gradually, I savored their sweet, delicious contents. It was very soothing to my throat.

When I woke up the next morning, another miracle had happened. My sore throat and my fever were gone. So the chain of events which I had thought were going to be fatal for me actually became my salvation. It showed me that in the worst situations in which we find ourselves, we should never lose our hope for God's help to bring a favorable change in our destiny and save us from destruction.

I prayed to the Almighty that we would not be checked before we left for work because I had the two empty jelly jars in my pocket. There was no way to hide them inside the barrack because every morning after we left for work, even our mattresses were searched. So the only way to get rid of my jars was to discard them on the streets of Bremen.

My prayer was heard because a very unusual thing happened. We were not checked on that particular morning. I was so relieved! Later on I deposited my jars among the ruins which we were clearing on the streets of Bremen.

I said my thanks to God for that. It was good that I recovered from my strep throat, because on the day following the terrible bombardment, there was lots of hard work facing us. We realized the horrendous damage created by the previous day's extremely intense bombardment. There was lots of rubble to clear, and dead bodies to pull from under the ruins. We witnessed so much tragedy. In some of the streets, all the houses were entirely gone. Many people had become homeless.

I wished for peace and the end of war and all the destruction created by it. Witnessing all that misery and loss of life, my thoughts were: *Why do we have wars? Why can't we live in peace with each other? The monsters of history create wars. I wish Hitler had never been born. He is destroying us and his people.* I had very strong feelings and hatred against wars. I expressed those thoughts much later in my life in the following poem:

War

War! Master of terror!
Hide your ugly face,
don't ever come back to our place!
Your sins shall never give you rest!
You are the killer
who tore away children
from the mother's breast,

slaying with your right hand,
smashing with your left.
Your crimes I will never forget.
You! Who destroyed mankind,
leaving tears, miseries, fright, sorrows,
empty ruined homes, and widows behind.
You! The carrier of pest and distress,
who cast your black shadow once upon us,
covering, shutting out lights, thus,
sharpen your ears,
open your senses,
listen to my curses:
I wish your death.
Your home should be Hell,
burn in its fires!
Hear, oh hear, you cruel wrath,
these are my true desires.
But I know, all is in vain.
Today you die,
tomorrow, you are born again.

At the end of the day we were exhausted physically and emotionally.

At dinner time, my comrade asked me, "What about my soup, do you still want it? It seems that you are feeling much better." I answered: "You can have it. I wouldn't like to deprive you of it now that miraculously I have recovered from my sore throat." I could see that she rejoiced in the annulment of our deal.

On that night I had a strange dream. In my dream I called for my father. I wanted him to help me get home from that awful and dangerous place where I was living. He appeared and listened intently to me as I told him how much I was suffering and how much I missed him and my mother. Then he looked at me and said, "My dear daughter, I can't help you anymore. From now on, you have to be able to help yourself." In my dream, I was very sad and desperate. I was thinking that my father had never abandoned me. What was happening that he decided to desert me? It was the first time that he had let me down.

When I woke up the following morning, I had an awful premonition. A terrible thought crossed my mind. *Maybe my father has been killed and, therefore, he can't help me anymore.* The idea that he might not be alive terrified me.

Chapter 17

The month of September came to its end. In October and November the weather got much colder. There were many rainy and humid days. We had no change of clothes. We were still wearing the flimsy dresses which we received in Auschwitz-Birkenau. Now and then some of us found some old, partly damaged clothes among the ruins and if we were lucky enough to have a good Wehrmacht guard with us that day, they let us keep them. I personally had only my long, blue, worn dress and the small raincoat, the one my friend Ilus found under the ruins on the Day of Atonement. It was nice to have that at least, although it didn't provide enough warmth, since I still didn't have any underwear.

We thought that the German officials would at least give us some warmer clothes for the cold months ahead, but we received nothing in return for our daily, hard, and stressful labor.

We constantly suffered from cold and hunger. Our small rations of bread and our soup, which contained a few vegetables, was totally inadequate food for us. It was of poor nutritional quality. We needed more substantial food, much richer in calories, to sustain us. Some people began to lose their teeth due to vitamin deficiencies. Every day I checked my teeth to see if they were moving, but fortunately they were still solidly anchored in my jaw.

Because of the cold weather, pneumonia became more prevalent among us. The people who ended up in the infirmary were not treated. After being there for a few days, they deteriorated even more and ultimately they were taken away and we never saw them again. They were probably eliminated, being not useful for work anymore.

The bombings in Bremen became worse as time went on. The Allied war planes dropped their bombs during the day and also at night. We often wondered if we could stay alive under those conditions. Yet we still had to go on and fight for our lives while it seemed that we were in an almost hopeless situation.

In December it started to snow. The winter weather created many aggravations for us. By that time, our shoes were wearing out. Working day after day in the rough ruins was hard on them and they were falling apart. Hard, stiff, wooden Dutch clogs were given to us which were too open and too cold. We didn't receive any socks. Therefore we were happy whenever we found any kind of rags under the ruins. We would wrap them around our feet inside our shoes in order to protect them to some extent from frostbite.

It was cold in our barrack. We were allowed to heat it only once a week on Sundays for only two hours. We eagerly awaited Sundays when we could warm ourselves for a short time.

The early morning hours in winter were very chilly. We had to walk with our wooden Dutch shoes on ice and snow to the trucks. It was so slippery that we practically had to skate. I was pleased that I was a fairly good skater and therefore I could handle the sliding better than many among us.

We traveled in open trucks to our work place, bracing against the cold wind. It was difficult to navigate with those shoes among the ruins. Even many years after my liberation from the camps, I could still see clearly on the screen of my mind our struggle walking with those wooden Dutch shoes and bearing the cold winds in Bremen. I expressed my feelings about the winter in Bremen much later as a free person.

The Streets of Bremen

Wearing wooden Dutch shoes,
our feet wrapped in rags,
we dragged ourselves
through the deep snow.
Icy winds freely cut their pathways
through our lightly covered,
shivering bodies.
We were tired, weak, and weary;
yet, we maintained our faith
and pride,
bearing with dignity
our solemn destiny.

> We were marked for death
> and stripped of liberty,
> waiting for the Allied Forces
> to set us free.

It was a cold and snowy day towards the end of December. We were taken to work on one of the streets in Bremen by the Wehrmacht guards. We looked forward to a better day because they were more kind and compassionate than our SS guards.

We were surprised to see some male prisoners working close by on the same side of the street. It was a small group consisting of about twenty to twenty-five men. Their guards were not so strict with them, which was unusual, considering how mean some guards could become. We could hear them talking among themselves, which was strange, because we were not allowed to talk while working. I realized that they were French prisoners because I spoke the French language. We noticed that their prison garb was in good condition and they appeared to be in much better shape physically than we.

During their lunch break they brought forth a very large kettle of soup and distributed its content among themselves. They also had spoons for their soup. To our great surprise they even offered some food to their guards who accepted it. It seemed that they were on pretty good terms. They had nice portions of bread along with their soup. Looking at them we realized that they were treated much better than we. They had more food and didn't look starved like we women prisoners.

We could see the warm vapors rising from the kettle and the smell emanating from it was exquisite. It had the pleasing odor of a beef stew—something we had been dreaming of. One male prisoner came over and spoke to our guards. It seemed they had some leftover food and they were wondering if they could share it with us. Surprisingly, our guards agreed. Maybe they also were hungry. There was not much food around in the city during wartime.

When the kettle was brought over to our side, the women in our group got extremely excited and were very eager to have some of it. They were pushing and shoving each other to get close to the kettle, fighting among themselves. I couldn't do that. I wanted to maintain some of my good manners. That kind of behavior was disgusting to me, even in those circumstances.

I always prayed to God in the camps to help me sustain my dignity and not let me alter my true nature and become ruthless and inconsiderate to others. I wanted to preserve my self-respect and not sink to the level of an animal. I was determined to hold on to the values and principles I grew up with. The end result of that was that I never managed to get any of the food because I always ended up the last one in the line. The others who were aggressive and rough got to enjoy their special treats.

It happened that we worked for several weeks on the same street where the French prisoners also worked.

Whenever we had kinder guards, they shared their food with us. I noticed that their guards, as well as ours, got ample portions of soup and nice pieces of bread from them. We were amazed at that. I had the impression that the good relationship with their guards and also with our guards was due to the fact that they had access to cigarettes and other attractive items and they probably bribed them. The whole thing was like a puzzle. We wondered how all these things were possible. We thought that perhaps because they were prisoners of war, they received food packages from some source, and had access to extra food and other items, like cigarettes. We respected them. They were kind and caring people who were willing to help us.

Every time when they brought over their kettle to distribute to us their leftover food, the scene was repeated. The women fought and pushed each other roughly in order to be first in line to receive a portion of soup. Due to my firm decision to act more civilized, I ended up the same way each time; when my turn came, there was no soup left in the kettle.

One day a very bizarre thing happened. On that particular day, like always, the Frenchmen brought over their leftover food and as usual, I was at the end of the line, when one of them came over to talk to me. He asked me, "*Parlez-vous français?*" ("Do you speak French?") I answered, "*Oui*" ("Yes"). He was pleased that we could communicate with each other.

To my surprise he told me, "My comrades and I were watching you and we were impressed that you didn't act like your other companions at the food distribution. You demonstrated lots of self-restraint and discipline, and there-fore, you distinguished yourself with an exemplary behav-ior, although it seems to us that you are the youngest among your companions. It shows to us that you grew up in a loving and gentle environment, where you were taught good manners. Your parents would be proud of you, just like we are. Therefore, we decided to give you some extra help. My name is Jean. Consider me a good friend who wants to help you. My family was killed. I had a sister who looked so much like you. I can't help her anymore because she was murdered. But I want to give you the help that I would give her if she were alive. You remind me so much of her. Tell me, what would you like to have?"

At first, I was speechless. I couldn't believe that what I was experiencing was real. I looked at him. He was an older man in his late thirties or early forties and he was of medi-um stature. He had a very short crew cut and dark hair. There was something very characteristic about his nose, which was big, protruding, and slightly curved downwards. His dark-brown eyes had a gentle and benign expression. He was close to my father's age and he reminded me of him.

He noticed my bewilderment and asked me again, "What do you need?"

Somehow, I didn't trust him, although he was very kind to me. I remembered the Polish prisoner I had encountered in Auschwitz who had brought me bread and turned out to be such a disappointment.

My answer was, "I don't think that I need anything from you." I was suspicious, wondering what he wanted in return, again questioning whether true good will, friendship, and kindness was possible in our environment.

Then he told me, "It seems to me that you don't know what you need and therefore my comrades and I will know what to do." After that he returned to his group.

On the following day, luckily, we had good guards. It was a cold and cloudy day. The Frenchmen were again working nearby on the same street to which we were assigned.

During their lunch break, as usual, the kettle with the leftover soup was brought over. I was, as always, standing at the end of the line. But Jean came to me and brought me a small bottle of milk and a white Kaiser roll. I couldn't believe my eyes. I had the impression that what was happening to me was only an illusion, but it turned out to be real. He insisted that I should take it. He stood near me, waiting to see me drink the milk and eat the roll. He even opened the bottle for me. My comrades next to me were amazed at what was happening. I couldn't eat those delicacies by myself. I shared it with some of them. He was very pleased that I accepted what he offered and that I trusted him.

It was miraculous that our guards were so lenient with us whenever the Frenchmen were around, and they left us in peace. They didn't even object when Jean was talking to me. I wondered who Jean really was, having so much influence on them, and who the Frenchmen really were. Their help was of utmost importance to all of us, considering our poor nutrition, our hard labor, and the cold winter when we needed more calories for our survival. The extra food they offered us was lifesaving.

I believe in miracles, because they happened to me in the camp. They can't be explained and they seemed unreal when they took place.

More miracles happened to me in the following weeks and months, which helped me to stay alive. It was strange and miraculous that throughout the cold month of January, we always worked on the same streets as the French prisoners and through them we could have some additional food.

Whenever it was possible, Jean brought me a small bottle of milk along with a white roll, which I shared with some of my comrades. One day, he approached me at the distribution of the leftover soup. I was standing at the end of the line. He was carrying in his hand a closed-up metal container, and he said, "Step out of your line and come along with me. I want to talk to you privately." I became suspicious, but I still trusted him. He proved to be a good man, trying to help all of us. We stepped aside from the others, and he said to me, "I brought this food especially for you. You don't look so good. You are losing too much weight. I am going to stand by and you have to eat this soup in front of me. I will not allow you to share it with anyone else. Everyone managed to have a share of the leftover food in the kettle except you. This is your portion, reserved for you."

He opened the lid. It was a wonderful surprise for me. I was in awe of what I saw in the container. It was a beef stew with some small pieces of meat, potatoes, and carrots. I was so hungry. He had also brought a spoon for me. He looked at me while I ate the food he brought for me. It was the first decent and tasty meal that I had in a very long time. I enjoyed every mouthful of it.

I knew that on that day a great miracle happened to me. God sent an angel in the form of Jean to save me. I felt that hope had entered my heart and soul. I felt that by having Almighty God at my side, I was protected and somehow, miraculously, I would survive. I would be able to tolerate my suffering and ultimately I would be saved from destruction and death.

The Frenchmen helped all of us throughout the cold month of January. Not only did they share their soup with us, but also their bread, and Jean came along time and time again with the extra food and bread reserved for me because he wanted to help me stay alive. He was like a loving, caring, and protective father to me. I thanked God for sending him my way. Who knows what would have happened to me without his assistance.

Unfortunately, our favorable situation didn't last long enough.

Towards the end of January, all of us women prisoners were looking forward to seeing the Frenchmen on our street. We had good guards and we were anticipating the extra help, but the Frenchmen were not there anymore. Our first thought was that maybe some of the more vicious SS guards might have denounced what they were doing and we were worried that they might have been punished for helping us. We wondered whether we would ever see them again.

♦ ♦ ♦

The month of February brought many hardships and disasters for us. Being so poorly and inadequately dressed for cold weather and having only wooden Dutch shoes and rags wrapped around our feet, not having any gloves except maybe some rags we found under the rubble of the ruins, we had little protection for our bodies and extremities during the cold, snowy, and icy winter weather. We were exposed to serious frostbite, the dread of every one of us, because it would lead to the loss of our extremities, which happened to some among us. It was horrible to experience that, because our so-called infirmary didn't give much help to those who were affected. The amputation of fingers or toes was a terrible thing by itself, but the greatest danger was that the person who had the misfortune to be in that predicament was declared not useful anymore for work. The infirmary where they were taken was just the entrance to the chamber of death. Whoever was in that situation was removed from there and one way or another was exterminated.

What saved me from severe frostbite was that from time to time, I would run in place, alternating with some jumps in place, in order to heat up my body and my extremities, thus preventing the development of serious frostbite which might incapacitate me.

My companions warned me not to continue doing that because I would be weakened by using up too much energy. But what they didn't know was that having been a competitive fencer since my early teenage years, I had developed tremendous endurance by practicing the constant quick movements and the continuous jumping back and forth required in fencing.

One very important part of the warm-up exercises in my training for elasticity and the ability to last throughout the many hours of competition was running and jumping rope. So I knew that under our circumstances I had to try my best and evoke within me the necessary strength and energy, no matter how difficult it was, in order to save myself from disaster. I had to be a strong fighter for my survival.

Despite all that I did, I still ended up with frostbite, but at least it didn't reach the severity to threaten the amputation of my extremities. We suffered from cold while we worked and we froze at night in our unheated barracks. Our blankets were too thin and didn't give us enough warmth. We eagerly waited for Sundays when we could have some heat in our barrack, at least for two hours.

We couldn't wash ourselves even in a minimal way. There was only ice cold water in the tap outside. We couldn't strip off our only clothing like during the warmer months of the year. We received no replacement clothing whatsoever.

I felt lucky to have my small raincoat with its two pockets, where I could warm my cold hands a bit once in a while. It also protected me to a small extent from the wet, snowy, windy weather.

All of us missed the warm meals and bread we had received from the Frenchmen. We had to revert again to the garbage can, if there was one around, to find food, and we searched among the ruins for buried morsels of some kind of food in order to appease our hunger.

The city of Bremen was heavily bombed by the Allied Forces. Our lives were in constant danger. More and more civilians moved away from the stricken city. We could see daily caravans of people running away, but we had to stay and clear the ruins and drag out the bodies of the aerial bombing victims. As time went on, the number of casualties increased. Many streets were completely gone after the big bombardments. We spent more time in the bunkers, and we could see the desperation and fright on the faces of the civilians who shared our bunkers.

Chapter 18

One day towards the end of February, we were taken to our place of work by some of the more cruel SS women guards. The most vicious among them, we named "The Raven." She was a tall, ugly, mean woman with jet-black hair and dark eyes. We knew that we would have a miserable time. Sure enough, she began to persecute us shortly after our arrival at our street. She noticed my small raincoat and yelled at me, *"Komm her du schmutziges Judisches Schwein."* ("Come here, you filthy, Jewish pig.") Then she said, "Take off your coat while you are working; you will work faster when you suffer of cold." She also ordered us to remove our rags from our hands. She was a true sadist and enjoyed looking at our terrified faces.

She was dressed in her warm uniform, high leather boots, and warm gloves. She didn't care if we lost our extremities by exposing them to the cold, icy temperatures without any protection. She exuded hatred toward us. Some of the women SS guards on that day were worse than their male counterparts.

All of us were silently praying for the Allied bombers to come to our rescue, and strangely, right after she commanded us to strip, the sirens blew and we saw the war planes approaching in the distance.

The Raven became panicky and she was the first one to run for shelter, not caring about anyone but herself. We realized what a coward she really was. She feared for her life, but she had no respect for ours.

On that day, repeated, heavy bombardments took place. We spent most of our time in the bunkers. Our guards were shaken up and decided not to stay in the city any longer. They were concerned about their safety and worried about our transportation facilities. They looked for our trucks in order to get back to our camp as soon as possible.

That particular day turned out to be almost a free day from work. We were lucky to be back and to be spared from further torture. We hoped that we would never see The Raven again. Fortunately, during the following weeks, she didn't show up. We thought she probably didn't want to expose herself to the dangers of the doomed city and had found herself a safer assignment.

It was towards the end of February. The many months of hard labor, the cold winter weather, our poor nutrition, and the constant threat of bombardment took a toll on all of the prisoners in Bremen. Our highly stressful life was weakening us emotionally and physically. We were losing weight and strength. It seemed that we were in a hopeless situation, being locked up in a city which gradually was being destroyed. We were caught in the midst of a bloody war.

The cold weather brought illness. Because we were so poorly clad and malnourished, our immune systems were weakened. Pneumonia became more prevalent among us. Because no medication was given to those of us who were stricken, the death toll was rising. Our sick inmates who entered the infirmary were taken away after a few days, and by then we knew well what would happen to them.

Our environment was demoralizing and yet we had to maintain our strong will to live and to survive, regardless of all the suffering to which we were constantly exposed. What aggravated our situation even more was that for awhile we had more SS women guards who were mean and totally oblivious to our weakened physical conditions and our lack of any nutritious solid food.

We dragged ourselves along the snow-covered streets, lifting heavy stones, bricks, and metal pipes, pulling out bodies buried under the rubble. We wished that the Frenchmen would show up and provide us with some food. We constantly talked about them and wondered what had happened to them.

Then on the last day in February, a miracle happened, which again elevated our somber moods and improved our morale.

We were working on one of the streets, clearing the ruins. Fortunately, for a change we had our Wehrmacht guards along. Around noon, Jean appeared quite unexpectedly. He was by himself, bringing bread to all of us. Naturally, the guards were also rewarded with bread and probably also with cigarettes, which always seemed a very important item for them. Jean knew what they wanted.

He came to me, carrying in his hands some bread and a pair of boots. When he looked at me there were tears in his eyes and he said, "My God, you look so thin. You have lost a lot of weight since I saw you last. I brought you bread and this pair of boots, to replace your wooden Dutch shoes so you can walk better."

I was so happy and deeply touched by his kindness towards me. I gave him a hug and told him, "Jean, you are my guardian angel. I am so happy to see you, and thank you for your most precious presents."

Then he said, "There are some things stuffed inside these boots: a pair of socks for you, a small piece of soap, and a comb. I noticed that your hair is getting longer. It is time to comb it. You will also find a message on a small slip of paper. Read it, then tear it up, but relate what I conveyed to you to your comrades. I can't stay longer. I have to leave right now."

I asked him, "What happened to all your comrades? Where are they?"

His answer was, "I can't tell you that. Take care of yourself. Don't lose your hope and courage. I will always remember you and all of your comrades. Have faith in God."

It seemed that for some reason Jean was in a hurry to leave. I was in a daze and wondered if I was dreaming. After he left, I took out the socks from inside the boots and also the comb and the soap, which I stuck in the pockets of my raincoat. Inside one of the boots, there was a small piece of paper on which was written: "Keep up your spirits, the liberators are close by." I tore up the paper immediately before the guards could notice it. Then I put on the socks. It was such a heavenly feeling to have a pair of warm, soft socks on my red, swollen, frostbitten toes. Then I put on the boots, which fit me perfectly. It was such a blessing to finally have some comfortable footwear. It was as though I were in a trance, wondering if what I had experienced was real. My socks and boots were a godsend from Jean, my guardian angel.

I felt that indeed God was protecting me and had performed miracles, helping me to survive. I wished that all my comrades could have gotten boots like mine, but it seemed that I was singled out by my Creator to have them. I thought that perhaps there was a purpose in all of that. Maybe I was destined to live and to do something in the future in exchange for those special privileges which were given to me.

I thanked God for the precious gifts which I received, and for sending Jean my way. Then I remembered that February 20, 1945, had been my 19th birthday. Jean's gifts were my belated, lifesaving birthday presents.

At the first possible moment, I eagerly related Jean's message to all my comrades. We rejoiced at the good news and we became more hopeful. Our morale was lifted. We realized that finally the war was coming to its end and Germany was facing defeat. On that day we felt more energetic finding out that the Allied Forces, our saviors, were coming to liberate us soon from our slavery and death.

During the first two weeks in March the situation in Bremen got worse. Bombers came day and night and we noticed increasing anxiety, fear, and restlessness amidst our guards and also among the population of the city. Bremen was a dangerous and deadly city. Everyday we were at risk of being blown up. Some of the underground bunkers, including the multi-story bunkers built above the ground, were hit, and we never knew when the shelters in which we huddled might be targeted.

The civilians in our bunkers were not as calm and relaxed as they had been at the end of July, 1944, when we had arrived in Bremen. Many of them were grieving the loss of family members and the destruction of their homes. They looked tired, desperate, and depressed. We also wondered if we would survive under those circumstances. Our workload increased and some of our SS guards became even more nasty and hateful towards us, perhaps because they knew that Germany was losing the war. We became the scapegoats for their anger and frustration.

On the third week of March, a sudden change took place in our camp. All of us were assembled outside in front of our barracks. We had to form rows of five and we were told that we were leaving our camp with our SS and Wehrmacht guards. We wondered where we would be taken. Again we were faced with fear of the unknown.

We marched with our guards for hours on a dirt road, leaving the outskirts of the city of Bremen. It was cold when we left in the early morning, but later on the weather got warmer. There were still patches of snow here and there on the ground.

Our most vicious guards came with us and we feared their cruelty. With dread, we recognized among them The Raven. Some of our kinder Wehrmacht guards were also with us.

It seemed that the Germans wanted to take us away from Bremen because the Allied Forces were closing in on the city. They feared the Allies and were running away from them, but in the meanwhile, they did not want to leave us there to meet the liberators. Perhaps they were about to derive pleasure from killing us somewhere, getting rid of us. We feared for our lives.

I was lucky to have my boots and socks. I felt sorry for my comrades who had to march with their wooden Dutch clogs and with only rags wrapped around their feet inside those stiff, hard shoes. We marched throughout the day, having only short periods of rest, following a dirt road leading into a forested area. We received no food nor drink during all that time.

At twilight we came to some primitive barn-like buildings. Then the guards broke our column into several groups and forced the groups into the single-room structures. They reserved some buildings for themselves. The structure into which I was pushed with other women was totally empty and bare. We had to sleep on its hard wooden floor. We were very crowded and pressed together. It was dark, there were no electrical lights, and we were locked inside for the night.

We were thirsty, hungry, and exhausted from our march throughout the day.

We had absolutely no provisions for our bathroom necessities—not even pails. We were forced out of necessity to use our metal soup bowls for that purpose. It was a horrible night, similar to those at Auschwitz. We were totally at the mercy of our guards, who treated us with roughness and brutality.

There were some rumors in the morning that during the night The Raven had intended to ignite our cottages. Apparently, someone prevented her from doing so.

At daylight, we continued our march. We were getting deeper and deeper into a heavily-forested area of birch trees.

On our second day some among us were weakened physically to such an extent that their feet, which had painful lacerations created by the hard, wooden clogs, couldn't take the stress of marching anymore, and they collapsed. Death was inevitable for them. They were mercilessly shot by The Raven and other vicious SS guards. Whoever couldn't march anymore was shot. That was the rule of the SS and they let us know.

Seeing my fellow inmates killed and left bleeding at the side of the road created in my heart an indescribable, deep sorrow. I will never forget their plight, trying to continue marching with us in agony. I wished that I had had the strength to carry them and help them survive. They were left on the road for the predators in the forest. The thought that some wild animals might devour them at night induced in me an almost unbearable emotional pain. I was horrified and so were my other comrades.

We asked ourselves: *Will that be the ultimate fate of all of us?*

Our march lasted for three days, during which we lost more and more comrades. There were also those among us who might have been physically strong enough to go on, but who were weakened emotionally and demoralized by depression resulting from witnessing the inhumane treatment of our fellow prisoners; they, too, were shot by the guards. It had seemed senseless to them to put up any further effort to go on. They had lost their desire to fight for their lives and wanted to die and find relief from their agonizing pain and suffering.

So again suicide became rampant among us, like in Auschwitz. It became an acceptable and desirable act, representing the only means of liberation from torture and pain.

You might ask what kept me going on that death march, saving me from falling into deep depression and meeting the fate of my fellow prisoners. What kept me walking in my severely weakened state? My strong and fierce determination to survive allowed me to last through that terrible ordeal. During my march, I had to evoke pleasant thoughts and create a series of self-suggestive positive images in my mind, which in turn gave me the fortitude to march against all the odds I was facing. In my imagination, I could be anywhere other than where I was. I could be everywhere I wanted to be. I could see myself liberated and at home with my family. I could see my mother lighting the candles of Sabbath on Friday night. I felt that as long as I could keep my spiritual freedom and create a better world in my mind than the one I experienced, I would stay alive. By shifting my focus from my miserable and life-threatening predicament, to pleasant thoughts and feelings, I overcame my fear of not being able to keep on marching. In other words, my positive attitude was my greatest tool of survival.

Sometimes I felt that I was halfway dozing, being exhausted, but somehow I was in a sort of trance and my feet were moving. I willed them to move. My faith in God was helping me. I had the feeling that in those instances when I almost fell asleep from exhaustion, God was carrying me. My Creator was at all times at my side, protecting me and giving me the strength and willpower to survive.

Finally, on the night of the third day, approximately half of us had survived the ordeal of the Death March and reached the gates of the Bergen-Belsen concentration camp. Fortunately, Pere, Jackie, Ilus, Lily, and Ilona had also survived and it was so comforting to have them along with me.

Part Four

Chapter 19

*T*he Bergen-Belsen camp was hidden in the midst of a birch forest and it was surrounded by a high, barbed-wire fence which was not electrically charged like the ones in Auschwitz. There were guards stationed by the fence in elevated watchtowers equipped with machine guns, just like in Auschwitz.

We came to a massive entrance gate with a guard post in front of it. One of the guards opened the gate, and our column of women passed through along with our guards. The gate was locked behind us.

As soon as we entered the camp, a terrible stench hit our nostrils. We were familiar with that nauseating odor. It was unmistakably the smell of corpses. It reminded us of Auschwitz.

It was a clear night and we could detect the outlines of some primitive barracks that looked like the shelters of Auschwitz.

Pere, Jackie, Ilus, Lily, Ilona, and I were standing at the end of our column. The guards divided our column into groups and started pushing them into the barracks. The inmates of those barracks were screaming because their barracks were already almost full and there was not much room inside for any more people. But the guards ignored that and forced more and more inmates into the buildings. Finally, there was no way to push in any more people. At that point, the guards ordered all of us who were at the end of the column to lie down wherever we were for the night.

Ilus, who always was very resourceful, noticed some tents close by. She said to me, "I would like to explore those tents. I didn't tell you, but I have a small candle and matches with me which I found in Bremen amidst the rubble of one of the houses. I have a way of making light so I can find out what is inside those tents."

I said, "Ilus, don't do that. You are going to get yourself in great trouble if one of the SS guards catches you."

But Ilus, who was a courageous and headstrong woman, was determined to carry out her plan. I feared for her life. She managed to get inside one of the tents. When she came out, she was very frightened. I asked her, "Ilus, what did you see in there?"

She answered, "Piles of corpses."

Taking into consideration what she witnessed and also the way we were treated, we drew the conclusion that probably we had been brought here to be executed. Unfortunately, we couldn't do anything to save ourselves.

We ended up spending the night on the ground and inhaling the awful stench. We had no other choice.

When daybreak appeared, we faced a most gruesome scene. The bare ground where we were sleeping was littered with unburied corpses in all stages of decay. The putrid stench of death and decay was almost unbearable. We were surrounded by decomposing corpses and we had been sleeping next to them.

The living women in the camp looked like walking skeletons clad in rags. Their eyes were deeply sunken into their sockets and they were wobbling around in a confused state of mind with a vacant look in their eyes. They reminded me of the *mussulmen* in Auschwitz. They were starved and dehydrated just like them, and they also manifested mental changes. We found ourselves in a place of horror. We had the terrible feeling that we would not survive because we had already been pretty much used up in Bremen. The question we asked ourselves was: *How much more pain and suffering can we withstand?* Death seemed imminent to all of us.

In Bergen-Belsen there was no roll call in the morning, and we didn't receive any drinks either. There was no running water and no electricity. The camp looked like an open cemetery with unburied, rotting corpses scattered all around on the hard ground.

The barracks were full of people with typhus. The corpses of the dead were lying among the living, and the living looked like the walking dead—emaciated and too weak to carry out the corpses of the dead. Many were dying of starvation and illness.

We newcomers were also greatly weakened, but we hadn't yet reached the final stage. Clad in rags, starved, and dehydrated, we were ordered by the SS guards to drag the dead bodies from the barracks and from the grounds outside and dump them into the existing deep ditches dug by former prisoners.

Heaps of naked bodies were stacked on top of each other in pyramids all over the camp. Dead bodies were lying all around the barracks, and we were surrounded by cruel and sadistic SS guards who had absolutely no compassion for us. We were there in order to drag our dead and dig the graves. There was no medicine for the sick people. There was no infirmary; no help of any kind. The camp was an extermination camp.

The barracks looked like cesspools. There was urine and excrement on the floors. Some barracks had narrow, three-tiered bunks occupied by sick and dying people. Tuberculosis was rampant, due to the horrible environment and unsanitary conditions.

In other barracks women were lying on the barren floor which had excrement, blood, and puss mixed into a horrible-smelling paste. That was due to the fact that many of the inmates were weakened to the point that they couldn't walk to the latrines. Some of the living ones had to live under nightmarish circumstances.

The barracks also were rat-infested. The people in them were covered with lice. It was a place of pestilence. Due to the terrible dehydration and lack of fluid, some were drinking their own urine. Some of the corpses which we had to pull out from those barracks were partly decomposed and chewed up by the rats. In other barracks, people who wanted to live resorted to cannibalism on the fresh corpses, eating the soft, fleshy parts and organs of the torsos.

Some among us newcomers broke down mentally, unable to tolerate the hellish environment in which we were trapped. It was hard for me to evoke positive thoughts in such an unbelievable, inhumane environment. I felt helpless and in great anguish. All of us new arrivals were in a state of shock. We couldn't believe that we were in such a horrific situation. It was one of the worst nightmares you could ever imagine.

We could see a gate leading from where we were to another part of the camp. I wondered if the conditions on the other side were more favorable, because our situation seemed unbearable.

We had been working for several hours, dragging corpses, when the gate was opened and we could see a number of women prisoners coming into our camp, carrying big kettles of soup. All of us were extremely hungry and thirsty by that time. The sight of food created a great agitation and excitement among us. We still had our metal containers with us, which we had received in Auschwitz.

We waited impatiently for the distribution. The soup in the kettles looked disgusting and had a foul smell, which reminded us of the soup received in Auschwitz, only it was much worse than that. It was a terrible concoction, consisting

297

of a strange, murky-looking fluid mixed with some grass and earth.

We wondered what kind of awful-tasting, poisonous substance they were feeding us. But as that was our only food for the day, we had to drink it, whatever it was, if we wanted to stay alive. But right after we got our small portions of soup, we were attacked by some of the starving women prisoners who had arrived at the camp before us, trying to snatch our bowls of soup from our hands. We were taken by surprise and had to defend ourselves against them.

Due to extreme dehydration and hunger, those inmates had lost all their inhibitions and human feelings. They wanted to live at all costs, not caring about what happened to their comrades if they were deprived of the extremely meager, life-sustaining fluid. They resorted to stealing food from others in order to stay alive. Starvation transformed many among us into beasts. I was lucky on that day that my bowl of soup was not grabbed from me.

It was a fierce fight for survival in our camp. No bread was given to us either. We wondered how long we could survive under those inhumane circumstances. Life expectancy was short in Bergen-Belsen. Hundreds of people died daily from starvation and illness.

My first nightmarish day in Bergen-Belsen was coming to its end. It was getting dark and it was time to go to sleep. But it was hard to do that considering that all of us who were at the end of the column of women at our arrival to the camp had to lie down outside on the ground next to the corpses. We carried the dead people during the day and slept next to them throughout the night. The smell of the dead was horrible and nauseating. But the situations in the barracks were also terrible, where the women lived in filth and with the dead bodies.

The only comforting thing was that Pere, Jackie, Ilus, Lily, and Ilona were sleeping next to me.

On that first night I had a frightening nightmare. I dreamt that I was walking on a country road. It was a beautiful day and I felt happy and free, when suddenly a strange-looking figure wrapped in a black cloak and wearing a mask barred my way. I wanted to turn back, but a cold, icy hand grabbed my arm and wouldn't let me go. I heard a voice say to me, "I am Death! I came to take you away to the world of the dead."

"It is not my time yet!" I said. "Please let me live a little longer."

"Look at yourself," the sinister apparition answered. "Don't you see that you are already dead?"

To my horror, I realized that I was a skeleton.

Suddenly, I woke up and felt very frightened. I was trapped in a distorted world of madness, amidst chaos and confusion, followed by ominous phantoms of delusion. I was worried that I was losing my sanity. I felt that I was slowly dying.

The following days in Bergen-Belsen were always the same. We were forced by our murderous, sadistic SS guards to perform the horrific work of dragging the dead bodies and digging graves. We were kept on a starvation diet and slept next to our poor, dead comrades.

The death toll in the camp reached staggering proportions. There were many new dead people in the barracks each day. Typhus raged throughout the camp as a result of starvation and the horrible, unsanitary conditions. It was transmitted from person to person by body lice which infested all of us. All kinds of other infectious diseases broke out. Dysentery became rampant.

In Bergen-Belsen, there were no gas chambers nor crematory ovens, but the Germans found another horrible way to kill us: through starvation.

Depression in the camp was replaced by exhaustion and apathy. Nobody had to resort to suicide anymore. Death came fast and naturally. There was no need for intervention.

Meanwhile, there were daily arrivals of new prisoners. Bergen-Belsen was the death terminal for thousands of prisoners, men and women who were taken there from the other German concentration camps when the Allied Forces came close. They wanted us dead, not liberated by the Allies. They made every effort to kill as many of us as they could.

In our camp there were women and men of many nationalities: Hungarians, Poles, French, Czechoslovaks, Russians, Gypsies, and others. Also pregnant women from the various camps in Germany were brought to our camp to die under the most horrible conditions. Our camp was the place of extermination.

The death toll was constantly escalating. After only a few days of being there, we newcomers began to deteriorate physically and mentally. We felt that we were becoming the living dead.

Sleeping night after night beside the decomposing corpses took a big toll on us. Some among us became mentally disturbed, falling into deep depression and utter apathy. The lack of adequate nutrition created mental problems.

Our SS female guards were even more vicious and heartless towards us than our male SS guards.

With all my good intentions to keep up my spirits, I found myself sinking more and more into depression. I felt helpless and forlorn, cast into a demonic world from which there was no possible escape.

I was fighting death and it seemed that ultimately the dark shadow of oblivion would be the winner. It was difficult to fight but I didn't want to sink into oblivion without leaving a trace behind me.

I expressed the feelings I had on those horrible nights and days in Bergen-Belsen years later in a poem

Forlorn

At my journey's end
in this mortal land,
I sink into time,
like footprints
in the dunes of sand.
I fight in vain
like a bird in a cage,
my trace is swept
by the winds of age.
I am free to live,

> but not for long,
> to eternity
> I can never belong.
> And yet, when death
> summons me to captivity,
> I beg and struggle for life,
> hour after hour,
> before I yield
> to its inevitable, absolute,
> and invincible power.

Living day after day in this horror, seeing my body gradually deteriorate from lack of food and water, becoming thinner with each day, looking more and more like a skeleton, created in me a feeling of loss, despair, and helplessness. I knew that I would have to do something before the symptoms of depression got worse, becoming life-threatening.

So, again like in Auschwitz, I had to somehow shock myself by taking some kind of action to prevent the onset of deep depression and establish in myself some positive, hopeful thoughts.

I came up with the idea of trying to escape and I became preoccupied with planning it, although in reality, it was suicidal to even consider it. I was convinced in my mind that I had nothing to lose, because probably I would die shortly. But while I still had some strength and could still walk, and before death took me along, I would try my best to save my life. So I began studying the possibility of escape, trying to figure out the best way to go about it.

I observed for a few days that the food carriers were the only people who could pass through the gate leading to our camp when they brought in our food, and also leave through the gate after the food was distributed.

I decided to try to smuggle myself somehow into the line of the food carriers and go along with them to the other side of our camp. Perhaps conditions were somewhat better there, and there would be more of a chance for me to survive, because where I was, the situation was unbearable and I couldn't stand it anymore.

I waited for the right opportunity. One day I decided to act on my plan. It happened that on that particular day, our food was carried in by Polish women prisoners. I watched them closely and when they were leaving our camp with their kettles, I sneaked into their line. It seemed that they accepted me. But I wasn't aware of the fact that they were counted before they passed through the gate leading to our camp by an SS woman guard. I was prepared emotionally to do whatever it took to escape regardless of the risk.

When our group arrived at the gate, an SS woman guard counted everyone. She knew from before that only twelve women had been chosen to carry the food. When she counted, she discovered that there was an extra person in the group. The guard immediately demanded that the thirteenth person step forward. I was terrified but I realized that if I didn't comply with her request, I would endanger the lives of the other prisoners, because she might very well shoot all of us, as a punishment. So I stepped forward. The SS woman got hold of me and was hitting and kicking me. I started retreating, but she continued following and hitting me. I was bleeding and in pain. When I came back, my friends were in awe. They told me, "You are insane, irrational, and suicidal to do what you did! She could have beaten you to death!"

My answer was, "What can I lose? I am going to die here anyway. I can't stand this anymore! Because of that, I will try to do it again. This is my last resort to maybe save my life."

It seemed that I was indeed suicidal, because I tried to escape the second time. Next time, when the food carriers' group consisted of French women prisoners, I sneaked into their line. I spoke French, so I could communicate with them. They were wonderful to me. They assured me that they would not betray me. If a guard came to the gate they would act like I was a part of their group.

I could have scored better with them, but unfortunately, when we had already passed through the gate, the same SS woman who beat me up before came and she recognized me. She pulled me out and she beat and kicked me even more than before. I thought that she probably would beat me to death. Then she told me in German, "If I catch you next time, I will kill you." I understand German and I knew that indeed she would kill me next time.

I was covered with blood and bruises. I was surprised that she didn't beat me to death. God was watching over me. I was in pain, but still alive. My wounds had to heal without any medication or treatment, and they did after awhile, but I was thinking: "At least I tried to do something to save my life as long as I still had some strength."

Regardless of the extreme adversities and suffering I experienced, I was still fighting all along to stay alive, even more than ever, because at that point, my life was in the greatest danger. I lived and slept with dead bodies and the thought that perhaps I would die shortly and some other prisoner would drag my corpse and push it into the mass grave horrified me. I realized the great value of life and I was determined to fight for it as long as my strength would allow me.

But later on towards the end of my second week in Bergen-Belsen, when I had barely recovered from my previous injuries, I had another close encounter with death.

One day, two SS women guards came along, telling us that they would take us into some barracks. We rejoiced at that. Anything was better than what we had to endure outside! Unfortunately, they guided us to the typhus-infested barracks. It was a good way to perish, by sleeping next to typhus-infected prisoners. It was clear that they wanted us to get sick and die.

So, what at first seemed to promise improvement in our conditions turned out to result in an even worse situation. As we arrived at the particular barrack, we saw a dying woman prisoner, infected with typhus, being thrown out of there, discarded like she was a piece of garbage. I will never forget her. She seemed delirious due to her high fever. She was lying helplessly on the barren ground, her eyes expressionless and glassy. It was a shocking experience. We were terrified, not knowing what would happen to us next.

Then, one of the SS women guards who accompanied us, started to push us brutally into the barrack, which was already full with 300 other women prisoners. The people were screaming inside because of lack of space, but she didn't care. Being placed in the typhus barrack was for us a death sentence because our immune systems were weakened to the point where our resistance to typhus was very low.

The SS woman who was pushing us relentlessly inside was short. She looked well-fed, mean, and carried a gun at her side. As I already looked extremely thin at that time, she singled me out of the crowd as we entered the barrack and tried to force me to climb up on one of the third tiers in the barrack and lie next to a woman who was dying of typhus. As I looked up at the sick and dying woman, I realized that the SS guard had condemned me to death by her action, exposing me directly to the terrible, devastating illness of typhus. I said to myself: *No, I am not going to do that! She wants to kill me. I have to fight for my life!*

I started running through the barrack, packed with prisoners who were constantly pushed in from outside by the second SS woman guard. The SS woman reached for her gun, ready to shoot me. I thought that this would be the end of me. She was going to kill me. But suddenly, she was immobilized by another wave of prisoners being pushed in from outside by the other guard, who probably didn't realize how many prisoners were already inside and that there was no more place whatsoever for others. She also didn't grasp what was happening to the guard inside, being pressed tightly together with the prisoners and unable to move.

I can't tell you what unearthly power took over me and gave me so much strength and courage to run away wildly from the SS woman, crossing through so many people and heading toward the end of the barrack, where I found an open window and jumped out. I remember the terror I felt, trying to hide myself outside, among the dead bodies. It was a miracle that I was not discovered. Escaping at that moment prevented a death sentence for me. I felt that on that day God protected me from death and guided me in the right direction. My faith in Him never faltered.

Later on, I looked for my friends. Eventually I found them. Luckily they had been spared from entering the typhus barrack, because the barrack got too full and they were ordered to stay outside. We were happy being together again. It was another miracle that we found each other.

On the following day Ilona was deeply depressed. We tried to cheer her up, but we didn't succeed. She felt that all our efforts fighting for our lives were in vain because there was no way of surviving in the camp. She was crying off and on throughout the night and said that she was losing her desire to fight anymore.

During the next day she seemed to be more introverted, silent, and immersed in her pessimistic thoughts. We were concerned about her.

At nightfall, as we were lying on the ground next to the corpses, we heard shots coming from somewhere in the forest. The shooting went on periodically throughout the night. We were terrified. Our first thoughts were that maybe our

SS guards were executing some prisoners there. Naturally, we couldn't sleep no matter how exhausted we were from our gruesome work during the day.

Ilona said to me, "Magda, I will die here before this camp is liberated. I will never be a free person."

I told her: "How can you say such a thing! We are all in the same situation, but we have to believe that we are going to be saved and we will still be alive when our liberators come to rescue us."

But she insisted that she would not be alive when the liberators came.

In the middle of the night she had to urinate. She wanted to go to the latrines. We were not allowed to use them at night. The guards were instructed to shoot anyone who would walk there during the night.

We begged our friend to empty her bladder on the ground where we were, but she insisted that she couldn't do that. We tried to hold her down but she broke away from us and ran towards the latrines. We heard a shot and a scream. We knew that she had been hit. She didn't want to live and suffer anymore and had decided to commit suicide.

Lily tried to scream when it happened. We covered her mouth, preventing her from doing that, because we were worried that the guards might shoot her, too. We tried to console her. She was crying and mourning her sister throughout the night. All of us became very depressed. It was very painful to lose our gentle and sensitive friend.

In the morning we removed her corpse from the place where she had been shot and brought her to Lily. She wanted to keep her body with us for a while. It was such a shocking experience for all of us. We wondered who would be the next among us to break down mentally and commit suicide in the same way.

At the end of my second week in Bergen-Belsen our soup was discontinued. We didn't receive any food anymore.

In our third week in the camp we were starving. We had no water, nor any other kinds of fluids. But still we were ordered to drag the corpses and dump them into the deep ditches regardless of our weak physical condition. Many among us collapsed and died next to the corpses stretched out on the ground.

Due to the lack of water, wounds broke out on our tongues from the dryness and it became hard to swallow. It also became more difficult to do our gruesome work.

I felt that each day my strength was failing. I was getting weaker and I thought that probably I had only a few days of life left. My death was inevitable. On the second night of the third week in Bergen-Belsen, while I was lying next to the dead bodies, I felt hopeless and depressed. I visualized death coming to get me and taking me to its place of eternal darkness, silence, and solitude.

I wrote the following two poems many years later to express the feelings and thoughts which I had on those nights in my third week in Bergen-Belsen, when I was preparing myself emotionally to meet death.

Unexpected Visitor

A faint call,
I tumble and fall.
Invisible hands
lead me in a trance
of no return.
Thoughts, passions, actions burn,
memories fade,
my fate I can't evade.
My life is at stake,
I shatter, and then break.
My time is up, no mistake.

Solitude

In the doorway of death
the lights stay shut
and the ties of life are cut.
No rays of hope penetrate
the thick walls
where doom and silence falls.
No distant cries and calls
are passing through
to stir the failing hearts
which once were new.

During this third week in Bergen-Belsen, my body rapidly
deteriorated. I was scared to look at myself. When I touched

my face, my cheeks felt hollow as though the fatty tissue and muscles were disappearing. I could mainly feel the structure of the bones sticking out. When I looked at my body, I could see all my ribs protruding. The muscles all over my body were shrinking and gradually their mass was disappearing, leaving behind thin, wobbly feet, thin arms, and skeleton hands.

It seemed like my body was consuming itself, not having any other nutrition to resort to, until it became a skeletal body of mainly skin and bones—the personification of death itself. It horrified me, becoming like the living dead.

I started looking like the corpses next to me. Towards the end of the third week, I felt so weakened that I had difficulty walking or even getting up from the ground. I felt that I was dying. I couldn't bear the thought that when I died, my body would be dumped into a mass grave. I would lie there and be forgotten forever by all. Nobody would ever visit my graveside.

In my imagination, I visualized my funeral taking place in the solemn and peaceful cathedral of my soul with angels around to honor me. I wanted to believe that even if my doomed body perished, my spirit would still live on. Some part of me would still be around—saved from oblivion.

A poem, which I wrote many years later, depicts the funeral which I was dreaming of, as my death was approaching at Bergen-Belsen.

Last Rites

There is a funeral
in the cathedral
of my soul.
The bells toll
their sinister tune,
and the solemn sound echoes
through grief-stricken shadows.
The tall candles are lighted,
while the cherubs of peace
circle around unsighted.
And by the pale flames,
death plays its old games.
Only the spirit is free,
escaping the doomed body,
rising above time and age,
standing on life's stage,
defying finality.

By the end of my third week in the camp, I could hardly walk anymore. I dragged myself to the trunk of an old birch tree, as our camp was hidden in a birch forest, and I collapsed there, next to the corpses. I was so weak that I could barely move or even speak because it was too exhausting. Total lethargy descended upon me.

I fought for my life all that time. But at that point, I felt that it was time for me to accept death as my inevitable fate. I was hoping to have a peaceful death. As I was lying there,

I was conscious of myself. Strangely, I didn't feel hunger or thirst anymore. I was beyond all that, but my mind was still active and I could think. My thoughts turned to God. I expressed to Him without words my silent wish to embrace life for the last time, to be buried next to a living thing and have my spirit lifted to Heaven. And I asked the Creator to grant me an easy, painless death

Then, a very strange and miraculous thing happened. As I lay next to the birch tree, surrounded by corpses, I looked up at the tree and I could see the fresh buds which appeared on the old branches. Those buds represented new life to me. I wished that I could embrace that tree, which was the only living entity around me, and that I could still hang on to life. Suddenly, I was possessed by a life force and I was able to crawl close to that tree and embrace the bottom of its wrinkled trunk. I thanked God for that privilege. I felt that God had granted my first wish to embrace life for the last time, and I was hoping that the Almighty would fulfill my second wish, for an easy death. Maybe I would be buried beside the trunk of that birch tree and I would become a part of its roots and be transformed into another form of life. I always loved trees and becoming part of one would not be so bad. Then maybe my spirit would survive and ascend to Heaven. I tried to have a positive attitude about death so that I could accept it peacefully.

Holding tightly to the trunk of my friend, the birch tree, who witnessed my agony, I looked ahead of me. At a short distance from where I was lying, there were stacks of naked corpses thrown on top of each other. We called them the

Pyramids of Death. We prisoners were forced to erect them. As many people were dying each day, there were fewer of us to drag the corpses and dig the graves. The death toll was rising so the corpses were accumulating. We were told to strip the dead of their clothing and then throw them on top of each other. These pyramid structures of naked corpses were widespread all over our camp. The bodies were left there unburied and deteriorating. The smell was awful. As time went on, we got used to it. We had to, because we couldn't get away from it.

Then I turned my eyes away from that horrifying scene and directed them upward, looking at the blue sky above and the shining sun. It was such a beautiful day in spring. It was so hard for me to say good-bye to life at age nineteen. I felt deep sadness, despair, and anger. I wondered: *Why were we condemned to starvation and death? Only because we were Jewish?* In those moments which I thought to be my last ones, I wished I could live longer. I realized the three most important things we should cherish are our life, our freedom, and our family, and so many times we take them for granted.

Finally, I closed my eyes, wondering what death would be like. I was prepared for it. I was even thinking: *Come death and take me. I don't fear you anymore. I am ready for you.*

Then, I heard a big commotion with joyful screams. I thought that I was dead and was hearing voices from the world of the dead. I was afraid to open my eyes, but the voices got louder, coming near me. Finally I opened my eyes. What I saw was hard to believe. The guards stationed on the elevated watchtowers in the camp disappeared with their machine guns, the gates of Bergen-Belsen opened, and the British troops rolled in with their tanks. The liberators had discovered our hidden camp accidentally. The British Forces liberating us were in awe of what they encountered.

A British soldier discovered me among the dead bodies, lifted me, and carried me away. I couldn't talk, and he was crying, filled with compassion. I felt sad that I was too weak to talk. I wanted to thank him and all the liberators for saving us.

As he carried me, I looked at the barren ground of Bergen-Belsen, littered with corpses, and I was filled with awe and sorrow, thinking that many of us were crushed by the unkind hand of fate. For so many of my comrades, the bells of victory had arrived too late. But I knew that if I did recover and survive, I would always keep alive the memory of all of those victims of persecution who were left behind.

My wish on that day of our liberation on April 15, 1945, was that somehow one day I should give all of them an honorable funeral and bury them in my heart, where they would stay with me as long as I shall live.

Many years later, I wrote the following "Requiem" in their memory, which expresses my thoughts and feeling of deep sorrow and pain while the British soldier carried me in his arms and I looked one last time at the dead bodies of my comrades.

Requiem

My eyes shed drops of tears
into the pools of years,
for those I loved and lost.
And like a haunting ghost
my spirit roams around,
searching for their unknown
burial ground.

They were the victims
of their faith,
sentenced to death
without a sin,
for worshipping
the only God
they believed in.

They died without protest,
without rebellion,
together with the rest
of six million,
innocent Jews
in the Nazi camps
of Germany.

O, Lord, please help me
to keep alive their memory.
They died in vain,

I witnessed their agony
and pain.
I heard their cries.
O, Lord, our God,
open for them
the gates of Paradise.
Let their souls
rest in peace.
Forgive mankind's atrocities.

Chapter 20

The British soldier carried me to a clean, empty barrack, probably a former SS barrack. He placed me on the floor, as there were no beds. I never knew his name, nor did I see him afterwards.

Soon after that, ten other women were brought in and placed on the floor. After awhile, British Army nurses entered and treated each of us with a white powder in an attempt to get rid of our body lice. Then they provided us with sheets, blankets, and pillows. Afterward, they fed us juice and water.

In the next three days that was the only nourishment I was able to tolerate. On the fourth day, I got my first solid food, which consisted of a cookie. I always liked sweets, so eating a cookie was enjoyable. Eventually, I was able to eat soups and soft food.

It took three to four days before my extreme weakness and confusion improved and I was more aware of my surroundings.

I found out then that the other ten women were also Hungarians and some of my friends were among them.

It took the better part of two weeks before I was able to get up and walk around, but I was still quite weak and wobbly. By that time, two of the women had become seriously ill with typhus. There were no places for them in the hospital which was already filled with typhus patients. They remained with us in the room. Two beds were set up for them in the middle of the barrack. We stayed on the floor at the side of the room.

The two women afflicted with the disease at first developed a high fever, followed by delirium, manifesting in a temporary psychosis. In that stage, each one of them was affected differently. One burst into sustained, uncontrolled laughing episodes. The other one had alternating spells of uncontrolled crying and uncontrolled laughing. Fortunately, both of them eventually recovered, and afterward they had no memory of their strange behavior.

One week later, Eva, another of our companions in our room, contracted typhus. Unfortunately, at that time there was no bed available for her because there was a great shortage of beds. So she had to lie on the floor of the barrack among us. No one in the room wanted to sleep next to her. I felt sorry for her and I volunteered to be the one. She also developed a high fever, but in her case the psychotic episodes that followed manifested in a different way. She had hallucinations. She spoke to me, visualizing me as her father, and as a Christian missionary, although she and her father were Jewish. At that time I still was very weak but I was feeling better. At least I could get up and walk around. I tried to help her. I held her hand, comforting her. Although I was concerned about contracting the illness, my strong desire to give her some comfort and assistance overrode my fear. Fortunately she also recovered completely. Like the two other typhus patients, she couldn't remember any of her delusions.

By that time, I was strong enough to leave the barrack and stand in line for the warm food distribution. We got a soup with meat and vegetables, bread, and cookies. I still didn't have all my strength and energy. It took some time to recover from the effects of starvation.

I was pleased that I didn't contract typhus, although I was so often exposed to it. One of the aftereffects of typhus is hair loss. Some of the women who had the illness became half-bald.

Once I could go outside, I could see what was happening in our camp. Our liberators had a very hard job on their hands and they were wonderful to us.

There were thousands of people, all in bad shape, needing immediate help. There was the job of delousing all of us. Many among us were suffering from typhus, dysentery, severe malnutrition, and other ailments. The sick people had to be isolated and taken care of, which was a tremendous task. New barracks and hospitals had to be erected.

Thousands of people died after liberation, either from typhus or from irreversible damage to their digestive systems due to starvation. They were unable to digest food anymore. The corpses had to be cleared from the ground. I found out that there were over 30,000 dead bodies on the ground of Bergen-Belsen.

Some of the SS guards, men and women, were caught and arrested by the British troops. The SS guards were forced to drag the corpses, dig the graves, and throw the bodies into them. They had to do the same horrible work they had forced us to do. It was finally the time of their punishment for their criminal actions.

The same SS woman guard who beat me up twice when I tried to escape from Bergen-Belsen was captured by the British Forces and she was forced, like the others, to drag the corpses and to push them into the mass graves. One of my friends spotted her and came to inform me about it. She said, "Guess whom I saw today? The SS woman who treated you so brutally. I know where she is. Come with me and beat her up! It is your turn to do that to her. She is loading and dragging the corpses. Remember how she injured you?"

So, I followed my friend. I wanted to get a good look at the cruel SS woman who beat me so mercilessly. But I couldn't harm her because if I had, I would have felt that I was no better than she. I couldn't harm anyone, and besides, I was thinking that she had already received her punishment from God. It was her turn to suffer for the crimes she had committed.

Because of the vast number of unburied corpses all over the camp, the British soldiers brought in bulldozers to dig mass graves and push the corpses into them. Then our whole camp was quarantined in order to prevent additional spreading of typhus. The clearing of the camp was a giant enterprise which took some time. The former SS headquarters, barracks, and hospitals were used for our living quarters and our extra-care units. British Army nurses and physicians exclusively were working in the hospitals and there were no more German personnel. The beds were removed from the former SS barracks because they were needed for the typhus patients in the hospitals. Probably that was why our barrack had no beds. It was impossible to give comfortable accommodations to so many people at the same time.

We heard that some of the high German SS officials in the camp were also arrested. Among them was Joseph Kramer, the commander of the camp, nicknamed "The Beast of Auschwitz and Bergen-Belsen;" Dr. Fritz Klein, SS physician and also a commander of the camp of Bergen-Belsen and previously, commander and SS physician of the women's camp in Auschwitz, as well as selector in Auschwitz for sending people to the gas chambers; and Irma Griese, the "Blonde Angel of Death," the most vicious and feared SS woman in Auschwitz and in Bergen-Belsen. Finally, justice caught up with them. Later on, Joseph Kramer and Irma Griese were hanged.

On May 20, 1945, the British set fire to all the prison barracks in the camp because they were contaminated and filthy beyond repair.

Meanwhile, eleven of us women were moved into a different barrack which was equipped with beds. Finally we could be more comfortable. There were also shower rooms established and it was indescribably wonderful at last to be able to wash ourselves with soap and warm water and to have towels to dry ourselves. We considered that a great luxury. Again, I was pleased to have some of my friends along with me.

After some time, as I was getting stronger, I felt the need to engage in some kind of activity whereby I could be useful. I volunteered to clean the barracks of the translators. Because in Bergen-Belsen there were so many men and women survivors of different nationalities, there was a need for people who were knowledgeable in various languages, especially English-speaking persons. The benefit of my cleaning job was that I received extra cookies for my services; extra food was very much needed. I kept on working for awhile in that job.

Then, one day, sometime in the month of July, 1945, about two-and-a-half months after my liberation, a miracle happened to me. On that particular day, I was waiting in line outside for my soup and bread, when I saw a man at some distance walking along our long line of people. His face looked familiar to me. When he came closer and passed by where I was standing, I recognized him. It was Jean. I broke out of my line, and followed him, yelling, "Jean, Jean!" He stopped, turned around, and recognized me. We were happy to see each other. We embraced and tears of joy rolled down our cheeks. It was so strange and miraculous to meet each other in Bergen-Belsen.

He looked well and was well-dressed, in civilian clothes. Jean was always a mystery man to me. I wondered, *How did he get into our camp?* He was always very secretive and never talked much about himself, even after our liberation from the camp.

He looked at me and said, "I don't like those rags on you and you look too thin, but you survived. That is the most important thing. But now, let's go back to your food line."

I told him, "Jean, I want you to have my whole portions of food today. This time I will watch you eat it. Remember that you did that for me in Bremen when you brought me that beef stew in that metal container?"

He answered, "No, I will not accept it because you have lost a lot of weight, and you need more nourishment in order to get stronger. Look at me. I look heavier than you so I need less food than you."

But I insisted that he accept my offer. In the end, he made a deal with me. He said, "Let us share it." I knew that the only reason he agreed to that was to please me and make me feel that I could do something in return for all his past kindness.

He wanted me to talk about myself and he accompanied me to my barrack. He came in and met all the women and my friends whom he knew before from Bremen. I asked him where he was staying, but he did not reveal it to me. He said that he would meet me again at our barrack in a few days. There were some things he had to do during that time.

I eagerly awaited his return. A few days passed by and as he promised, he showed up at our barrack at midmorning, carrying a small suitcase in his hand. He handed me the suitcase and said, "This is for you! Open it!"

I couldn't believe my eyes when I opened the suitcase. The following things were enclosed: a pretty, multicolored dress, a pleated, Scottish-style skirt, a white blouse with a ruffled collar, some underwear, two pairs of higher-heeled shoes, a comb, a piece of soap, and a handkerchief. All the women in our room were surprised and somewhat envious, but they were pleasant to Jean, who was like a father to me and an angel sent from heaven. I felt that God was watching over me. I was so deeply touched that I could hardly talk. I cried and thanked Jean for all his kindness and caring.

He visited with my friends and me for a short while. Then he came with me to the food line and again we shared my food. When he parted he said that he would come back the following day to see me in the dress he brought me.

The next day I took a shower and combed my hair, which was getting longer at that time and had natural waves in it. It was surprising, because before I always had very straight hair. Then I put on the underwear, my colorful dress, and my higher-heeled shoes. Everything fit me perfectly. For the first time in a long while, I felt proud of myself. I turned again into the young teenage girl from before. Jean made that all possible. I thought that he was an exceptionally kind and good person, and I felt lucky that he came my way.

Jean came to our barrack just as he said, close to noon. He was very pleased that everything he brought me looked so good on me. He said, "Finally you are decently dressed and you look well. I am so happy to see that!"

I left our barrack with Jean to stand in the line for the distribution of our food and again I shared my food with him. Afterwards, he asked me, "What are your plans for the future? Do you intend to go back to your native country?

Or, if that is not possible, maybe you should consider staying in Germany and going to Hamburg." He said that he had a friend there who had a factory and could give me a job. He handed me a letter, which he addressed to his friend asking him to be helpful to me and to give me a job in his business.

Then he accompanied me to my barrack and he said good-bye to me. We hugged each other and I asked him, "When are you going to be back?"

He answered, "I can't tell you. But whatever happens, you should know that there is a brother who will always be thinking of you wherever you may be and will watch over you."

Jean left after that and I never saw him again. He was there to help me when I needed him and then he disappeared. I have often wondered who he really was. His presence remains an unexplainable mystery.

Shortly after Jean left, I volunteered to work in the typhus hospital, even though I had not yet recovered my strength completely. My friends and companions advised me against doing that.

They told me, "It is unwise to expose yourself to the typhus patients. Be happy you haven't gotten the illness so far. Keep in mind that you might not be entirely immune to it."

My answer was, "God was protecting me all along and helped me to survive. I feel that I have to do something for being given that privilege. I have to assist others who are in need of care."

I worked for three months in the hospital and I never regretted it. I fed the sick, I washed them, carried their bedpans, and comforted them. I listened to their wishes and desires.

There were those who recovered from the illness. There were others who didn't overcome it and died. I listened to their stories and their confessions before they passed away. I felt like a rabbi. I closed their eyes after that. When I couldn't do anything else for them anymore, I said a silent prayer, asking God to let their souls rest in peace in Heaven. I felt such sadness for those who suffered and survived the pain and the terror of the Holocaust, and then died after their liberation without being able to enjoy better times.

I will never forget the tragic death from typhus of one of my fellow former prisoners. She and her sister were with me all along through Auschwitz, Bremen, and Bergen-Belsen. One of the sisters had attended one year of medical school. She didn't get typhus after liberation, but unfortunately her sister did and she had the privilege of being hospitalized. It looked like she was getting better, but then her condition deteriorated again and her high fever returned along with delirium. Her psychotic episodes manifested in hallucinations, visions similar to the effects of LSD. She imagined that she was a bird and could fly. She jumped out of a window from the second floor of the hospital and died instantly. It was something totally unexpected. Everyone was very sad, feeling guilty for not keeping a closer eye on her. But the whole thing was a highly unusual happening. I felt very sorry for her and also for her sister who was deeply disturbed.

I also remember the tragic story of another typhus patient in the hospital. She and her daughter were fortunate to be together all along in Auschwitz and also in Bergen-Belsen. The mother contracted typhus after liberation and she was lucky to be hospitalized. Her daughter was at her bedside all the time, watching over her and praying for her mother's recovery.

After a few days, the mother was miraculously recovering, and her daughter was feeding her fluids and soft foods, because she was too weak to take care of herself. Both of them seemed happy. Everything looked good. Watching them, I thought how privileged they were to have each other. It didn't happen very often that mother and daughter got to stay together in the camp and also survive. I wondered what had happened to my mother. Maybe I would never see her again. I felt such a sadness.

Then, one day when I was at the bedside of another patient, the daughter came to ask my help. She seemed to be in great despair and very agitated. She said, "Please come quickly, there is something wrong with my mother! She looks so strange! I think that something stuck in her throat while I was feeding her."

I followed her to her mother's bedside and I saw that her mother was dead. Sometimes typhus patients seemed to recover, and then suddenly died of some unexpected complications. I told her that her mother had passed away.

She screamed, "No! No! It is not true! You are lying to me! Help her to swallow her food!"

I called the physician who pronounced her mother dead. Even then she didn't want to believe it. She yelled, "She is alive! She is alive! Don't you see that she is moving? Please help her!"

It was heartrending to witness her suffering. She couldn't accept that she had lost her mother after liberation and couldn't cope with the loss and pain. She had a mental breakdown and had to be sedated and kept under observation. Eventually she recovered, but her depression never lifted. She was badly harmed emotionally and she was never the same person as she had been before the tragic event.

There were many other tragic occurrences during the three months of my work in the typhus hospital. Although I was exposed to the typhus patients, I was protected from the illness. God was watching over me. I felt all along that I was doing the right thing by giving assistance and comfort to my companions who needed care.

In the course of time, a movie theater was created in the camp to provide some entertainment for the British troops and for the survivors. I never attended the movies because one could only go if one was accompanied by a British soldier or officer. I felt that after all we had gone through, we should not have these kinds of restrictions. In my opinion, that represented an infringement on our freedom, which was humiliating.

But many of the women had a different feeling about that. They took advantage of being courted by the British soldiers and officers and went with them to the shows. Some of the women, even among those in my barrack, went beyond that. There were those who sometimes took their pillows and blankets and disappeared in the forest among the birch trees for the night with some soldiers. Naturally, they had some benefits from those nightly escapades, like receiving chocolates, cigarettes, food items, and even some special clothing. Maybe the other reason for doing it might have been to prove their femininity and to reinforce the feeling that they were still attractive and desirable. Maybe in that sense one shouldn't be too critical of their behavior.

However, when some of the women in my barrack tried to encourage me to do the same, I became very resentful. I had my own values, concepts, and principles, and I wouldn't allow anyone to interfere with them. Because they couldn't influence me in that respect, they started making fun of me, calling me "The Old Maid." Although that nickname was very offensive to me, I was determined to ignore it. The more I did, the more they kept aggravating me. That started to spoil my relationship with them. Even Pere and Jackie started taunting me and I resented them for that. Only Lily was supportive of my principles. She was close to my age, while all the other women in our barrack were quite a bit older and couldn't fully understand my feelings.

I was busy working in the typhus hospital and I felt great compassion for all my sick and dying comrades who suffered a great deal. My thoughts were with them.

One day I met a young woman in her twenties in the camp, from another barrack, who was a former resident of my native city. She was an artistic person and had been an actress there. She didn't attend the movie house either for the same reason that I didn't. Her name was Judith. She had the idea to organize a theater group, consisting of Hungarian women interested in acting and participating in her project. She intended to get permission from the British to allow us to occasionally use the movie house to perform some well-known Hungarian plays and also some classical ballet dancing, which might be of interest to everyone. She asked me if I would be interested in helping in her project. I told her that I would be delighted to do so and I also mentioned my strong interest in acting, which I developed early in my childhood.

We started working on our project and we got the approval from the British to perform in the movie house. My friend Judith selected for our first performance, the famous play of the well-known Hungarian playwright, Madács Imre, *The Tragedy of Man*. I had a dual role in it. I was the narrator, and also played the role of Mephisto (The Devil), which was the main role in the play. Our performance was very successful and it was repeated several times. Later on, some dance performances also took place. One of them was *The Dance of the Elves*. The music for it was composed by the famous Norwegian composer, Edward Grieg.

I tremendously enjoyed being involved in the theater plays. As our group became more successful, some of the women in my barrack became mean, teasing me endlessly, saying, "Here comes the 'Old Maid'." They started persecuting me. I took refuge from them by walking in the birch forest among the old birch trees. I felt that the trees were my true friends. I talked to them and they knew how lonely I felt. Sometimes while I was among them, I recited the poems of my favorite Hungarian poets, like Ady Eudre and Petofi Sándor.

I liked Judith. She became my best friend. She understood my feelings. One day she asked me, "Would you be interested in writing a new play for us?"

She knew that I had enjoyed writing since I was ten years old. I took the challenge and for the first time in my life, I wrote a play. I worked on it devotedly and hid my manuscript under my mattress. I didn't want anyone in my room to read it.

Often when the weather was nice I sat on the grass among my favorite trees in the forest, working on my play. Finally, I completed it and hid it as usual under my mattress before I left for work in the hospital. I had in mind to present it to Judith after work.

When I got back from work, I went to retrieve my finished play from under my mattress. It was there, but torn into pieces. I never found out which one of the women did that. I felt like a part of me had been torn into pieces and I was bleeding from emotional pain. Whoever did it was an evil and jealous person who wanted to hurt me. From then on, I felt that I had no friends in the barrack. I felt such anger, loneliness, and betrayal.

Towards the end of the summer of 1945, a great event took place in our camp. Jehudi Menuhin, the great Jewish violinist, came to Bergen-Belsen to perform for us. I will never forget that day. It was a beautiful, sunny day and the concert was scheduled for the afternoon, outside, so that everyone could attend. A platform was erected for the artist and chairs were provided for us. A huge crowd attended the concert. Brigadier General Glen Hughes, head of the Second British Army, which liberated us, was present, along with officers and soldiers of the British Army.

Jehudi Menuhin appeared in simple attire. He wore a white shirt with rolled up sleeves, blue slacks, and black shoes. He introduced himself and told us how privileged he was to perform for us survivors and our liberators.

Then he placed his violin under his chin and took his bow in hand. When he touched the strings of his musical instrument, heavenly music resounded in the air. Haunting and beautiful melodies emerged. Many of us cried while listening.

The music touched the depth of our souls. I realized what an exceptionally great artist Menuhin was. He put his heart into his playing and was able to mesmerize all of us. It was such a wonderful, kind gesture on his part to come and play for all of us. I thought how fortunate I was to survive and experience the great performance of a world famous violinist like Jehudi Menuhin.

Part Five

Chapter 21

I was in Bergen-Belsen for six months after my liberation. At the end of that period, I had to make a very hard decision about what I should do with my life. We were repatriated with the help of the American Jewish Joint Distribution Committee (JDC), but I had to wait for the Hungarian transport to my native city. I also had the choice to go to the United States. The JDC helped young people like myself immigrate to the USA. I also had relatives in Palestine (the present state of Israel) which was at that time under British mandate. I wrote a letter to my mother's cousin, Rózsi Krochmal, who was living there with her husband and child, asking her what to do, but I didn't get an answer. The postal communication was very poor. I decided to go back to my native city of Kolozsvár, which after World War II reverted to Romania, and was renamed Cluj. My letter to my relatives in Palestine arrived after I left Bergen-Belsen to return home with the Hungarian transport, which included a relatively small group of about fifteen to twenty women.

I felt that my decision to go home was the right one. I wanted to look for the survivors of my family. I didn't know if my parents had survived, but I had to find out what happened to them. I was scared. The thought that I might not find anyone alive terrified me.

The day of departure arrived. The transportation facilities were terrible after the war. We traveled by freight train, sometimes in railroad cattle wagons, which reminded me of the railroad cattle cars in which I had been transported to the concentration camps with my family. The odor of the wagons evoked in me horrible memories of our journey to the camps. Somber and depressed thoughts crossed my mind.

It took a long time to get home, about two weeks, because many times we had to stop and wait in different cities in order to acquire transportation so that we could continue our journey. During that period, the JDC, who organized our repatriation, also provided us with food and with some primitive accommodations throughout our trip home.

The Red Cross and the JDC distributed packages of food to us during our entire journey. The German cities through which we traveled were in ruins, looking like cemeteries with only parts of buildings visible, giving the impression of tombstones. Hitler surely destroyed us, but also his own country and his people.

Our last stop before reaching Cluj was Budapest, the capital of Hungary. We arrived there in the morning. We were notified that we would have to stay there throughout the night until the next day, to wait for the arrival of a freight train to take us further. So again the Red Cross and the JDC provided us with food and accommodations.

After we were settled, we were instructed to go to the Distribution Center a few blocks away from our accommodations to pick up our packages of food. So I left my room with a group of women to pick up my package. As we walked on the street towards our destination, there were two non-Jewish Hungarian women strolling behind us, listening to our conversations. We overheard them talking to each other: "Look at these fat Jewish women. All those stories about how badly the Jews were treated in the German concentration camps are a bunch of lies."

Those women thought we were fat, while in reality we still were bloated due to water retention, an aftereffect of starvation. Even though it was half a year since we were liberated in Bergen-Belsen, we still were not completely recovered from the side effects of starvation.

It was upsetting and sad to realize that there still was anti-Semitism in the hearts of the Hungarian population. It also was hard to tolerate knowing that after all our suffering and our tremendous losses in human lives and properties, many of the Hungarian people still hated us. The Holocaust did not stop that.

Two of the women next to me got very enraged and told me, "We will teach a lesson to these two anti-Semites by beating the hell out of them."

I said, "It is a bad idea; don't do it! It will get us into trouble and delay our trip home!"

But they were determined to do it anyway. So, they turned around and faced them, ready for the attack. But the two Hungarian women got scared and ran away.

I was thinking how futile it would have been to beat them up. There was no way of changing their views about us. We probably would have been arrested by the police on battery charges, which in turn would have interfered a great deal with our journey home. I was grateful the Hungarian women had run away.

After I got my package of food, I decided to walk back by myself to the place where we were settled in for the night. I wanted to have privacy and figure out what I would do with my life in case I did not find anyone at home. I was deep in thought and was not paying attention to where I was going. At one point, I realized that I was lost and had ended up on unfamiliar streets. I got confused and upset about not knowing where I was. I had no idea how to get back to our accommodations.

I was determined to ask for help from the first person who came my way. The street where I was walking was nearly deserted, but I was pleased to see a person coming towards me on the opposite side of the street. It was a man, and as he came closer it seemed to me that his face was familiar. I had the impression that I had seen him before. As he came closer I recognized him. He was our Jewish next-door neighbor who had lived in our same apartment house before we were taken to the concentration camps.

He also recognized me and said to me in astonishment, "Magda, you are alive!"

I answered, "I am so happy that you also survived! I am so pleased to see you. What a coincidence! I had to get lost in this city in order to meet you!"

He said, "How happy your mother will be to see you come back from the camps!"

I asked him, "When did you see my mother?" I couldn't believe that my mother was alive.

Then he related to me the following:

"When I returned to Cluj from the camps, I found out that all my family was killed in the Holocaust; nobody returned. I couldn't stay in that city because the memories were killing me. So, I moved to Budapest. But while I was in Cluj, I met your mother one day at our city's square, by the Statue of King Matthias and his warriors. I walked her home and we reminisced about the times when we were living happily with our families. I know where she lives and can give you her address."

He tore out a piece of paper from his small notebook of addresses and wrote down my mother's address.

I was thoroughly shocked and I realized that I had to be in a certain place at a certain time in order to hear the first wonderful news about my mother. So after all, there was a purpose in losing my way. Our former neighbor accompanied me to our accommodations and we said goodbye to each other.

When I entered our room, I was still dazed and excited by the wonderful news. The other women in the room noticed my strange look. They thought that something unpleasant must have happened to me and they looked worried. I said to them, "Today a miracle happened to me. I found out that my mother survived and I have her address!" I told them about my strange encounter with our neighbor. They were happy to hear the good news. They hoped that some wonderful unexpected surprises might also come their way, and they would find some members of their families alive when they returned.

I couldn't sleep that night. I still couldn't believe it was true. The next morning we continued on our journey to Cluj. We arrived in the late afternoon. I looked at the paper with my mother's address. One of the women in my transport who was also from Cluj wanted to come along with me, in order to witness the reunion with my mother and to give me moral support.

We came to a big apartment house which had a gate equipped with a bell. You had to ring the bell so that somebody from inside the building could open it. My knees were shaking from my strong emotions when I touched the bell. I told myself: *Now you are going to find out the truth.*

I rang the bell and a window opened on the second floor. I heard my mother's voice, "Who is there?"

I said, "It is your daughter coming home!"

My mother and I both started screaming hysterically due to our indescribable joy.

My homecoming was a total surprise to my mother. She ran down the stairs to greet me and opened the gate in a hurry. We embraced and kissed each other. Our uncontrolled screaming was followed with fits of crying. My companion was crying too, and finally she left, saying good-bye to us, hoping that this miracle which she witnessed would also happen to her. Unfortunately, as I found out later, it wasn't the case. Her mother didn't survive.

After our very emotional meeting, I walked up the stairs with my mother to her very small apartment. It consisted of one big room which served as a bedroom, a dining room, and a small kitchenette. My mother worked in a restaurant as a cashier at that time. Her salary was small; therefore she couldn't afford a big place for herself. But she was a very neat, hard-working person and the apartment was cozy and pleasant, with homemade curtains and tablecloths.

Among the belongings she had managed to salvage from our former, looted home was my Spinet piano. It was amazing that no one had taken the piano from our home. I was so happy to see it because I loved to play the piano. Music was one of my passions.

When I entered our small, but neat little home where I was free and surrounded by the love of my mother, I kneeled down and kissed my piano and some of the old familiar pieces of furniture. My mother looked worried, asking me, "Are you alright? You never did such strange things before."

I told her, "Mother, these are my old friends from our former home. I grew up with them. I am so happy to see them again."

I looked at my mother. She looked so thin and tired and her beautiful, jet-black hair had many strands of white in it. Suffering and not knowing whether we were alive had taken a toll on her.

A mother is irreplaceable. I came home in rags, dirty from all that travel. I stripped off my clothing. She prepared warm water for me to wash myself. On a chair she kept a set of secondhand clothing, which was prepared for me in case I came home. In a cupboard she had stored three boxes of chocolates reserved for me, which she purchased from her meager savings, knowing how much I liked chocolates.

It was such a wonderful feeling to have white, clean sheets on the bed, which we shared because she couldn't afford a second one.

Finally, after a modest dinner of scrambled eggs, cheese, and white bread with butter, which seemed like a feast to me, we went to bed on that first day of my homecoming and we talked almost throughout the entire night. There were so many things we wanted to talk about.

During that night she told me all about her survival. I found out what had happened to her after she was taken from the ghetto to the hospital because she was gravely ill.

At that time I had been desperate and thought that I would never see her again. There had been rumors in the ghetto that even the sick Jewish people would be removed from the hospitals and deported to the German concentration camps.

Later on, when I was in Auschwitz, I learned that all the sick people who were taken there were killed shortly after their arrival in the killing facilities of Auschwitz-Birkenau.

Mother told me that shortly after her arrival at the hospital, she lost consciousness. She couldn't remember how long it took before she woke up. When she finally awoke, she found herself on a hospital bed with Dr. Hainal standing next to her. She felt very ill and weak. Dr. Hainal said to her: "Don't be afraid. As long as I am here in charge of the Department of Internal Medicine, nothing bad is going to happen to you. I am going to take good care of you." And he did. He tried to administer all kinds of treatments to my mother. She couldn't digest food for a long time, so he placed a feeding tube in her so she could get some nutrition. My mother was in critical condition for many months, but she gradually started to recover and she survived. Dr. Hainal kept her hidden in the hospital until the end of the war.

The Gendarmes (Hungarian police) came several times to take the Jews from the hospital. But they never succeeded in getting any of the Jews hidden by Dr. Hainal. In order to keep my mother safe, he told them that he needed her for experiments. He knew that they would agree to that. They considered it normal and appropriate to use Jews for medical experiments. The Nazis experimented medically on Jews in the concentration camps. Dr. Hainal was also hiding three Jewish families at the psychiatric ward of the hospital. He was a brave and compassionate man. If the Gestapo had found out what he really was doing, he would have been shot or deported to Auschwitz.

On one hand, there was someone like Dr. Hainal who risked his life to save Jews, and I am sure there were also other good and compassionate people who were hiding Jewish families, risking their lives. There were also those who would have liked to help but were afraid to, because they didn't want to endanger their families. This is understandable.

But on the other hand, there were many anti-Semites among the population who welcomed the opportunity to rob the Jews and to announce their hiding places.

Although Dr. Hainal assured my mother that he would always protect her and would not allow anything to happen to her, my mother lived in constant fear at the hospital. There were two anti-Semitic nurses who threatened her, telling her that they would inform the Hungarian authorities about her. Surprisingly, one of them was a Catholic nun. But they never did turn her in. They used that as a form of emotional torture on my mother. It was very evil to do that, considering how ill and desperate my mother was. They aggravated her condition by keeping her in constant fear. I hope that later on in their lives they got punished for their cruelty.

In contrast to that, there were the other nurses who tried to help and console my mother. Like anywhere else, there were good and bad people amidst the population of our city.

After the end of the war, my mother left the hospital and faced total economical disaster. Everything we owned had been lost. She didn't have any money or any place to go. Before she left the hospital, Dr. Hainal gave her some money so that she could help herself for a few days. I am eternally grateful to him. I would like to keep alive the memory of the late Dr. Hainal, an outstanding human being.

My poor mother didn't know what had happened to me or to my father. She had lost a great deal of weight due to her extended illness and she was very depressed. She looked for a job and luckily found one at a frame shop where she was a salesperson, waiting on customers. Having a warm and pleasant personality, she was very much liked.

She rented a small, one-room apartment on the second floor of a large apartment house in the city. She went to our old home, which had been looted, and found a few furniture pieces left there. That was helpful because she couldn't afford to buy any furniture. She could barely exist on the small salary she earned. She started looking for a better-paying job so that she could maintain her apartment and pay the monthly rent and her living expenses.

Fortunately, later on, she found another better-paying job. She was hired as a cashier at the sophisticated Hungarian restaurant owned by Mr. and Mrs. Nice. The owners were wonderful and kind people. They liked my mother, who did a good job for them. They felt sorry for her and tried to help her in any way they could. She could eat there free of charge. That was important because she could spend less money for food—that helped a lot.

Meanwhile she waited anxiously for the return of my father and for me, her only daughter. She prayed and cried a lot, hoping that we were alive.

After the end of World War II, in 1945, the people from my native city who survived the camps were gradually returning to their homes, coming back by train. My poor mother went every day to the railroad station as the transports of people came in, showing them my photo and the photo of my father. She asked the people if they had seen us and if they had any news about us, but she was unable to get any information of our whereabouts. She hadn't received any signs of life about us until the day I showed up, totally unexpected.

In the morning, we ate our modest breakfast, a big treat for me after all the deprivations I had experienced in the camps. Fresh bread with butter and jelly, and coffee with milk seemed to me like a king's feast.

It was the end of October. It got quite cold in our city at that time of the year, since we were surrounded by the Carpathian Mountains. In our room we had a tall, decorated, ceramic heater which was fueled by wood. My mother started the fire and fed the heater with pieces of wood. She wanted me to feel warm and comfortable in our home. After she did that she gave me a big kiss and left for work.

After I was left alone, I realized that the impossible dream I had in the camps had come true. When we were constantly hungry, starving, and suffering of cold and hard labor, we prisoners talked incessantly about food and dreamed of being free and in a comfortable, warm place at our homes with our family members. Often my fellow prisoners asked me, "Suppose that you survive and return home, what would be your favorite dish? What will you do on your first day at home?"

My answer was, "There is no question in my mind—my favorite dish would be chocolates!"

I also visualized numerous times what I would do on my first day at home in Cluj. I would sit by the fireplace, enjoying the warmth, reading a good book, having a box of chocolates at my side, and savoring the delicate sweets from the box, gradually consuming all its contents.

At that time, my vision had seemed an impossible dream. And yet there I was, sitting by the fireplace, reading a book, and savoring my chocolates. I felt like such a lucky person, waiting for my mother to come home from work.

Mr. and Mrs. Nice were very helpful to me, too. They insisted that I also could eat at their restaurant free of charge. Mr. Nice took me to the kitchen and told their chef to feed me well, and to give me the best food available. My mother and I were fortunate to have such caring and compassionate people around us.

I was very happy that I had found my mother, but then I found out that my father and many of my family members were killed in the Holocaust. The great emotional pain of losing my father hit me on the first Friday night at home. I remember that day.

On that particular Friday night, the other impossible dream I had in the camps materialized. That dream followed me throughout my captivity. When the pain of suffering reached an almost intolerable level, I would evoke in my imagination a positive, happy image of being at home on a Friday night. I could see my mother lighting and blessing the Sabbath candles. I would feel the happiness and the anticipation of our festive dinner. I could visualize my father saying a prayer before the start of our dinner, then taking the white challah (egg bread), breaking it, and giving a piece to my mother, to me, and a piece to himself. Then he would pour a glass of wine for each of us, reciting a prayer. After that ritual, the dinner would be served by my mother. She was a great cook. She always prepared the tastiest fish dishes as appetizers for every Friday night.

My favorite was the gefilte fish, which was followed by chicken soup, fried potatoes, cucumber salad or kosher, homemade pickles, roasted duck, and naturally, some fancy, homemade cakes as dessert. While I was dreaming in the camps of all these delicacies, I could almost taste these special dishes and feel the presence of my loved ones. The evocation of those happy, peaceful scenes kept me alive in the camps by reinforcing my desire to keep on fighting for my life so that I could return and experience once again those joyful times with my parents and family.

And there I was, at home again and this time, everything was real on that particular Friday night.

I watched as my mother took our Jewish candelabra and lit the Sabbath candles, uttering softly the words of the prayer of benediction:

"Blessed art Thou,
Oh, Lord, our God,
King of the Universe,
Who has sanctified us
by Thy Laws
and commanded us
to kindle
the Sabbath light."

She wore on her head a hand-crocheted prayer shawl while she performed the ritual.

I gazed at my mother. I couldn't believe that my dream had come true. I felt such joy seeing her. So many times in the camps I gave up hope that I would ever see her again. While I was enjoying those happy feelings and thoughts, suddenly the empty chair where my father used to sit was staring at me. It felt like somebody had thrust a knife into my chest, and I would bleed and die of grief. I felt the deep pain of a terrible loss. My father was not with us anymore. I realized that I would never see him again. The thought that his remains were dishonored and buried in a mass grave was agonizing.

I wanted to find another honorable burial place for my father. I buried him on that Friday night deep in my heart and he will stay with me as long as I live. I also buried there all my family members who died in the various German concentration camps and all my fellow prisoners who perished there. All the victims of the Holocaust are buried in my heart forever.

The following "Eulogy" to my father was conceived on that Friday night but was born only much later when I became a writer.

Eulogy
(in memory of my father)

My dear father,
you left us forever.
You had a heart of gold,
you were kind and clever.
Why didn't you survive?
I am heartbroken, but alive.
Back from the German
concentration camps,
but you are buried there.
I will mourn you forever.
Why were you treated so brutally?
Only because you were a Jew.
What was our sin?
Our religion.
We were condemned
to persecution.
Your last words
still ring in my ears
after so many years.
"My child, my dear daughter,
soon we will be separated
from each other.
I may never return—
Be strong, don't cry.
Let the candle of hope burn
in your heart.

Take care of your mother,
cherish and respect her.
Don't forget your loving father.
Remember to follow
the broad, countless streets
of knowledge,
and beware the dark,
narrow alleys
of ignorance.
Practice the art of love,
forgiveness, and tolerance ..."
Father, my dear father,
I can never forget you.
Your words are deeply carved
into my memory.
Beloved Father,
rest peacefully.

The Aftermath of the Holocaust
Coping with Loss and Grief

I was happy and grateful to have my mother around, to be alive and free, walking again the familiar streets of my hometown. It seemed a miracle. Yet, at the same time, it was painful and agonizing to pass by the homes of my family members who hadn't survived the camps. It was hard to cope with the overpowering feelings of loss and grief. It felt like a part of myself was torn out, and I was bleeding profusely from my emotional wounds. The realization of my losses seemed unbearable and I wondered if I would ever recover from the wounds of the Holocaust.

Wounded

I walk in pain
through memory lane
with the fragments
of past painful passages
piercing my brain.

As the hours pass
I roam aimlessly
on the pavement, on the grass,
until the night
dims my sight.

Darkness covers my thoughts,
but my heart burns with fever
and lights up the dark sky.
Will I ever recover?
Or will I die?

I could still hear the cries of my suffering and dying fellow prisoners. The shadows of the gas chambers, crematory ovens, and death pits were still haunting me. The images of the dry, charred bones of the innocent victims lining the pits were permanently imprinted in my memory. Those were the remains of the brave Jewish martyrs. Many of my family members, including my beloved father, were among them. They should always be honored and remembered.

The Valley of Dry Bones
(In the memory of my beloved Uncle Eugene,
Uncle Jacob, his wife Ilona, Uncle Ernest, his wife Ethel,
Aunt Rachel,
and all the members of my family who were killed by
the Nazis in Auschwitz).

In the valley of dry bones
there are no graves, no tombstones.
The petrified remains
of the innocent victims of persecution
covered with bloodstains,
are scattered around,
casting horror and awe
upon the clay ground.
I witnessed their unjust execution.
They were taken by force
to their chambers of extermination.
Kicked and beaten by cruel fists,
they wore tattooed numbers on their wrists
and the Shield of David on their chests.
They met death
by uttering their sacred prayer
in their last breath:

"HEAR, O ISRAEL, THE LORD OUR GOD
THE LORD IS ONE!"
Brave Jewish martyrs,
members of my family,

my fellow prisoners,
many years have passed by
since you are gone.
But, I remember your desperate cry:

"Our bodies will decay,
our flesh will be rotten,
if you survive Auschwitz,
please, don't let us be forgotten!"

My life was spared
by God's intervention.
I know that the purpose
of that heavenly protection
was to return with the memory
of your sufferance and pain,
to make sure you didn't die in vain,
to fulfill your last wish;
not letting your courageous spirits ever perish.

After coming home from the camps, besides coping with loss and grief, which were so hard to tolerate and made me very depressed, I also had to deal with my physical discomfort, an aftereffect of my captivity. I had frostbite on all of my fingers and toes from the cold I had to endure throughout the winter in Bremen, where we had to work on ice and snow-covered streets all day long without gloves or adequate shoes.

When I came home, all my fingers were red, painful, and swollen, and I developed purulent wounds on my toes. My mother tried to treat them with the old home remedy, which involved roasting onions in the oven and then placing the warm onions on my toes. It was believed that they would drain the pus. We had no access to antibiotics at that time. I was lucky not to get gangrene. Ultimately, I had to be medically treated, because the onions didn't do the job, although, they proved to be somewhat helpful.

My other problem was the water retention resulting from the harmful effects of starvation. I looked swollen. Actually, my mother was surprised to see that. When I came home, she expected me to look quite thin, but I looked fuller than she had visualized because of that metabolic malfunction. It took a year to overcome all these health problems. Eventually, I was cured of all of them.

But the emotional wounds of the Holocaust are long-lasting. They are the invisible wounds, which are much harder to cure. It took me many years to heal. A Holocaust survivor, even if she or he is healed, carries the scars of it for a lifetime. A tendency toward depression is one aftereffect of the horror-filled experiences in the camps. This haunts the lives of the survivors of the Holocaust, along with a hypersensitivity to emotional hurts.

After my return, I also suffered from horrible nightmares, which continued for many years. The traumatic and shocking experiences to which I had been subjected were still living in my subconscious mind and they were activated, manifesting themselves in my dream world, in which they were intertwined into strange stories, where reality and fantasy were so strongly interwoven that they merged into each other.

I had difficulty suppressing the gruesome and terrifying memories of the Holocaust. I couldn't forget them because they were etched deeply into my soul. But I realized that if I wanted to survive, I had to accept them and live with them.

Also I knew that I had to recover from my intense grieving period and overcome the dark, somber, depressive thoughts which festered in my soul.

I prayed to God to relieve me from my relentless, tormenting memories.

My state of mind during the first month after my homecoming is expressed in a poem that I wrote at a later stage of my life.

The Soul of a Holocaust Survivor

The dark, ominous clouds of depression
are descending upon me,
killing my joy,
and robbing my spirit's liberty.
The phantoms of past shocking
and painful experiences
are haunting my body and senses.
They follow me closely everywhere with persistence,
through the years of my existence.
I can't run away
from the shadows of my inner being,
I must keep on fighting and living.

Where is the path of my destiny?
My thoughts are void of clarity,
am I heading for insanity?
I beseech the Lord
to eradicate my confusion,
to dissipate the thick vapors
of my delusion.
To clear my judgment and reason,
to free me from the prison
of emotional torture,
and to spare me in the future
from the intrusion of cruelty,
death, and destruction.

I have seen life's nakedness.
I endured agony, distress,
and unjust slavery
hurled by merciless Fate at me,
during my captivity
in the extermination camps in Germany.
Where I was threatened daily
by the Devil's delegates ...
I lived behind the Gates of Hell,
the looks of it I can never dispel.

I am a survivor of the Holocaust.
Will the wounds cast upon me
forever last?
The deep sores and suffering

are still kept alive within me,
by the ghosts of memory.
They never leave me,
they hang on to my side,
whether I am awake, or asleep,
or when I rest, walk, or drive.
Invisible keepers of reminiscences
are depleting my senses.
All that's left behind
are the blind forces of passion,
and the representatives of anger,
hatred, resentment, and aggression.
They follow me with no hesitation
till my life's cessation.

Will I ever recover completely
from the wounds inflicted
in the annihilation camps of Germany?
Will I ever stop mourning
the murdered members of my family?
And the suffering and death
of six million Jews like me?

Only God knows
life's secret codes, its rules and woes,
and what for me the future holds.
Only He can tell
when for me will toll the bell.
To the Almighty I pray

at the end of each day,
asking the Creator
to cease my distress,
to restore my peace and happiness.
To heal my injuries,
and to liberate me
from relentless, tormenting memories.

My mother had much compassion for my feelings and depression. She tried to be helpful, but she was worried, seeing me so introverted and withdrawn into my sad thoughts. She knew that I needed some time to recover and to accept the losses I experienced. I missed my father and my Uncle Eugene, who was such an inspiration to me.

I tried to find comfort in the realization that although their physical bodies were deeply buried in the ground, their spirits were with me. I had dreams about my father, my uncle, and my lost family members.

In my dreams, they seemed real and alive. I told myself that I could still communicate with them in my dream world. I had to believe in the survival of the spirit. How could I otherwise accept the loss of my loved ones? I had to believe that although my loved ones were not with us anymore, their physical bodies didn't survive because "from dust we emerge, to dust we return," but their spirits escaped their bodies and rose above time and space, standing on life's stage, defying finality.

These thoughts helped me to accept the things I couldn't change and gave me courage to focus on the positive changes I could introduce in my life. I knew that before I could accomplish that, I had to find some peace within myself and stop my self-torture.

The period of grieving can last a long time, but the intensity of it gradually diminishes. However, we can never forget our departed loved ones.

I felt that if I wanted to survive my losses, I had to divert my thoughts from my inner mind and turn them outwards, towards beneficial, external solutions of my troublesome problems and great emotional upheavals. Only then could I go on with my life and introduce the necessary changes for my survival.

So, after a month of being deeply depressed and being withdrawn into myself, not feeling the need to communicate with other people, feeling comfortable in my solitude, having my loving mother at my side, being enclosed in our modest, but cozy, one-room apartment, sitting by thefireside, eating

Photo 18 – Magda 19-years-old

chocolates, and reading books, my mother sat down one day by my side and told me: "I love to look at you eating these chocolates, but do you have any plans about what else you would like to do? Do you have any goals which you would like to achieve in your life?"

The questions of my mother were like a wake-up call for me.

My answer was, "There is no doubt in my mind what I would like to do. I would like to fulfill my long-term wish to go to medical school."

My mother's answer was, "After all you went through, I am surprised that you are so unrealistic. You are aware that we are very poor and we can't afford to pay for that."

I said to my mother, "There is a way! I could apply for a scholarship."

From that day on, I was on my way to recovery. I again became a fighter, and this time for my education. I felt that if I succeeded in my fight for life in the camps, there was no doubt that I would be successful in my fight for education.

Photo 19 - Medical School!

So, at the end of November, 1945, I began studying. I had to pass many exams before I could apply for medical school. First, I had to finish the eighth grade of my high school (we called it gymnasium). At the time of our deportation, I had just completed the seventh grade of my high school.

I borrowed all the necessary books of the required subjects and studied them day and night. I took exam after exam. In the spring of 1946, I received my certificate of baccalaureate, after a grueling, three-day, written and oral exam, conducted in our city by a special commission

After that, I had to pass a very tough medical school entrance examination. Again, I studied day and night for that big exam. There were 900 students participating in it, out of which only 150 passed the exam and were admitted to medical school. I was one of those who passed. I also had a high grade-point average and qualified for a full scholarship.

Photo 20 – Magda's medical student Carnet (identification card)

During the summer of 1946, I met a medical student who was in his last year of medical school. He was very helpful to me. He offered to tutor me, knowing how difficult the entrance exam would be and how important it was for me to pass it and attend medical school on a full scholarship. In the process, we fell in love with each other.

In the late fall of 1946, we got married and at the same time, I began to attend my first year of medical school on a full scholarship. My seemingly impossible dream came true.

My husband, Dr. Eugene Herzberger, became a neurosurgeon, and we have been happily married for the past 58 years.

Photo 20 - The wedding picture of Magda and Eugene Herzberger taken in 1946.

Epilogue

I was an eyewitness to the Holocaust. I am an eyewitness to a new dawn, the rebirth of a new life, my second life, my second chance. Now I have my family, my beloved husband, my son, my daughter, and my grandchildren. I cherish my family. *What is the meaning of life?* I ask myself after all my experiences. The meaning of life is to live life fully, to bring out all the beautiful treasures buried within your soul. The meaning of life is to love, to share, to be.

The meaning of sufferance I have learned, too. Sufferance makes us eligible for God's blessings. Through sufferance we grow. Sufferance, agony, and disappointments kill something within us. Something is put to sleep within us and yet, something new is born at the same time. There is always a twilight and a new dawn. Day is followed by night and night is followed by day. A resurrection takes place within us each day. We remember the past, it belongs to us; and yet, we have to learn from the past so that we can grow in the future. After the dark night there is daybreak.

Daybreak
(to my husband)

Come, my love,
the night is gone.
Yesterday slipped away
on the Milky Way,
and the purple dawn put on
its sapphire crown,
ushering the new day
and making way
for the rising sun.
Let us resume
our daily course
on life's terrain.

Let the returning light
illuminate our sight
and start a new episode.
Let us decipher a part
of the hidden code
of creation,
on our temporary
earthly station.

Photo Descriptions

Photo 1   Magda in her second year of life. Photo was taken in 1927 in Cluj, Romania.

Photo 2   Magda's mother, Serena Daszkal, at age 17, with two of her cousins. Picture was taken in 1918 in Kolozsvár, Hungary (later Cluj, Romania). My mother, Serena Daszkal, is on the left with a black bow in her hair. Both of her cousins were later killed in the Holocaust.

Photo 3   Three-year-old Magda with some family members. Photo was taken in 1929 at Turda, resort town in Romania, located at a distance of 20 miles from the City of Cluj, Romania. One of her mother's uncles resided there with his family. In the picture Magda, as a small child, stands in the front row at right, next to her mother's cousin Margot (in the center), who was the youngest daughter of Moritz Salamon. Next to Margot, at her left, is her older sister Irene, with her daughter Bubetza standing in front of her. Behind Margot is her other sister Dora. Next to Dora are two other family members. Only Magda and Margot survived the Holocaust. All the others in that group were killed in Auschwitz.

Photo 4   Magda at age 4. The photo was taken in the summer of 1930 at the resort town of Felix, Romania, where her parents spent their vacation at that time.

Photo 5   Magda at age 5 with her parents, Herman Mozes and Serena Mozes. The picture was taken in 1931 in Cluj, Romania.

Photo 6   Magda's uncle Eugene, Romanian fencing champion, in his swimming trunks. Photo was taken at the resort town of Felix, Romania in 1930.

Photo 7   A portrait of Magda's uncle Eugene. Picture was taken in the city of Arad, Romania located at a distance of about 250 miles from the city of Cluj, Romania on August 24, 1930.

Photo 8   Magda at age 6 after the performance of her solo dance, during kindergarten, is bowing to the audience after a curtain call. Photo was taken in 1931 in Cluj, Romania.

Photo 9   Magda at age 6 in a dance group of children at the kindergarten. In the photo which was taken in 1931 in Cluj, Romania, after the performance of a dance, Magda is standing at the extreme right. She is the first boy clown holding a girl clown.

Photo 10 Magda at age 6 in a group picture taken in 1932 in Cluj, Romania, after one of the kindergarten plays in which Magda had the main role. She is sitting in the first row at the right, dressed in the national Romanian outfit. All the children in this picture, both boys and girls, are clad in national Romanian attire.

Photo 11 Magda at age 16 in a group photo with her classmates and some teachers at the Jewish girls' gymnasium, taken in 1942 in Kolozsvár, Hungary (former Cluj, Romania). In this picture Professor Antal Mark, director of the two Jewish gymnasiums (one for girls, the other for boys), is sitting in the second row, the first person on the right. The third person at his left is Winkler Janka, the principal of the Jewish girls' gymnasium. In the photo, Magda is standing in the back row behind Antal Mark to the left. Mainly her head is visible, with a white bow in her hair.

Photo 12 Dr. Moshe Carmilly-Weinberger, Chief Rabbi of the Neolog Synagogue in Kolozsvár, Hungary (former Cluj, Romania) during the period of 1934 to 1944. Dr. Carmilly-Weinberger was the founder of the Jewish gymnasiums (one for boys and one for girls) in Kolozsvár, Hungary in 1940.

Photo 13 Magda at age 16 with her piano teacher, Mr. Stern, and his pupils. This picture was taken in 1942 in Kolozsvár, Hungary (former Cluj, Romania). In the photo Mr. Stern is sitting in the middle of the second row. Magda is standing behind him in the third row. She is wearing a white sweater with some decorations on it.

Photo 14 Portrait of Magda's father, Herman Mozes. Picture was taken around 1940 in Kolozsvár (former Cluj, Romania), Hungary.

Photo 15 Magda's uncle Eugene with his fiancée Pere. Picture was taken sometime in the early 1940's in Kolozsvár, Hungary (former Cluj, Romania).

Photo 16 Roll call at Auschwitz in front of the Hungarian women's barracks. The picture was published in The Auschwitz Album in 1981 by Random House, page 129. This book was based upon an album discovered by a concentration camp survivor, Lili Meier.

Photo 17 Enlarged section of Photo 16. Magda Herzberger is centered in this photo.

Photo 18 Magda at age 19. Photo was taken in 1945 in Cluj (former Kolozsvár), Romania sometime after Magda returned from the camps.

Photo 19   The Cover for Magda's medical student Carnet, see Photo 20.

Photo 20   Magda's medical student Carnet (identification card) confirming her registration in the second year of medical school (1947-1948) at Regele Ferdinand I (King Ferdinand I) University in Cluj (former Kolozsvár), Romania.

Photo 21   The wedding picture of Magda and Eugene Herzberger taken in 1946 in Cluj, Romania. At that time Eugene was a medical student in his last year of medical school and Magda was enrolled in her first year of medical school.

Recommended Reading

Auschwitz: A Doctor's Eyewitness Account, by Dr. Miklos Nyiszli. Published by Arcade Publishing, New York, 1993. Originally published by F. Fell, New York, 1960.

Children of the Flames: Dr. Josef Mengele and the Untold Story of the Twins of Auschwitz, by Lucette Matalon Lagnado and Sheila Dekel. Published by William Marrow and Company Inc., New York, 1991.

Escape from the Holocaust, by William S. Ruben and Paul Ruben. Published by Manor Books, Inc., New York, NY, 1978.

I Was a Doctor in Auschwitz, by Dr. Gisella Perl. Published by Ayer Company Publishers, Inc., North Stratford, New Hampshire. Reprinted edition, 1997. First published in 1948.

80629: A Mengele Experiment, by Gene Church. Published by Sharon Kimberly Damon Publishing Company, Richardson, Texas, 1986.

Man's Search for Meaning, by Victor Frankl. Published by Washington Square Press, Publication of Pocket Books, New York, NY, 1984.

Shoah: An Oral History of the Holocaust/ The Complete Text of the Film, by Claude Lauzmann. Preface by Simone De Beauvoir. Published by Pantheon Books, New York, a division of Random House, 1985.

Survival in Auschwitz, by Primo Levi. Published by A Touchtone Book, Simon and Schuster, 1996. First published in 1958. Translated by Guilio Einaudi by Orion Press.

Inspirational Poetry (unpublished), by Magda Herzberger, copyright © 2001 by Magda Herzberger.

Antal Mark Memorial Volume, edited by Dr. Moshe Carmilly-Weinberger Mozes. (Kolozsvár, 1943).

A History of Hungary, Peter F. Sugar, General Editor, Peter Hanák, Associate Director, Tibor Frank, Editorial Assistant. Published by Indiana University Press, 1990. Second printing paperback edition, 1994.

Eyewitness to Holocaust, by Magda Herzberger. Published by Modern Images, Mattoon, Illinois, 1985, 1987, 1990.

Five Chimneys by Olga Lengyel. Published by Ziff-Davis Publishing Co., 1947, and by Academy Chicago Publishers, Chicago, 1995.

God Saved Me for a Purpose, by Magda Herzberger. Published in Sisters in Sorrow. (See No. 16 below.)

Memorial Volume for the Jews of Cluj-Kolozsvár, edited by Dr. Moshe Carmilly-Weinberger, formerly Chief Rabbi of Kolozsvár and Professor of Jewish Studies at the Yeshiva University in New York. The book was published in 1970 (1st edition), and in 1988 (2nd edition) by Sepher Hermon Press, Inc., New York for Alumni Association of Jewish Schools in Kolozsvár.

Sisters in Sorrow: Voices of Care in the Holocaust. Compiled by Roger F. Ritvo and Diane M. Plotkin. Published by Texas A and M University Press, College Station, Texas, 1998.

Survival in Auschwitz: the Nazi Assault on Humanity. By Primo Levi. Translated from Italian by Stuart Woolf.

The Road to Life: The Rescue Operation of Jewish Refugees on the Hungarian-Romanian Border, by Moshe Carmilly-Weinberger, New York, 1994.

The Auschwitz Album. A book based upon an album discovered by a concentration camp survivor, Lili Meier. Text by Peter Hellman. Published by Random House, New York, 1981.

The Romanians, a History by Vlad Georgescu, edited by Matei Calinescu, translated by Alexandra Bley Vroman, published by Ohio State University Press, Columbus, Ohio, 1991 (2nd edition). Originally published as Historia Romanilor in 1984 by the American Romanian Academy of Arts and Sciences.

The Yellow Star. The Persecution of Jews in Europe, 1933-1945, by Gerhard Shoenberner. Translated from the German language by Susan Sweet. Published by Bantam Books by arrangement with Transworld Publication, Ltd., 1979.

The Waltz of the Shadows, by Magda Herzberger. Published by Philosophical Library, New York, 1983.

Will to Freedom: a Perilous Journey through Fascism and Communism, by Egon Balas. Published by The Syracuse University Press, 2000.

Magda Herzberger's Biography

Magda Herzberger was born and raised in the city of Cluj, Romania. Being of Jewish faith, she and her family were deported to the German concentration camps in 1944 when Hitler occupied her native city. She is a survivor of three death camps: Auschwitz, Bremen, and Bergen-Belsen. Most of her family members were killed by the Nazis. Her mother survived; she passed away ten years ago at the age of 93.

Magda is a poet, lecturer, and composer. *Inspirational Poetry* is one of her unpublished manuscripts consisting of a selection of her best writings during the 38 years of her writing career. This book contains thoughts on life, faith, hope, love, her feelings as a Holocaust survivor, and a variety of other subjects. Behind each of her poems there is a story to be told and experienced.

She is also the author of four previously published books: *The Waltz of the Shadows* (an autobiography in poetry form), *Eyewitness to Holocaust* (an autobiographical essay consisting of prose and poetry), *Will You Still Love Me?* (a collection of love poems dedicated to her husband), and *Songs of Life* (a poetry book with a variety of subjects).

Magda has numerous musical compositions. Among them is "Requiem," dedicated to the memory of all the victims of the Holocaust (composed for baritone solo, soprano solo, choral and piano accompaniment). It was performed and televised numerous times throughout the years.

More than 300 of her poems are published in anthologies, poetry journals, newspapers, etc. She also has an

378

unpublished manuscript containing short stories, poetic narratives, as well as a manuscript of fairy tales for children. Thirty-seven pages of her memoirs are featured in *Sisters in Sorrow: Voices of Care in the Holocaust*, memoirs of women survivors of the Holocaust compiled by Roger A. Ritvo and Diane M. Plotkin. Published by Texas A&M University Press, 1998.

Magda was a marathon runner, skier, and mountain climber. She and her husband, Dr. Eugene Herzberger, who is a retired neurosurgeon, reside in Fountain Hills, Arizona. They have a daughter Monica, a son Henry, and two grandchildren.

For the past 31 years, Magda has been lecturing about the Holocaust and reading her poetry in schools, universities, church organizations, nursing homes, literary organizations, etc. She has also participated in many TV and radio programs, including national TV Channel 9, WOR, New York.

Being an eyewitness to the Holocaust, she was invited by the Shoah Survivors of the Holocaust Visual History Foundation, which is sponsored by Mr. Steven Spielberg, to give her testimony as a survivor. Her interview took place at her home in Fountain Hills, Arizona on November 17, 1995. It was conducted by Mrs. Louise Bobrow, interviewer for the Foundation. She received the videotapes of her interview accompanied by a personal message from Mr. Steven Spielberg himself. It demonstrates Mr. Spielberg's personal interest in each survivor's testimony. She also has been a contributor to the Shoah Foundation's quarterly newsletter, *Past Forward* (1996-1998).

This volume, *Survival*, her autobiography, and most recent publication, was published by 1st World Library, Inc. of Austin, Texas, 2005. Two additional book manuscripts: *How to Survive During Hard Times and Depression* and *Survival in the Holocaust* are currently in process.

Magda's primary goals are to instill love for poetry in the hearts of people through her work, to keep the memory of the Holocaust alive through the presentations of her experiences in the death camps, and to show the beauty of life through her writings and music. Her philosophy of life: Have faith, hope, and love in your heart—Believe in impossible dreams and make them come true—Cherish each moment of life—Never take anything for granted.

Magda may be contacted at the following email address: magdaherzberger@yahoo.com